Community Development Practice in Africa

Putting Theory Into Practice

Community Development Practice in Africa

Putting Theory Into Practice

Editors

Charles Gyan
McGill University

Linda Kreitzer
University of Calgary

Somnoma Valerie Ouedraogo
MacEwan University

INFORMATION AGE PUBLISHING, INC.
Charlotte, NC • www.infoagepub.com

Library of Congress Cataloging-in-Publication Data

CIP record for this book is available from the Library of Congress
http://www.loc.gov

ISBNs: 979-8-88730-718-3 (Paperback)

  979-8-88730-719-0 (Hardcover)

  979-8-88730-720-6 (ebook)

Copyright © 2024 Information Age Publishing Inc.

All rights reserved. No part of this publication may be reproduced, stored in a retrieval system, or transmitted, in any form or by any means, electronic, mechanical, photocopying, microfilming, recording or otherwise, without written permission from the publisher.

Printed in the United States of America

CONTENTS

Editors' Introduction ix

SECTION I: HISTORICAL AND THEORETICAL FOUNDATIONS OF COMMUNITY DEVELOPMENT IN AFRICA

1. Unveiling Ghana's Community Development Tapestry: An Exploration through Time
   Charles Gyan and Linda Kreitzer 3

2. Contribution of African Traditional Knowledge to Community Development Theory and Practice in Africa
   William Abur 23

3. Community Development in Uganda: A Historical Inquiry in the Practice of Meeting Community Needs
   Venesio Bwambale Bhangyi and Senkosi Moses Balyejjusa 35

4. Analysis of Villagization Model of Rural Community Development in Tanzania Mainland Through Ubuntu Lens
   Meinrad Haule Lembuka 51

SECTION II: MODELS AND APPROACHES TO COMMUNITY DEVELOPMENT IN AFRICA

5. Asset-Based Community-Driven Development (ABCD) as an Approach and Model to Address the Challenges of Africa
   Hanna Nel 67

6. Self-Help Group as a Community Development Platform for Rural Households in Kenya
   Atieno Paul Okello, Oino Gutwa Peter, and Atieno Obara Rebeccah Chawiyah 85

7. African Centered Community Development in Social Work: Exploring Imbewu Youth Empowerment Centre as an Asset-Based Community Informed Project
   Thembelihle Brenda Makhanya 99

SECTION III: COMMUNITY ENGAGEMENT IN AFRICA

8. Community Development Practice in Africa: An Autoethnographic Reflection of Development Through the Bikpakpaam (Konkomba) Example in Ghana
   Matthew Gmalifo Mabefam 117

9. Community Engagement in Improving Agricultural Production: Lessons for Community Development Practice
   Shamiso Mandioma and Abdulrazak Karriem 131

10. Engaging Traditional Leadership as a Key and Practical Approach to Community Development: The Jatropha Project in Puriya Community as a Case Study
    Eunice Abbey and Vyda Mamley Hervie 149

11. Community Development Associations and Fundraising for Self-Help Projects in African Suburbia for Rural Development
    Babatunde Ayoola Fajimi 163

SECTION IV: SUSTAINABLE AND ETHICAL COMMUNITY DEVELOPMENT IN AFRICA

12. Exploring the Problem of "Justice" in a Context of Community Development in Africa: A Dialogue Between Philosophy and Politics
    Irene Ayallo 181

13. Interactions of Community Development and Legal Reforms in Rehabilitating Juvenile Offenders in Zambia
    Chilala K. Sheilas, Chikampa Victor, Moonga Fred, and Hamauswa Shakespeare 197

14. The Collective Path to Sustainability: Leveraging Community Systems for Positive Change
   Rosemary Anderson Akolaa 211

15. Sustainable Community Development Practice in Africa: Cultural Competemility and Professionalism Informed Approach
   Paula Ugochukwu Ude 227

Conclusion
   Somnoma Valerie Ouedraogo 243

Contributors 247

Index 255

EDITORS' INTRODUCTION

Community development is the core of every society. It nourishes and sustains the collective spirit of any community. In the African context, this concept of community development has roots that stretch back thousands of years, intricately woven into the fabric of pre-colonial Africa. In these ancient times, various methods of community development evolved in accordance with the preferences of African cultures. However, these indigenous community development practices and methods, both positive and negative, underwent a transformation with the arrival of the colonial powers on the continent. Community development was strongly impacted by colonialism, which stripped thousands of years of indigenous community practices and imposed onto these countries new and artificial borders, languages, and Western community development norms and practices. Unfortunately, most of these Western community development norms and practices served the colonizers' interests with little regard for the people living in these indigenous communities. For example, infrastructures such as roads, bridges, and services were strategically built near harbors and colonial settlements, instead of focusing on rural areas that would benefit from access to services. Colonizers not only exploited Africa's resources but also used hard labor practices to construct these infrastructures and extracted these resources in often inhumane ways. As the colonizers continued living in these countries, Western community development structures were introduced, local people were sent to the Western world to be trained to administer these services to their people. To add insult to injury, indigenous methods of serving the population were unjustly deemed uncivilized.

The struggle for independence in many African countries brought forth a Pan-African movement, determined to dismantle the foreign structures and pave the way for an authentic African approach to community development. However, so entrenched were these systems that little progress

Community Development Practice in Africa: Putting Theory Into Practice, pp. ix–xvi
Copyright © 2024 by Information Age Publishing
www.infoagepub.com
All rights of reproduction in any form reserved.

was made, compelling most African countries to continue down the path of modernization and westernization. By 1950, President Truman of the United States stated, "we must embark on a bold new program for making the benefits of our advances and industrial progress available for the improvement and growth of the underdeveloped areas (Rist, 2008, p. 17). This sets the stage for the dichotomy between "developed" and "underdeveloped" countries, making these terms into political agenda, and casting Africa as "underdeveloped." Neoliberal economics were introduced with a promise that all countries would rise to an affluent level of living with the elimination of poverty.

Underdeveloped countries were identified as needing help from the Western world, totally ignoring the fact that the very resources stripped from Africa were the reason why one could be "developed the western way." As the World Bank and the International Monetary Fund (IMF) introduced structural adjustment programs, it became evident that these neoliberal policies were not universally beneficial. Unfortunately, this top-down approach to development was used as the common way to approach developing communities and has continued to be used by international non-government organizations and governments. This approach fosters dependency on external aid agencies while sidelining the voices of community members in decisions regarding the development and growth of their communities. This dependency has left African communities distrustful of foreign intervention, yet they remain dependent on external support to "help" them strengthen their community. This creates despondency, fait accompli, and a lack of confidence to change anything without outside help.

According to Walsh (2010) "the very idea of development itself is a concept and word that does not exist in the cosmovision's conceptual categories and languages of indigenous peoples" (p. 17). That is, indigenous worldviews do not encompass the concept of "development" as it is known in the Western contexts. The notion of development as it exists today was a construct of Western thinking and as a result communities in Africa are relooking at how communities should develop, emphasizing a participatory approach to development. Decolonizing Western institutions and listening to communities is growing in the world of community development. As Kreitzer (2012) states:

> Development, so far, has had mixed success. What is missing is that people in the western world do not listen to the people. Listening, really listening, building relationships, and advocating for full participation of the community or group is essential. Promoting self-awareness, encouraging people to come up with their own solutions and working towards a dynamic approach to development is a way forward. (p. 126)

Encouraging self-awareness and empowering people to devise their own solutions while embracing a dynamic approach to development is the way forward. The scholars who contributed to this book are exemplars of this progressive vision. Their innovative community development practices set in motion a groundswell of change, with communities taking the reins through a bottom-up approach. However, much work needs to take place for communities to decolonize institutions and create new, indigenous ones that authentically serve the needs of their community. This book delves into these transformative processes, offering a deeper understanding of the dynamics of community development in Africa and the imperative of embracing the participatory path towards meaningful change.

This book includes 15 chapters concerning the intricate world of community development in Africa and organized into four sections: (1) Historical and theoretical foundations of community development in Africa; (2) Models and approaches to community development in Africa; (3) Community engagement in Africa; and (4) Sustainable and ethical community development in Africa. Each section provides a unique lens through which to explore the dynamic field of community development in Africa. The chapters are written by African scholars representing Ghana, Tanzania, Uganda, South Africa, Sudan, Nigeria, Zimbabwe, Kenya, and Zambia. Our goal for this book is to present grassroots community development initiatives in various parts of Africa, woven together by threads of history, theory, methodology, engagement, sustainability, and ethical practice. We have produced a dynamic and exciting book which introduces new thinking on community practice as well as confirming present practices that seem to work in the African context. With this in mind, we begin with a deep dive into the historical and theoretical foundation of community development in Africa.

Chapter 1 begins with a historical view of community practice in Ghana, a country the authors have had the privilege of living in and engaging in community development. The chapter divides this historical journey into three eras: (1) pre-colonial; (2) colonial times; and (3) modern day Ghana. In pre-colonial Ghana, community was the heart of the country and festivals, communal labor, and other cultural events strengthened community engagement. However, colonial rule introduced a different paradigm and system of community development, which favored infrastructure that helped build Ghana for colonial interest, including building roads, bridges, and communication. Most of rural Ghana was left out of this process. After World War II and independence, community development took on a different approach, mainly educational. The authors question the origins of community development in Ghana, whether it is a traditional system or a colonial legacy. The chapter concludes by providing insights into the current landscape of community development in Ghana.

Chapter 2 brings together the concept of community development and the Ubuntu philosophy and values through an example of a local Sudanese development project. The chapter critiques the conventional top-down approach to community development and proposes Ubuntu philosophy as a holistic, indigenous, and bottom-up alternative in Africa. Drawing from the author's own extensive experience as a community worker, social worker, and teacher, the author highlights the strengths and challenges of both approaches. The author advocates for valuing indigenous knowledge through a decolonization of community practice. While offering some practical stages of community development, they challenge us all to reflect on and integrate Ubuntu values in community development practice.

Chapter 3 presents qualitative research using a systematic literature review and secondary data analysis concerning community development in Uganda. Comparative thematic analysis of the literature and documents were conducted with sub-themes and themes identified. The authors begin by exploring the historical roots and contemporary influences on community development, including a conceptualization of community development in Uganda. The authors explore the public and non-public sector's role in Ugandan community development, highlighting challenges and opportunities for strengthening communities to be sustainable and integrated into the national and local government planning. They conclude by identifying four recommendations for policy and practice in relation to community development. They advocate for a bottom-up approach where community members have their voices heard and stakeholders listen.

Chapter 4 takes readers to Tanzania and the villagization model of rural community development. The author gives a historical account of villagization beginning with pre-colonial strong community villages to Tanzania's villagization model introduced by Nyerere under the Ujamaa policy. The chapter draws on secondary data and research articles and uses the Ubuntu philosophy while critiquing this villagization model. The author takes readers through the rise of the villagization model, linking it to the Ubuntu model. The author offers a discussion about the rise and eventual dissatisfaction with the villagization model when people moved to towns and cities. To conclude, the chapter offers lessons learned from the villagization model, including how it impacted the local, national, and global agenda. The chapter concludes by reflecting on the relevance of this model in modern African community development.

Chapter 5 begins the section on "Models and Approaches to Community Development in Africa." The author takes a deep dive into Asset-Based Community-Driven Development (ABCD) in which she has been involved for many years. Beginning with a critique of an African worldview and Ubuntu, she then offers an extensive practical understanding of ABCD by explaining the purpose and principles of this approach to community development. The different phases of the ABCD process are described, giving examples of tools to use in each phase. The chapter offers examples of ABCD's implementation in South African communities, addressing model limitations and showcasing its benefits in community development practice.

Chapter 6 introduces another kind of model, that of self-help groups. The authors begin with an extensive exploration of self-help groups in Kenya, underpinned by a comprehensive literature review. The authors define self-help groups, unraveling their significance, purpose, and typology, such as savings groups, women's health groups and farmers' groups. Each of these groups is explained in detail and the importance they have played in Kenya's communities. The chapter emphasizes the theory of collective action within the framework of self-help groups, outlining obstacles to and recommendations for enhancing participation.

Chapter 7 offers an understanding of how pandemics and colonialism have shaped community development in South Africa. The author emphasizes the role of racism, and apartheid and how community development was used in political movements to erase oppression. The chapter presents a holistic view of the community development process, intertwining Afrocentricity and decolonialism through ABCD. A practical example from the Imbewu Youth Empowerment Centre in South Africa illustrates the integration of Afro-centric and ABCD approaches. The chapter concludes by offering some lessons learned using ABCD with Imbewu Youth Empowerment Centre.

Chapter 8 begins the third section of the book called "Community Engagement in Africa." This chapter comes from Ghana, written by an author, using autoethnographic reflections, who has worked in community development projects run by different agencies for many years. The author's critique of community development and its history in Africa challenges us to think reflectively about the history of community development as written from a different perspective, many of whom have paid little attention to community development pre-colonization. The chapter presents an indigenous approach to community development by delving into the Bikpakpaam ethnic group's practices in Ghana. It concludes by encouraging community workers to appreciate multiple community development approaches to determine the most suitable one for the specific community they are serving.

Chapter 9 looks at community development practices in Zimbabwe through the NGO called Development Aid from People to People (DAPP). This research project employed a qualitative case study methodology, incorporating semi-structured interviews, to investigate the factors contributing to the decline in farming production levels and to explore strategies for supporting farmers in adopting sustainable farming methods to enhance food security. The authors bring together a philosophical approach to community development, followed by principles of community development. The chapter discusses the agricultural policy, community engagement and DAPP's role in empowering farmers, ultimately ensuring food and nutrition security in Zimbabwe.

Chapter 10 integrates the concept of community development with the pivotal role of traditional leaders in Ghana. The authors explain the important contributions traditional leaders make across many African regions. Exploring the concept of community development, these authors introduce the concept of participatory theory or people-centered development in the context of a Jatropha project in Puriya, Mion District in the Northern Region of Ghana. The project is part of the Ohayo Ghana Foundation, a Japanese organization using a biofuel plant (Jatropha) for soap, lamp, fuel, and so forth. Engaging traditional leaders in this project led to the successful building of a factory to produce these resources, which involved the whole community throughout the process. However, the project had a pre-mature ending, and the authors reflect on what happened to this promising project. They conclude with important lessons for future community development projects.

Chapter 11 introduces the role of Community Development Associations (CDA) for developing rural communities in the context of Nigeria. The author defines CDAs, discusses their purpose, and explores their various theoretical approaches. The author also examines the role of different stakeholders, including government, philanthropists, NGOs, corporate organizations, and international agencies in funding CDAs. Practical examples are included that show how CDAs and self-help projects can collaboratively empower communities, reducing the need for external funding in community engagement and action. The chapter concludes by highlighting some challenges of funding self-help projects in rural communities, including capacity development. The chapter advocates for building capacity that will strengthen and empower communities to fulfill their dreams of a thriving community.

Chapter 12 begins our last section focusing on "Sustainable and Ethical Community Development in Africa." The chapter explores the complex issue of "Justice" in the context of community development through research in Kenya. Beginning with a short description of community development in Africa, the author introduces the concept of justice, critiquing Western theories of justice that are problematic to the African context. The chapter shows these problematic issues through practical examples of the justice system in Kenya. The chapter highlights the significance of ubuntu, public participation, and the notion of impartiality as important elements of justice in Kenya. The author concludes with a diagram showing

Editors' Introduction　xv

the critical elements of a multi-disciplinary concept of justice tailored to the African context, emphasizing public dialogue and a focus on centering the margins.

Chapter 13 discusses the whole concept of juvenile delinquency in relation to Zambia. The chapter provides an introduction to Zambia and defines juvenile delinquency on a global scale. The chapter elaborates on the Zambian juvenile justice system, critically examining its challenges. It highlights the introduction of the National Juvenile Justice Strategy and Action Plan (2022–2026) and its implications for managing juvenile delinquents in Zambia. The authors give a description of the institutionalized model of rehabilitation and the community-based correctional model (CBM) identifying specific strategies for CBM. The chapter concludes by addressing the strengths and challenges to these models.

Chapter 14 presents research conducted in Ghana looking at how community systems impact sustainable development, comparing two communities, one in northern Ghana and the other in southern Ghana. Using an ethnographic research design guided by the theory of the change model, the author assessed the existing systems and structures, examining the effectiveness of district political-administrative structures and indigenous administrative structures. The chapter provides an in-depth exploration of the findings, accompanied by a clear chart and thematic analysis. The author concludes by emphasizing the importance of the theory of change in assessing communities, advocating for a reduction of government and political intrusion, and an increase in the involvement of traditional leaders and elders in decision-making.

Chapter 15 introduces two vital concepts, cultural competemility and professionalism, for effective community development and engagement in the African context. A brief history of both concepts is described, including four key elements important to these concepts. Each concept is then applied to community development practice and how social workers can use these concepts in African localities and communities. The chapter outlines the three stages of implementing these concepts and provides practical examples of each stage. It discusses the policy implications of cultural competemility and professionalism, considering their economic and educational implications. The author addresses challenges related to the application of these concepts in community development and provides a diagram showing their application within communities.

We conclude this book by highlighting some of the important concepts that weave their way into most of the chapters; that of the importance of Ubuntu and that community needs to be the driving force behind community development initiatives. Community development has a complex history in Africa with many different stakeholders in the past and present "doing" community development, with mainly unsustainable results. The authors in this book were courageous enough to share those setbacks and challenges, offering recommendations and lessons learned to continue improving this knowledge base of community development. Many of the chapters are research projects, something that needs to be encouraged to continue the growth of a healthy knowledge base concerning community development and practice in Africa. Decolonization of social work in Africa continues to challenge the profession to critique theories and practices that are Western based and developing more appropriate practices relevant to Africa. It is imperative to nurture the evolution of practices that are contextually relevant to Africa, ensuring a harmonious fusion of global insights with local wisdom. This does not discount the value of Western community development models. In fact, the ABCD model was developed in the United States and has been effective in the African context, as demonstrated by several of the authors in this book. Challenging, critiquing, and developing new models strengthen the decolonization process. We hope this book will inspire and encourage us all to practice community development in a sustainable, humble, and competent way.

Charles Gyan
McGill University

Linda Kreitzer
University of Calgary

Somnoma Valerie Ouedraogo
MacEwan University

REFERENCES

Kreitzer, L. (2012). *Social work in Africa: Exploring culturally relevant education and practice in Ghana.* University of Calgary Press.

Rist, G. (2008). *The history of development* (3rd ed.). Zed Books.

Walsh, C. (2010). Development as *Buen Vivir*: Institutional arrangements and (de)colonial entanglements. *Development, 53*(1), 15–21.

SECTION I

HISTORICAL AND THEORETICAL FOUNDATIONS OF COMMUNITY DEVELOPMENT IN AFRICA

CHAPTER 1

UNVEILING GHANA'S COMMUNITY DEVELOPMENT TAPESTRY

An Exploration Through Time

Charles Gyan and Linda Kreitzer

ABSTRACT

The sense of community and communal living are greatly prized ideals and beliefs of traditional Ghanaians. Collective effort toward developing communities have always been part of the African culture before colonialism. Hence, the principles behind community development are not foreign to Africans. The purpose of this chapter is to reflect upon the history of community development in Ghana, starting from pre-colonial up to the current perspective and to discuss future ways forward. During the pre-colonial period, communities in Ghana relied on forms of cooperative labor to meet their needs as well as setting up community development initiatives. During the colonial period, communal labor metamorphosed into forced labor due to the way it was administered. Mass education was introduced by the British as a means of colonizing the minds of the Indigenous people. After independence, community development became a major function of the Government of Ghana and was implemented through various forms of decentralization and local government policies. In contemporary Ghana, the key community development actors include the government, non-government organizations, international non-government organizations, civil society organizations and community-based organizations along with community members themselves. In conclusion, the history of community development in Ghana is not a history of stages, in which later forms of community development are entirely

Community Development Practice in Africa: Putting Theory Into Practice, pp. 3–21
Copyright © 2024 by Information Age Publishing
www.infoagepub.com
All rights of reproduction in any form reserved.

replaced by former policies, but a history of supplementations, in which early forms and strategies continue to thrive with some transformations alongside later ones.

Keywords: community development, history, Ghana, cooperative labor, festivals

Introduction

Ghana is recognized as one of the more stable countries in West Africa, with rich natural resources (Throup et al., 2011). Despite this, the country is characterized by high levels of poverty. Outside of the main urban centers of Ghana, government institutions and public infrastructure are not well-developed (Diao et al., 2019). Authors theorize that most rural communities in sub-Saharan countries, including Ghana, have been sidelined in the provision of infrastructure and basic social amenities (Akkoyunlu, 2015; Atuahene & Owusu-Ansah, 2013). However, community development is part of Ghana's overall strategic development plan on a broader scale to sustain and increase the development benefits associated with rural development (Akudugu & Laube, 2013).

Community development is a concept frequently used by geographers, social workers, and others in the 21st century that has been in existence for centuries (Schenck et al., 2010; Weyers, 2011). The concept of community development is not self-evident or transparent. It is highly contested and, depending on how it is defined, its practices shift over time. Community development with regards to this chapter involves the organization and mobilization of local resources, community members, local and international organizations, and other stakeholders (Gyan & Baffoe, 2014).

The nature of the community development system in Ghana of centuries ago was not the same as today. However, understanding the current state of community development in Ghana can be difficult, if not impossible, without reference to the past community development processes. Any inquiry into contemporary community development system must take inspiration from the past. Therefore, the purpose of this chapter is to provide the history of community development in Ghana starting from pre-colonial times to current perspective and future ways forward.

History of Community Development in Ghana

The sense of community and communal living are greatly prized ideals and beliefs of Ghanaians. Throughout ages, collective efforts underlie the equilibration of Ghanaian and African societies in general (Nukunya, 2003;

Ogbujah, 2014). These collective efforts can be seen from the persistent usage of "we'" and "ours" in the everyday speech of traditional Ghanaians. A Ghanaian believes that: "I am because we are, and since we are, therefore I am. This is a cardinal point in the understanding of the African view of man" (Mbiti, 1990, p. 106).

Community Development in Pre-Colonial Ghana

Collective efforts toward developing communities have always been part of the African culture before colonialism (Bondarenko, 2014). Hence, the principles behind community development are not foreign ideologies to Africans. Festivals, "nnoboa"[1] and communal labor are some of the means through which Ghanaians have embarked on community development projects.

During the pre-colonial period, festivals constituted one of the major strategies around which community development and African traditions revolved (Donkoh, 2011). Therefore, the history of community development in Ghana will not be complete if the roles of festivals are neglected. Festivals are essential to the development of Ghanaian communities. They are occasions for community development decision-making and fundraising (Donkoh, 2011). During festivals, citizens living outside their home villages may either go back or send resources to support various development projects. Bonye (2011) argues that celebrating festivals over the years in Africa has played two major roles—traditional and contemporary—in development. He contends that festivals are used for the preservation of culture. In recent times, the traditional role of festivals (preservation and maintenance of culture) continues to exist alongside the contemporary community development roles (action plan, accountability, and advocacy). With the current role, there are three major activities—drawing of action plans, holding traditional leaders as well as local government representatives accountable and advocating for community development projects (Bonye, 2011; Gyan & Baffoe, 2014).

In Ghana, there has also been a tradition of customary arrangements, where people exchange labor for farm work (Nnoboa) (Amanor et al., 1993). Community members helped each other by using their strength in a program of rotational labor to raise their quality of life and standard of living (Amanor et al., 1993). Communal spirit was one of the motivation factors for local Ghanaians to adopt this mutual aid technique of ensuring sustainable development. The use of this technique was also necessitated by the idea that the general good of the communities could not be realized individually (Chirwa et al., 2005). Afriyie (2015) argues that capitalism and Western civilization have made the local culture of communal sustainable development (nnoboa) system sluggish. He advocates for "sankofa"—the re-adoption and improvement of this system to help propel the contemporary Ghanaian society other than relying exclusively on the Western notion of community development.

Another strategy adopted during the pre-colonial period in Ghana for community development was communal labor. The Ghanaian community during this period used communal labor to ensure the setting up of projects. Okia (2012) argues that the use of communal labor in Africa as a community development technique was instrumental in offsetting the state's labor cost. Most villages in Ghana and some parts of Africa had community farms where residents had to devote a day within the week to work on the village farm. On a regular circulating schedule, every adult in the community provided the necessary labor to build local infrastructure or work on village farms (Okia, 2012). Participation in the Ghanaian communal labor system was mandatory, but because the local people made the decisions, they willingly engaged in it. According to Okia, "in theory, the colonial state construed communal labor as a relic from the 'tribal' past that was deemed part of the traditional work obligation of an ethnic group and, hence, a communal responsibility" (p. 2). The influence of colonialism continued through indirect colonial activity.

Community Development in Colonial Ghana

The colonial masters adopted the communal labor system and manipulated this communal obligation. Through the revitalized traditions such as communal labor, the colonizers connaturalized and socio-politically put certain indigenes into leadership positions which gave new meaning to their relationship with the colonized (Okia, 2012). Addo-Fening (2008) argues that the imposition of colonial rule on Ghana changed the traditional governance structure from the customary-based political governance to an outlandish "remote-controlled" system. This foreign system and its associated classification of the people by the British led to the misuse of power by the chiefs and headmen (Addo-Fening, 2008). Disreputable forced labor policies emanated from the communal labor system and forced the communities to intermittently organize the local people to work on the colonial infrastructure (Tsey & Short, 1995). For instance, the development and expansion of roads and railways in Ghana after the British defeated the Asante confederation led to the promulgation of several road maintenance laws (such as the Roads Ordinance, The Road Maintenance Rule), which gave the chiefs' power to recruit indigenes. Okia (2012) found that several forced laborers were recruited for road maintenance projects in 1910. This was not peculiar to only anglophone West Africa. In francophone West Africa, the general decree of 1912 instituted the corvée,[2] which put the development of infrastructure in the hands of the indigenes (Okia, 2012). This labor, which was organized by the local authorities, was supposed to meet the felt needs of the local communities. Most authors, however, argue that the reinvented traditions in both francophone and anglophone West Africa were fraught with a myriad of abuses (Akurang-Parry, 2000; Okia, 2012).

Another key community development strategy that was adopted after the Second World War (WWII) in Ghana was mass education. During this period, mass education became synonymous with community development (Du Sautoy, 1958). The British Colonial Development and Welfare Act of 1945 (Smyth, 2004) and the 1951 Gold Coast Plan for Mass Literacy and Mass Education (Du Sautoy, 1958) legally brought into the landscape of community development a scheme of state-sponsored social welfare initiative. The mass education strategy was geared toward addressing issues such as poverty, apathy, diseases, illiteracy, and ignorance. According to Du Sautoy (1958), the strategy was to teach the people how to live and read. The program was delivered in four parts—educating women on home management and childcare, adult literacy, extension campaigns and self-help project work.

Community development practice after World War II concentrated mainly on modifying the people's way of life—beliefs, thoughts, and behavior. This was an ideological strategy targeting Africans to accept that their way of life was inferior. This notion was captured by James MacQueen, who indicated, "If we really wish to do good in Africa, we must teach her savage sons that white men are their superiors" (Falola, 2007). As introduced by the colonial offices, community development practice targeted mostly cultural, attitudinal, and value change, with little or no focus on economic aspects (Dunham, 1970).

The introduction of mass education was perhaps the British means of colonizing the minds of the native people. Said (1978) states that to have knowledge of an object is to control or have power over it. The implementation of this mass education scheme as a community development strategy and having authority over the colonies were in an era when the indigenes, particularly the products of the British education system, had a growing sense of consciousness about the negative effects of colonialism. Smyth (2004) argues that the implementation of the mass education scheme was constrained by growing African nationalism around the 1950s. Though African nationalism became triumphant over colonialism in Ghana in the late 1950s, the community development thought, and practices used by the colonial masters were not totally abandoned. They were to be transformed to reflect and address the felt needs of Africans and Ghanaians. In a 1957 speech, Dr. Kwame Nkrumah, first President of Ghana, indicated:

> We must seek an African view to the problems of Africa. This does not mean that Western techniques and methods are not applicable to Africa. It does mean, however, that in Ghana we must look at every problem from the African point of view. (McWilliam & Kwamena-Poh, 1975, as cited in Akyeampong, 2007)

In recent discussions of the roots of community development, a controversial issue has been whether community development is a colonial legacy or not. According to Smyth (2004) community development practice in developing countries is a colonial heirloom. From this perspective, the notion of community development was born out of colonialism. That is, the colonial administrators became very concerned about the use of local resources in the various colonies to develop them. On the other hand, some argue that community development has never been a new concept for developing countries before colonialism, it is rather interwoven in the heritage of developing countries' culture. As Mapuva (2015) argues, colonial rule and its associated legislation have, however, impacted the current state of community development in developing countries. He further posits that globalization and the need to diversify pushed the colonialists, after exploiting the colonies, to transform the traditional community development strategies which were interwoven in the culture of the people. For instance, the transformation in Zimbabwe was from the reliance on agriculture and forestry as a means of community development to "mining, tourism and manufacturing" (Jephias, 2015, p. 144). Du Sautoy (1958) also argues that the techniques and principles behind the practice of community development in Ghana are not new, but rather it is their concerted and thoughtful execution in terms of policy, which is new. These arguments presuppose that community development is not a new concept to the global south because it has been part of the culture of the people.

Our own view is that community development has its roots in the global south, and it was embedded in the way of life of the people. The recent notion of community development, the top-down approach to community development and the institutionalization of the practice of community development in Ghana can be considered colonial legacies which date back to the establishment of the Department of Social Welfare and Community Development in the 1940s by British colonial administrators (Abloh & Ameyaw, 1997). However, it is important to remember that Ghanaians used and continue to use local community development strategies such as communal labor, nnoboa, and festivals during the pre-colonial, colonial, and post-independence periods to meet the felt needs of their communities. That is, the bottom-up approach to community development is deeply rooted in the traditional self-help and mutual aid techniques prevalent within traditional African and Ghanaian communities, both prior to and during the colonial era.

The Modern-Day Community Development Practice in Ghana

The history of community development in Ghana is a history of supplementations, in which early forms and strategies continue to thrive with some transformations alongside later ones. However, not every community development practice or principle has changed. The nnoboa and communal labor are still in practice, and festivals continue to be held. The major changes that have taken place are the critical roles being played by governments, NGOs, sister cities, CBOs, and community members.

Government involvement in community development predates Ghana's independence. After independence, community development became a major function of the Government in Ghana. According to Batten (1957), community development as a key function of governments in tropical countries (including Ghana) before the middle of the 20th century concentrated on developing communication networks and exploiting material resources with little or no focus on the welfare needs of the local community members. Thus, most community development programs focused on economic development rather than social development (Midgley et al., 1986).

The rapid increases in the needs and wants of local communities have led to the decentralization of government power to ensure a more effective and efficient mobilization and management of community resources to meet the needs of the local communities (Dejenie, 2003). In the case of Ghana, the scarcity of resources and the need to involve local people in community development decisions were the motivation for the adoption of a decentralized system of government (Dejenie, 2003).

After independence, successive Ghanaian governments implemented various forms of decentralization policies. Efforts geared toward a decentralized system were introduced over the years. For instance, in 1961, 1983, 1988, 1992, 1993, and 2016, different laws and decentralization policies were promulgated (Kuusi, 2009). The Local Government Act 54 of 1961 was the first to establish a local government system that ensures locality development (Abakah, 2018). Another key effort was the Local Government Act (Act 462) of 1993, which strove to facilitate a holistic approach to the decentralization process (Abakah, 2018).

Present Day Community Development Structures

The prevailing decentralization program, which started in 1961 (Abakah, 2018), was sanctioned by Ghana's Fourth Republican Constitution in 1992 (Kuusi, 2009). The 1992 Constitution of Ghana (1992) states that "Ghana shall have a system of local government and administration which as far as practicable be decentralized" (article, 240(1)). Therefore, the development of the local areas by the local government can be examined in the context of the decentralization principles and practices instigated by the Local Government Act, 1993 (Act 462) (Government of Ghana, 1993). The structure and powers of the Metropolitan, Municipal and District Assemblies (MMDAs) are prescribed in the Local Government Act of 1993 (Act 462) (Government of Ghana, 1993). The main legal instruments relating to the local government system in Ghana are: 1) The Local Government Act 54; 2) Civil Service Law 1993 (PNDCL 327); Local Government Act 462; National Development Planning Act 480; National Development Planning Commission Act 479; District Assemblies' Common Fund Act 455; Local Government Service Act 656; Institute of Local Government Studies Act 647 (Der Bebelleh & Nobabumah, 2013) and Local government Act 936.

The Government's involvement in community development and the management of local resources in Ghana hinges essentially on the level of decentralization of government machinery (Ayee, 2003). Effective government sponsored community development projects can be attributable to the success of the decentralization program. Thus, implementing an effective decentralized system is a catalyst for greater participation of the citizenry, the facilitation of government sponsored community development programs, and ensuring equitable development throughout the country (Ayee, 2003; Offei-Aboagye, 2004). Offei-Aboagye (2000) contends that Ghana's decentralization desired to "provide more responsive, equitable and participatory development, bring government and decision-making nearer to the people as well as quicken the process of decision-making, serve as a training ground for political activity" (p. 2). However, the local government system in Ghana has limited capacity to take many initiatives (Arthur, 2016). The MMDAs depend on the national government for both financial and, to a large extent, human resource. Apart from the Assembly members, over 30% of the members of the MMDAs are government appointees who are more accountable to the president than the local people (Lentz, 2006). This lack of accountability to the people has recently ignited a debate as to whether the District, Municipal and Metropolitan Chief Executives should be elected or appointed by the president (Debrah, 2016). Nevertheless, the decentralization system in Ghana has reinforced clientelism and neo-patrimonial rule (Lentz, 2006). The sub-districts that are supposed to stimulate and drive community development have remained non-functional.

A recent development in the community development landscape in Ghana is the introduction of the sister cities program. Town twining is a program established through a social and legal agreement between geographically and politically distinct cities. These agreements seek to promote development, cultural exchange, and commercial ties between the cities (Clarke, 2011). According to Clarke (2011), there were over 2,500 sister cities partnerships in over 90 countries as of 2011. In Ghana, some of the cities have entered into sister cities agreement with cities in the West. These agreements include Columbia, Maryland and Tema, Ghana (established in 2014) (Michaels, 2015); and Accra and Columbus, Ohio (est. 2015) (Evans, 2015).

These programs contribute significantly to the development of communities involved. Economists argue that cultural differences can thwart trade and, as a result, city twining is meant to address these differences. Cremer et al. (2001) found sister cities program to offset the cultural distance that serves as a barrier to local economic development. For instance, through the cyber sister city program between Agogo (a rural community in Ghana) and Fort Lauderdale (a city in Florida), an ICT Training Center has been set up in Agogo to provide the members of the community access to the world of online information. Within the sister-city relationships, there are benefits that the cities in the Western countries also get from the cities from the global south. Most authors agree that these relationships expose the citizens of the Western cities to different cultures and help them function effectively in a globalized world (Dai, 2008; Villiers, 2009). Despite all benefits associated with these reciprocal relationships, the power dynamic of the Western cities may dictate community development initiatives for the cities in the global south.

Sister city programs are ideally supposed to promote interdependence and mutuality (Lawson, 2007). There is an ongoing debate on whether proximity counts in caring and responding to one another. When it comes to the topic of the global north and south relationships and the practicality of caring for one another, most of us will readily agree that no one enters a relationship without any interest. However, where this agreement usually ends is on the question of whether the sister cities program can foster a relationship of mutuality. Some are convinced that one can best provide community development support or care in situations of proximity (Friedman, 1991) and that people are more likely not to care much about the other "when distance comes between them, either in absolute space or via the distancing technologies and architectures of modernity" (Bauman, 1989, as cited in Clarke, 2011, p. 12), Singer (1972) and other neo-singers such as Arneson (2004) and Cullity (2007) maintain that on moral grounds people (sister cities) ought to contribute to the relief of the misery of distant needy strangers around the globe. They further argue that distance should not be a barrier to providing support to the distant stranger. That is, help should rely on both a moral premise, the principle of benevolence (Singer, 1972) and on empirical premises, in the sense that there are global developmental problems and disasters, and the presence of means through which providing support has the potential of providing relief for people (Weiner, 2003).

Over the years, governments and communities have not been able to single-handedly meet the needs of their citizens and residents (Mansuri & Rao, 2004). In response to the unmet needs of citizens in Ghana, the incorporation of companies, NGOs, and INGOs in community development has risen into prominence (Mansuri & Rao, 2004). These stakeholders have seen recent pressure from communities and civil societies to assume even greater responsibilities for revenue generation and distribution, transparency, and capacity building in local communities. These responsibilities, when coupled with those of communities, government, and civil societies, become powerful drivers and lead to important partnerships (World Bank, 2010).

In the 20th century, Ghana, and sub-Saharan Africa, in general, witnessed a massive growth in community or rural development-focused NGOs (Bratton, 1989). One key factor that led to this significant increase in the NGOs in Ghana is the Structural Adjustment Programs (SAPs). Ghana's attempts to enhance its economic prospects and lessen her loans with the International Monetary Fund (IMF) led to the adjustment of Ghana's economy through the implementation of neo-liberalized SAPs (Boafo-Arthur, 2018; IMF Conditionality, 2018). The Government's emphasis on reducing the state's control of social services have led to the increase in the number of local and international not-for-profit actors in community development programming in Ghana (Abdulai, 2016). In 1996, there were 320 registered NGOs (Bob-Milliar, 2005). By 2009, there were more than 4,463 registered NGOs in Ghana (Government of Ghana, 2009). The presence of these organizations has added a new approach to community development in Ghana. They engage in various community development activities ranging from advocacy, agriculture, public education, food security, microfinance, extension services, women empowerment, and provision of social amenities (Bob-Milliar, 2005; Government of Ghana, 2009).

There is a growing body of literature that suggests that the involvement of these organisations in community development has been alleviative for poor countries. The Organisation for Economic Cooperation and Development (2008) posited that the NGOs' approach to community development has been the most effective way of meeting the needs of the "poor or socially excluded" (p. 2). It has become common today to argue that NGOs have access to the vulnerable groups at the grassroots level; hence, their activities have improved the lives of vulnerable groups (Adjei & Arun,

2008). For instance, in World Vision International's quest to empower women in the Northern part of Ghana, the NGO has provided women with loans and skills training through its gender and development program (Kyei, 1998). According to Kyei (1998), this program has built the income generating capacity of women and, in turn, increased their access to basic services.

As it is right that NGOs in Ghana have been key players in the promotion and advancement of the socio-political and economic lives of the people in rural communities, there is also the need to reassess the popular assumption that they are "top-down" in their approach to community development. According to Seini and Nyanteng (2003), most NGOs in Ghana are "urban-based and have little or no contact with the grassroot farmers" (p. 21). "In spite of the community-based character of local NGOs … they are run by local elites … would rarely challenge the existing social hierarchies" (Crook, 2003, p. 80). Holmen (2010) sums this up by arguing that the activities of NGOs in rural Africa have not made any meaningful impact. Although we agree most of the NGOs are urban-based and have not been able to contribute to the development of rural communities in Ghana as expected, it must be admitted that there is no magic bullet to address the developmental challenges of African nations. NGOs being urban based does not necessarily mean they have lost touch with local people. Most NGOs may have their headquarters in the cities, but their project sites are situated in the villages. It is often easy to raise funds and mobilize resources in the cities to supplement the efforts of the people at the grassroots level; hence, most NGOs set up their head offices in the urban areas (P. Oduro, personal communication, April 16, 2016).

Moreover, post-independence Ghana has witnessed the adoption of communal labor principles as the heart of community development policies. These policies are based on the belief that the sustainability and ownership of community development projects can be ensured when community members commit to the initiation and implementation of projects (Gyan & Baffoe, 2014). Therefore, the system of division of labor makes the government responsible for the provision of technical expertise while the community members provide labor and resources (Abloh & Ameyaw, 1997; Gyan & Baffoe, 2014). Ghana's Labour Act (Government of Ghana, 2003) recognizes the importance of communal labour when it states: "A period during which a worker is absent from his or her normal duties … on account of the worker's participation in voluntary communal work … shall not be counted as part of the worker's annual leave" (Act 651, Part IV, section 23).

Present Perspective of Community Development

Community development in Ghana continues to see the involvement of communities and their members. Modernization and social change continue to pose social, political, technological, and economic challenges and demands on Ghanaians. The existing cultural values and practices in Ghana have been the vehicles through which people negotiate the complex demands and challenges associated with modernization. Governments and various stakeholders of community development in Ghana and Africa at large have in recent times recognized the importance of incorporating the African traditional community development strategies into the contemporary community development process. Nukunya (2003) indicates that state actors over the years have made efforts to create policies that ensure the use of traditional ceremonies, such as festivals, as the platforms or strategies to involve local Ghanaians in the development process. These occasions give ordinary citizens the opportunity to express their views in the development process of the community. Communities have, therefore, used these traditional institutions or events as an effective way to draw action plans, hold their leaders accountable, and advocate for community development projects (Bonye, 2011). Traditional festivals continue to be one of the main pillars of community development and the sustenance of the Ghanaian community (Bonye, 2011). Traditionally, communities in Ghana continue to rely on forms of cooperative labor to meet their needs and set up community development initiatives (Nukunya, 2003). This cooperative labor—communal labor—tradition makes it incumbent on community members both living in or outside the community to take up the responsibility of developing their own community.

Due to rural-urban migration, most citizens of the rural communities in Ghana are non-resident—live outside the communities. These non-resident members of the communities often provide resources to support community development initiatives in their ancestral communities. The community members living outside the communities at times get exposed to happenings in different communities and different ways of perceiving issues, thereby looking at the development challenges of their ancestral communities with a different lens. This kind of exposure makes them assume the role of initiators and the main financial contributors to community development in their ancestral communities. Tsey (2010) argues that the value placed on the performance of one's funeral in their ancestral village regardless of where they reside at the time of their death establishes a social expectation among non-residents to contribute to the development of their village of origin. Thus, community development participation through communal labor reconnects physically disconnected citizens back to their community of origin (Tsey, 2010). On the other hand, all able-bodied resident members of the communities pool together their resources occasionally under the aegis of the traditional leaders to initiate and implement projects in their various communities. However, it should be noted that festivals, funerals among others, are becoming an increasing financial burden for community leaders. The burden is growing, and non-resident members of the communities are becoming unhappy about it, particularly those who now live in the urban areas and have little connection to their community except when those ceremonies take place.

Future Directions of Community Development

The long history of community development efforts in Ghana has not translated into expected improvement of quality of life of underprivileged and marginalized people (Gyan & Ampomah, 2016; Gyan & Baffoe, 2014). Considerable efforts need to be exerted to incorporate innovative and creative ideas by the community development organizations for the betterment of vulnerable people.

One key issue that needs to be considered by community development practitioners and researchers in Ghana is the influence of globalization. Globalization influences the political, socio-cultural, and economic aspects of the individual, community, and the Government. It leads to rapid changes in infrastructure, labor process, and many traditional sources of income. It has the potential to both strengthen and weaken the local communities depending on the area that it influences most. This, at times, creates new challenges that require innovative ways of addressing them. However, with "globalization" also comes new opportunities which must be capitalized by community development organizations. People and organizations are now interconnected globally, thereby paving the way for international collaboration for the initiating of successful strategies for solving local problems. This "glocalization" of community development must be interrogated by practitioners to address the issue of westernization. This interrogation will help in making community development more transnational and reflective of the realities of the unique context of Ghana.

Considering that communication is the key element of any successful community development, the use of social media and social networking as tools for community development has enormous potential to make far-reaching changes in the field. Social media and networking offer a simple and inexpensive method for building relationships, communicating, and reaching several audiences. However, to reap the full benefits of social media and networking as tools for community development in Ghana, there is the need for measures to be put in place to overcome its associated challenges, including both digital divide and learning digital divide.

These challenges could be mitigated by providing more digital platforms for community development. However, in rural areas, given the lack of infrastructure (consistent internet services), knowledge about such technologies, training sessions must be incorporated to enhance their ability to get maximum benefit from such technological advancements.

Collaborative relationships and partnerships are of paramount importance. Community development projects' sustainability and ownership are dependent on community members' commitment to the development of the projects. Consequently, priority must be given to bottom-up approaches instead of top-down approaches while making decisions. Furthermore, in the decision-making process, involvement of all segments of the community must be ensured.

Traditionally, the focus of community development efforts is to improve material living conditions of people of a particular community through empowering them and building harmonious relationships among different stakeholders. However, the relationship between people of the community and their natural physical environments has been neglected. For instance, community development practitioners in Ghana do not consider wildlife conservation and deforestation. Besides focusing on improving the material living conditions, community development approaches in Ghana should also consider people's attitudes toward the environment by introducing environmentally friendly practices to tackle the harmful effects of climate change. Because in the long run, the survival of human beings is dependent on the sustainability of the environment they live in. Therefore, conservation of livelihoods is a very important consideration for community development practitioners, researchers, and programs in Ghana.

Conclusion

The historical perspective of the community development provided in this chapter revealed that the history of community development in Ghana is not a history of stages, in which later forms of community development totally replaced earlier ones, but a history of supplementations, in which early forms and strategies continue to thrive with some transformations alongside later ones. Furthermore, economic development remains a key issue addressed by the community development programs with little or no focus on human development and social development aspects.

Traditionally, communities in Ghana continue to rely on forms of cooperative labor to meet their needs and set up community development initiatives (Nukunya, 2003). During the colonial period, communal labor transformed into forced labor due to its administration. After independence, community development became a major function of the

Government of Ghana. Successive governments implemented various forms of decentralization and local government policies. The key actors of community development in contemporary Ghana include the Government, NGOs. INGOs, CSOs, and CBOs, along with community members themselves. Consequently, community development practice in contemporary Ghana has been given assistance from individuals as well as governmental and non-governmental institutions. Therefore, there has been the institutionalization of a system of division of labor where the government is responsible for the provision of technical expertise while the community members provide labor and resources.

REFERENCES

Abakah, E. (2018) Participation without a voice? Rural women's experiences and participation in local governance activities in the Abura–Asebu–Kwamankese district of Ghana. *Cogent Social Sciences*, 4(1). https://doi.org/10.1080/23311886.2018.1549768

Abdulai, A. G. (2017). The political economy of regional inequality in Ghana: Do political settlements matter? *The European Journal of Development Research*, 29(1), 213–229. https://doi.org/10.1057/ejdr.2016.11

Abloh, F., & Ameyaw, S. (1997). Ghana: A historical perspective on community development.In H. Campfens (Ed.), *Community development around the world: Practice, theory, research, training* (pp. 279–288. University of Toronto Press.

Addo-Fening, R. (2008). The relevance of traditional governance. In B. Agyeman-Duah (Ed.), *Ghana: Governance in the Fourth Republic* (pp. 32–57). Digibooks Ghana Limited.

Adjei, J. K., & Arun, T. (2009). *Microfinance programmes and the poor: Whom were they reaching'? Evidence from Ghana*. Brooks World Poverty Institute Working Paper Series, 7209, 265–291.

Afriyie, O. A. (2015). Communal non-formal financial market system development: A model for nnoboa market system. *European Journal of Accounting Auditing and Finance Research*, 3(3), 48–60.

Akkoyunlu, S. (2015). The potential of rural-urban linkages for sustainable development and trade. *International Journal of Sustainable Development & World Policy*, 4(2), 20-40. https://doi.org/10.18488/journal.26/2015.4.2/26.2.20.40.

Akudugu, J. A., & Laube, W. (2013). *Implementing local economic development in Ghana: Multiple actors and rationalities*. ZEF Working Paper Series, No. 113, University of Bonn, Bonn. https://www.econstor.eu/handle/10419/88371

Akurang-Parry, K. O. (2000). Colonial forced labour policies for road building in southern Ghana & international anti-forced labour pressure, 1900–1940. *African Economic History*, 28, 1–25. https://doi.org/10.2307/3601647

Akyeampong, K. (2007). *50 years of educational progress and challenge in Ghana*. CREATE. http://www.create-rpc.org/pdf_documents/PTA33.pdf

Amanor, K., Denkabe, A., & Wellard, K. (1993). Ghana: Country overview. In K. Wellard & J. G. Copestake (Eds.), *Non-governmental organizations and the state in Africa: Rethinking roles in sustainable agricultural development* (pp. 183–194). Routledge. https://doi.org/10.4324/9781003421740-20

Arneson, R. (2004). Moral limits on the demands of beneficence. In D. K. Chatterjee (Ed.), *The ethics of assistance: Morality, affluence, and the distant need* (pp. 33–56). Cambridge University Press.

Arthur, D. D. (2016). Examining the effects of governance challenges in Ghana's local government system: A case study of the Mfantseman municipal assembly. *Journal of US-China Public Administration, 13*(7), 454–465.

Atuahene, F., & Owusu-Ansah, A. (2013). A descriptive assessment of higher education access, participation, equity, and disparity in Ghana. *SAGE Open, 3*(3). https://doi.org/10.1177/2158244013497725

Ayee, J. R. A. (2003). Decentralization and local governance: The Ghanaian experience. In N. Amponsah & K. Boafo-Arthur (Eds.), *Local government in Ghana, grassroots participation in the 2002 local government elections* (pp. 19–47). Uniflow.

Batten, T. R. (1957). *Communities and their development*. Oxford University Press. https://doi.org/10.1017/S1373971900078471

Boafo-Arthur, K. (2018). Structural adjustment, policies, and democracy in Ghana. In K. Konadu-Agyemang (Ed.), *IMF and World Bank sponsored structural adjustment programs in Africa* (pp. 241–271). Routledge.

Bob-Milliar, G. (2005). Non-governmental organizations in Ghana: Profit making organisations. http://www.ghanaweb.com/GhanaHomePage/features/NGOs-In-Ghana-Profit-Making-Organisations-80271

Bondarenko, D. M. (2014). Communality: A foundation of the African historical, cultural, and socio-political tradition. In A. M. Vasilliev (Ed.), *Society and politics in Africa: Traditional, transitional and new* (pp. 680–681). HSE.

Bonye, S. Z. (2011). The role of traditional festivals in action planning, advocacy and social accountability. *World Journal of Young Researchers, 1*(3), 32–39.

Bratton, M. (1989). The politics of government-NGO relations in Africa. *World Development, 17*(4), 569–587.

Chirwa, E., Dorward, A., Kachule, R., Kumwenda, I., Kydd, J., Poole, N., Poulton, C., & Stockbridge, M. (2005). Walking tightropes: supporting farmer organizations for market access. *Natural Resource Perspectives, 9*, 1–6.

Clarke, N. (2011). Globalising care? Town twinning in Britain since 1945. *Geoforum, 42*(1), 115–125.

Cremer, R. D., De Bruin, A., & Dupuis, A. (2001). International sister-cities: Bridging the global-local divide. *American Journal of Economics and Sociology, 60*(1), 377–401.

Crook, R. C. (2003). Decentralisation and poverty reduction in Africa: The politics of local-central relations. *Public Administration and Development: The International Journal of Management Research and Practice, 23*(1), 77–88.

Cullity, G. (2006). Beneficence. In R. E. Ashcroft, A. Dawson, H. Draper, & J. R. McMillan (Eds.), *Principles of health care ethics* (2nd ed., pp. 19–26). John Wiley and Sons. https://doi.org/10.1002/9780470510544.ch3

Dai, L. (2008). Reducing CAGE distances through international sister cities: a relational view of strategic alliances. *Competition Forum, 6*(1), 168–181.

Debrah, E. (2016). Decentralization, district chief executives, and district assemblies in Ghana's fourth republic. *Politics and Policy, 44*(1), 135–164. https://doi.org/10.1111/polp.12146

Dejenie, M. (2003). Module III: Urban financial management prepared for MDP programme. Adisa Ababa, ETH. https://docplayer.net/18856913-Module-iii-urban-financialmanagement-prepared-for-mdp-program.html

Der Bebelleh, F., & Nobabumah, A. S. (2013). Political decentralization and local participation in Ghana: Perspectives from the upper west region. *Public Policy and Administration Research, 3*(11), 12–25.

Diao, X, Magalhaes, E. & Silver, J. (2019). Cities and rural transformation: a spatial analysis of rural livelihoods in Ghana. *World Development, 121,* 141–157. https://doi.org/10.1016/j.worlddev.2019.05.001

Donkoh, W. J. (2011). The developmental and HIV/AIDS-fighting roles of traditional rulers: Agency of festivals. In D. I. Ray, T. Quinlan, K. Sharma & T. A. O. Clarke (Eds.), *Reinventing African chieftaincy in the age of aids, gender, governance, and development* (pp. 121–147). University of Calgary Press.

Dunham, A. (1970). Community development—Whither bound? *Community Development Journal, 5*(2), 85–93. https://doi.org/10.1093/cdj/5.2.85

Du Sautoy, P. (1958). *Community development in Ghana.* Oxford University Press.

Evans.W., (2015). *Columbus becomes sister city to Accra, Ghana.* Columbus Underground. https://www.columbusunderground.com/columbus-sister-city-accra-ghana

Falola, T. (2007). The Amistad's legacy: Reflections on the spaces of Colonization. *Fourth* Annual Distinguished AMISTAD Lecture. *Central Connecticut State University, 14*(2), 6–7. https://web.ccsu.edu/afstudy/upd14-2.html#Amistad

Friedman, M. (1991). The practice of partiality. *Ethics, 101*(4), 818–835. https://www.jstor.org/stable/2381666

Government of Ghana. (2009). *Department of Social Welfare: NGO registration.* Ministry of Employment and Social Welfare.

Government of Ghana. (2003). *Ghana Labour Act, 2003 (Act 651).* Government of Ghana.

Government of Ghana. (1993). *Local Government Act, 1993 (Act 462).*

Government of Ghana. (1992). *The 4th Republican Constitution of Ghana.*

Gyan, C., & Ampomah, A. O. (2016). Effects of stakeholder conflicts on community development projects in Kenyase. *SAGE Open,* 1–8. https://doi.org/10.1177/2158244016635254

Gyan, C., & Baffoe, M. (2014). "I Feel Like I Don't Exist in This Community": Stakeholders' thought on their noninvolvement in community development initiatives in Kenyase. *Public Policy and Administration Research, 4*(12), 1–8.

Holmen, H. (2010). *Snakes in paradise: NGOs and the Aid Industry in Africa.* Kumarian Press. https://www.tandfonline.com/doi/abs/10.1080/02589001.2010.499237

International Monetary Fund [IMF] Conditionality. (2019, March 5). *IMF Conditionality.* https://www.imf.org/en/About/Factsheets/Sheets /2016/08/02/21/28/IMF-Conditionality

Jephias, M. (2015). Skewed rural development policies and economic malaise in Zimbabwe. *African Journal of History and Culture*, 7(7), 142–151. https://doi.org/10.5897/AJHC2015.0269

Kuusi, S. (2009). *Aspects of local self-government: Ghana North-South local government cooperation program*. The Association of Finnish Local and Regional Authorities.

Kyei, P. O. (1998). *Non-Governmental Organisations and Poverty Alleviation in Nadowli District: Views from the Rural Poor*. GTZ.

Lawson, V. (2007). Geographies of care and responsibility. *Annals of the Association of American Geographers*, 97(1), 1–11. https://doi.org/10.1111/j.1467-8306.2007.00520.x

Lentz, C. (2006). Decentralisation, the state and conflicts over local boundaries in Northern Ghana. *Development and Change*, 37(4), 901–919. https://doi.org/10.1111/j.1467-7660.2006.00506.x

Mansuri, G., & Rao, V. (2004). Community-based and -driven development: A critical review. *Policy, Research Working Paper; no. WPS 3209*. World Bank Group. http://documents.worldbank.org/curated/en/399341468761669595/Community-based-and-driven-development-A-critical-review.

Mapuva, J. (2015). The controversies of devolution in Zimbabwe. *International Journal of Political Science and Development*, 3(5), 183-192. http://www.academicresearchjournals.org/IJPSD/Index.html

Mbiti, J. S. (1990). *African religions and philosophy*. Heinemann.

Michaels, A. (2015). *Columbia to celebrate sister city of tema during Ghana Fest 2*. https://www.baltimoresun.com/maryland/howard/columbia/ph-ho-cf-ghana-fest2-tema-ca-1105-20151030-story.html

Midgley, J., Hall, A., Hardiman, M., & Narine, D. (1986). *Community participation, social development and the state*. Methuen.

Nukunya, G. K. (2003). *Tradition and change in Ghana: An introduction to sociology* (2nd ed.). Ghana Universities Press.

Offei-Aboagye, E. (2000). *Promoting the participation of women in local governance and development: The case of Ghana Institute of Local Government Studies, Legon, Ghana*. Maastricht Press. https://ecdpm.org/wp-content/uploads/2013/10/DP-18-Promoting-Participation-Women-Local-Governance-Ghana-2000.pdf

Offei-Aboagye, E. (2004). Promoting gender sensitivity in local governance in Ghana. *Development in Practice*, 14(6), 753–760. https://doi.org/10.1080/0961452042000283987

Ogbujah, C. (2014). African cultural values and inter-communal relations: The case with Nigeria. *Developing Country Studies*, 4(24), 208–217.

Okia, O. (2012). *Communal labor in colonial Kenya*. Palgrave Macmillan. https://doi.org/10.1057/9780230392960

Organization for Economic Cooperation and Development (OECD). (2010). *Civil society and its effectiveness: Findings, recommendations and good practice, better aid*. https://doi.org/10.1787/9789264056435-en

Said, E. (1978). *Orientalism*. Pantheon.

Schenck, R., Nel, H. & Louw, H. (2010). *Introduction to participatory community practice*. Unisa Press.

Seini, W., & Nyanteng, V. (2003). Afrint macro study: Ghana macro report. *Institute of Statistics, Social & Economic Research, ISSER, Legon, Ghana*. http://www.keg.lu.se/en/sites/keg.lu.se.en/files/a5.pdf

Singer, P. (1972). Famine, affluence and morality. *Philosophy and Public Affairs, 1*, 229–243.

Smyth, R. (2004). The roots of community development in colonial office policy and practice in Africa. *Social Policy and Administration, 38*(4), 418–436. https://doi.org/10.1111/j.1467-9515.2004.00399.x

Throup, D. W., Cooke, J. G., & Downie, R. (2011). *Ghana: Assessing risks to stability*. https://www.csis.org/analysis/ghana.

Tsey, K. (2010). The role of customs and beliefs in legitimating community development participation in Botoku, rural Ghana: Implications for substance abuse prevention. *Forum on Public Policy*, 1–13. https://www.forumonpublicpolicy.co.uk/

Tsey, K., & Short, S. D. (1995). From head loading to the iron horse: The unequal health consequences of railway construction and expansion in the Gold Coast, 1898–1929. *Social Science and Medicine, 40*(5), 613–621. https://doi.org/10.1016/0277-9536(95)80005-5

Villiers, J. C. (2009). Success factors and the city-to-city partnership management process—From strategy to alliance capability. *Habitat International, 33*(2), 149–156. https://doi.org/10.1016/j.habitatint.2008.10.018

Weiner, L. (2003). What we owe to distant others. *Philosophy, Politics, and Economics, 3*, 283–304. https://doi.org/10.1177/1470594X030023001

Weyers, M. L. (2011). *The theory and practice of community work: A southern African perspective*. Keurkopie.

World Bank. (2010). *Mining community development agreements—Practical experiences and field studies*. www.sdsg.org/wpcontent/uploads/2011/06/CDA-Report-FINAL.pdf

ENDNOTES

1. It is the traditional self-help and mutual aid techniques used by cocoa farmers during the pre-colonial and colonial period.
2. It is an unpaid labor which was intermittently done by citizens of French colonies during the colonial period.

CHAPTER 2

CONTRIBUTION OF AFRICAN TRADITIONAL KNOWLEDGE TO COMMUNITY DEVELOPMENT THEORY AND PRACTICE IN AFRICA

William Abur

ABSTRACT

This chapter discusses the concept of community development, the role of the community development workers in relation to the Ubuntu philosophy and values. The chapter is a critical reflection based on work experiences, reflection, and teaching content in community development subject. It is argued that Ubuntu values and principles are important for community development approaches. Ubuntu principles and values are focused on vulnerable populations and are very much aligned with the bottom-up community development approach. These principles and values are essential for community development practitioners that want to invest their time and skills in working with vulnerable community groups. Ubuntu philosophy is an indigenous philosophy that offers a different perspective and approach around the world. This philosophy is useful for decolonizing the top-down approach, which is often forced on vulnerable community groups by the aid workers or colonizers. Devaluing local community knowledge and skills has been one of the biggest problems in Africa. This is one of the reasons why many projects failed to meet the needs of the community groups. There is still more work to be done to eradicate the use of the top-down approach among international and governmental organizations that work with vulnerable community groups. This chapter presents Ubuntu concepts and values as an alternative way of doing community development work with community groups in Africa.

Keywords: African knowledge, Ubuntu philosophy, community development, theory and practice

Introduction

Working in the community development space is about engaging with local community groups and community members in the process of identifying local issues and delivering services to these communities. The concept of community development is about working with communities to create projects that benefit the needs of local community groups. The deliberate engagement of community members in the discussion of fundamental activities and services, such as family and child welfare, farming, community leadership/governing, human rights issues, and small business start-up, is critically needed in communities in Africa. The general aim of community projects is to engage people in the development process to create healthy communities and to allow community members to take ownership of community projects through participation in discussions, decision-making and/or leadership. It is about bringing people together and empowering them to serve themselves, their families, and their community members. Community development approach and practice from the Ubuntu perspective is deeply rooted in human connection. Connection from individual to individual, family to family, and community to community; these interconnections promote support and empowerment among community members. This Ubuntu spirit exists in many African societies, with individuals helping each other in the spirit of humaneness and solidarity.

Ubuntu Philosophy

Ubuntu philosophy has become an important theme for education in community development, social work, and others. It is a centered on African knowledge and has received a global recognition as indigenous African philosophy with a holistic worldview about humanity and environment (Abur & Mugumbate, 2022; Mugumbate et al., 2023).

> Africans believe in something that is difficult to render in English. We call it Ubuntu, Botho. It means the essence of being human. You know it when it is there and when it is absent. It speaks about humaneness, gentleness, hospitality, putting yourself out on behalf of others, being vulnerable. It embraces

> compassion and toughness. It recognizes that my humanity is bound up in yours, for we can only be human together. (Tutu & Tutu, 1989, p. 71, as cited in Koen, 2021)

In many African cultures, Ubuntu values are present in community practices that involve group work, such as farming, community celebrations, community gatherings, family meetings, youth teaching and other important events. Ubuntu values are best practiced when community elders gather under big trees to discuss community issues, socialize, and tell stories to younger generations as a way of passing on knowledge and skills (Mugumbate & Nyanguru, 2013). In other words, Ubuntu values are well promoted in many African community groups through communal meetings and sometimes in a spiritual form rather than in individualist and materialist forms (Charles, 2007; Mungai, 2014).

Ubuntu philosophy is embedded in community development, social work, and community welfare with an emphasis on humanity and care for the community rather than politics. However, war and conflict have significantly impacted community development practices in some parts of Africa. War has truly disrupted community harmony and has indeed reduced the principles and practice of Ubuntu. There is a great need for the promotion of Ubuntu values and principles to bring harmony to societies that are affected by war and conflict. The community spirit and social fabric have been uprooted and diminished in many African countries affected by war and conflict.

> A person is a person through other persons. None of us comes into the world fully formed. We would not know how to think, or walk, or speak, or behave as human beings unless we learned it from other human beings. We need other human beings in order to be human. (Tutu, 2004, p. 25)

There are many positive aspects of African societies and communities that should be promoted locally and internationally. The concept of community is one of the strongest philosophies in many African societies. In reference to the above quotation, community development can be understood in terms of human development. A person can be a person through other people in his or her life (Abur & Mugumbate, 2022). The African concept of Ubuntu is rooted in the well-being of people and the development of people, including through raising children and young leaders in the community (Abur & Mugumbate, 2022). A person can only be strong and fully grown when she or he is supported by the community. Politicians cannot be politicians without the community behind them. Children and youths are raised by the community and mentored by the community. Therefore, the roles of community elders such as aunties, uncles and community leaders are very powerful in African communities (Abur & Mugumbate, 2022).

Elders in the community have the important role of taking care of vulnerable people, including children. For instance, when a person misbehaves in the village by acting in a way that threatens community harmony and unity, the elders are likely to call it out and take action to prevent threats to the community and future bad behavior (Buqa, 2015). When the community is threatened, the elders must come together to find a solution to protect the community and the individuals in it. Ubuntu philosophy is about helping one another to grow and supporting community development for the progression of society. Ubuntu values are expressed through compassion, dignity, humanity, reciprocity, social justice, communalities, and mutuality in community building (Buqa, 2015; Lutz, 2009).

Community Development

Traditionally, in Africa, community development activities often took place during farming seasons and harvesting periods. Communities would come together to assist each other on their farms to ensure that no one was left behind. The research evidence suggests that, prior to this, different community groups were engaged in community development work by working together on farms to support themselves. Villagers used to come together to meet and discuss welfare issues in families and the community (Eweje, 2006). In recent decades, the concept of community development has focused on assisting individuals in developing their skills and knowledge. The primary aim of community development is to support the development of local community members and build the capacity to implement projects that bring economic benefits and social development to the community. It is about empowering community members to make use of their local resources and knowledge to deliver services to their vulnerable community members, such as children, youths, the elderly, and women. In some cases, community development is about mobilizing resources, such as organizing fundraising for projects and assisting community members with the planning and implementation of projects. The Western approach to community development came later, with communities expected to work with organizations on developments such as schools, clinics, water projects, feeding projects, and road projects. However, these organizations sometimes failed community members by not empowering them with sustainable knowledge and skills (Mugumbate et al., 2022). This is particularly problematic for international organizations involved in community development work in Africa. Most of these international organizations use a top-down approach instead of a bottom-up approach when working with community groups in Africa (Mugumbate et al., 2022; Sindima, 1990). Africans define community as a group of members that come together, do things together, speak a common language or have a common interest and are either related by blood, marriage, or share a common environment (Mugumbate et al., 2022; Sindima, 1990). More importantly, in traditional African values, community members protect each other from common enemies. Community development helps community members to achieve their social goals and group aspirations and contributes to human development, environmental protection, business development, and so on. Community development work can assist local community groups in maintaining their community values by supporting community members to pass on their knowledge, skills, and experience to the next generation through education and other activities. The concept of being together as a community makes life meaningful for community members by creating projects or activities that can support the community to grow. Community activities should create a sense of connectedness and togetherness (Mugumbate et al., 2022; Sindima, 1990).

Example of Community Development in South Sudan

In the author's village in South Sudan, community development involves community members supporting each other during the farming season. Community members also come together to discuss leadership roles and responsibilities as a way of governing themselves. Villagers come together as members of a village to help each other on farms. This is where the practice of the community takes place, where people take responsibility to protect children in a village by ensuring that every child is raised by the entire village. Children are taught by the entire village to become a responsible citizen. This is where the great work of community development practice is rooted in African traditional knowledge.

These practices are based on Ubuntu values and practices in many parts of Africa. As a social worker who has worked in the community development space and has taught social work and community courses, the traditional community development concept is strong in many parts of Africa, particularly in remote villages where people come together to connect, perform cultural celebrations and rituals, and are empowered to protect their villages and cattle camps from enemies. This is a significant contribution of African traditional knowledge to community development theory and practice.

Community Development Approach From the Ubuntu Philosophy

Community development is driven by a people-centered perspective (Mugumbate et al., 2022). Community development from the Ubuntu perspective is based on the following working values and principles:

- Development that supports all people by displaying respect and promoting the dignity of the local people.
- Families are valued.
- Respect for the communality or collective approach.
- Aspirations for the present and next generation.
- Addressing present issues and future issues.
- Respect for culture and the beliefs of the people.
- Allowing people to initiate or be part of the co-design and co-production processes (Mugumbate et al., 2022).

These principles are based on a bottom-up approach or inside-out development approach which prioritizes local knowledge and skills. This approach encourages community members to work side-by-side with non-government organizations and government organizations to address community development issues together.

Decolonizing Community Development Practices

Now is the time to decolonize community development by rejecting the top-down approach used by international development workers when working with local community groups in Africa and other developing countries. Forced labor occurred between (1900–1946) in many African communities that were controlled or colonized by colonizers. Force labor was a total exploitation and dehumanization of African Ubuntu values/principles (Abur & Mugumbate, 2022). Forced labor contributed to increase the industrialization of the colonizers' interests and their countries, but careless about the people and community groups in Africa. This was tragic to many community groups in Africa. It is the right time now to move away from forced labor and top-down approaches when working with community groups in Africa (Mugumbate et al., 2022).

Top-Down Approach

Research indicates that the top-down approach is derived from a colonization view and does not respect local community knowledge and skills (Abur & Mugumbate, 2022; Mugumbate et al., 2022). The following are some examples of the top-down approach observed within the international community development approach:

- Planning of projects without the involvement of local community members.
- Treating local community members as incapable.
- Forcing ideas or initiatives for local community groups.
- Prioritizing the needs of funding bodies or expertise outside of the community.
- Assuming that development can be handed over to local community groups.
- A lack of respect for local knowledge and skills (Mugumbate et al., 2023).

The use of the top-down approach within developing communities must be dismantled as it is not useful for many local community groups. Instead, it serves those holding power and positions in governments and other non-governmental organizations by addressing their interests instead of those of vulnerable community groups (Bubar et al., 2022; Mugumbate et al., 2022). There are many consequences of the top-down approach for local community groups, as this concept is heavily rooted in the colonization approach and often neglects the needs of vulnerable populations, such as indigenous community groups (Bubar et al., 2022; Mugumbate et al., 2022).

Bottom-Up Approach

The community development approach from the Ubuntu philosophy is the opposite of this top-down approach. It is about taking care of vulnerable populations and the natural environment without chasing power. Moreover, the Ubuntu approach works against racism and discrimination because the Ubuntu approach is an inclusive practice based on humanness, togetherness, wellbeing of the people, and care for the community and environment (Mugumbate et al., 2022; Mugumbate et al., 2023)

Top-Down Versus Bottom-Up Approach

It is very important for community development practitioners to be aware of both top-down and button-up approaches to community development. The top-down approach comes from the leadership development space and occurs when leaders in positions of power make decisions without consulting or engaging with junior staff members. This approach has often been used by international community development organizations when making important decisions on behalf of vulnerable community groups. People who use the top-down approach think that a decision about a community development project can be made quickly without wasting time on the consultation process with local community groups or community members.

In contrast, the bottom-up approach is about engaging local community members in decision-making about projects that are of relevance to the local community. The advantage of this approach is that community members or teams within local community groups are given the opportunity to voice any concerns about community development projects. They are also given the opportunity to participate in designing community development projects and to guide the delivery of services according to the needs of the community (Emery & Flora, 2006). The bottom-up approach ensures that local community members or community groups work collaboratively with international organizations or government organizations in a power-sharing or balanced way. The bottom-up approach promotes team building and community engagement among local community groups or members. The problem with the bottom-up approach is that it is time-consuming due to the detailed steps that need to be taken to engage local community groups in these projects. However, it is less risky, or problematic compared with the top-down approach, from a community development perspective (Mugumbate & Nyanguru, 2013; Mugumbate et al., 2023).

Working With Communities and Groups

It is essential that community development workers understand how to work with communities and groups. All community practitioners need to have well-developed skills for community work. One of the important skills for such workers is the ability to facilitate a community forum or group discussion. The facilitation of small community groups is fundamental in community development work (Mugumbate et al., 2013). The facilitator of community groups should consider the differing skill levels of community members. Some people may bring high levels of skills and experience, while others in the group may be inexperienced (Abur, 2020). The job of the facilitator/s of the group is to ensure that all members in the group are well supported to participate effectively. There are several stages of working with groups. These stages are forming, storming, norming, performing, and adjourning (Tuckman, 1965, 2001).

1. **The forming stage** begins with orienting the group and testing the dependence of the group.

2. **The storming stage** is when there is resistance to the influence of the group, especially when there are task requirements.
3. **The norming stage** is when the members of the group are open to discussion. For example, they start to discuss the topic or start introducing new topics.
4. **The performing stage** is when group discussion reaches a constructive stage and action can occur based on the topic of discussion.
5. **The adjourning stage** is when the group becomes disengaged in the discussion. This stage can be uncomfortable for some group members because of anxiety, separation, and termination. Some group members may experience sadness because the group is ending.

Valuing Indigenous Knowledge

Local communities have a wealth of knowledge, including in relation to environmental management (Abur & Mugumbate, 2022; Mugumbate et al., 2023). This local knowledge is often neglected by organizations working with community groups; instead, these groups impose foreign concepts of development on local communities. This is something that all emerging community development workers need to avoid by considering the local knowledge in any given community. Many concepts of community development used in many countries in Africa are based on the work of colonizers (Abur & Mugumbate, 2022). Ubuntu approach is one of the community development concepts that valued local knowledge when working with local communities. Local communities have vast indigenous knowledge and systems that can be utilized in community development initiatives. Local community knowledge is passed from generation to generation by community elders or leaders (Abur, 2018). This is often achieved through storytelling, arts, and intuitions (Mugumbate et al., 2022). Local knowledge includes traditional knowledge of the environment, traditional knowledge of leadership, traditional knowledge of farming, local knowledge of technical matters, local knowledge of conflict management, local knowledge of child-rearing, and local knowledge of science and medicine (Iloka, 2016). It is very important to value local knowledge from the planning phase of community development initiatives through to the end of the project. Local community members are more likely to take ownership of the project or initiative when they see their ideas being incorporated into the project (Abur & Mugumbate, 2022; Mugumbate et al., 2022). Local knowledge is useful in providing communities with ways to address local problems; community members know what is needed in their present situation. For example, in some countries in Africa, local community members know the time for the cultivation of crops and the rearing of livestock based on their indigenous knowledge (Mugumbate et al., 2023).

Challenges in Community Development Work

Working with community groups can be exciting and challenging at the same time due to the different needs of community groups. My work experiences with different community groups taught me enough to know some of the challenges in community development work (Emery & Flora, 2006). The key challenge in working with community groups is developing trust for the project and among community members (Abur, 2018). A community development worker should start by engaging community members to build trust (Shevellar & Westoby, 2018). Other challenges for community development work include managing competing priorities and balancing differences, assumptions, beliefs, values, and power within community groups (National Research Council, 2009). A lack of community development skills and approaches can be problematic and can cause serious mistrust and a lack of participation in initiatives (IvyPanda, 2022; Shevellar & Westoby, 2018). Community members can be disengaged due to mistrust. Sometimes, the work of community development practitioners involves persuading community members to participate in development initiatives. This can be achieved through the dissemination of information about development projects and raising awareness using community language and channels of communication (Shevellar & Westoby, 2018). Community education and awareness raising are part of community empowerment. Communication must be clear and simple for community members to understand. This can help community members to feel that the development initiative is for them instead of viewing it as a project for outsiders and not requiring local contributions. When engaging community members, it is essential to understand that community members not engaged in development initiatives are a significant source of knowledge about issues facing the community (Bradshaw, 2007; IvyPanda, 2022). They may already know the solutions to their local problems, such as youth issues or crime-related issues (Shevellar & Westoby, 2018).

Conclusion

This chapter presents community development concepts and the role of community development worker using Ubuntu philosophy as a way of decolonizing the community development concepts which were brought by the colonizers to Africa. The biggest problem with the top-down approach is that community members are often excluded from decision-making on issues that are of concern to their lives or community groups. This approach is opposite to the Ubuntu values that are rooted in caring for humanity. Community development workers play a significant role in providing essential services to improve the lives of people in cities and villages. The role of a community development practitioner is to connect people with services and community groups by creating activities that bring community groups together to share their knowledge on important community issues. This is the foundation of community development work. Community development work is also about helping people to express their needs and concerns on political matters that are related to their local environment and community. Students within the field of community development should have a passion for social justice issues, a passion to help other people, good communication skills, good leadership skills, and be willing to work with community organizations to promote positive change in people. Readers of this chapter are encouraged to reflect on Ubuntu values and to try to express compassion, dignity, harmony, humanness, gentleness, hospitality, kindness, and empathy to vulnerable people in their community work and beyond.

REFERENCES

Abur, W. (2018). *Settlement strategies for the South Sudanese community in Melbourne: An Analysis of employment and sport participation* [Doctoral dissertation, Victoria University]. http://vuir.vu.edu.au/36189/

Abur, W. (2020). Teaching resilience skills to social work students and others. *African Journal of Social Work, 10*(2), 23–31.

Abur, W., & Mugumbate, J. R. (2022). Experiences of Ubuntu and implications of African philosophy for social work in Australia. *Advances in Social Work and Welfare Education, 23*(2), 21–37.

Bradshaw, T. K. (2007). Theories of poverty and anti-poverty programs in community development. *Community Development, 38*(1), 7–25.

Bubar, R., Kelly, T., Souza, C., Lovato-Romero, L., & Bundy-Fazioli, K. (2022). Disrupting settler colonial microaggressions: Implications for social work. *International Journal of Social Work Values and Ethics, 19*(2), 47–77. https://doi.org/10.55521/10-019-206

Buqa, W. (2015). Storying Ubuntu as a rainbow nation. *Verbum et Ecclesia, 36*(2), 1–8.

Charles, E. (2007). *How can I bring Ubuntu as a living standard of judgement into the academy? Moving beyond decolonisation through societal reidentification and guiltless recognition* [Doctoral dissertation, University of Bath]. United Kingdom.

Emery, M., & Flora, C. (2006). Spiraling-up: Mapping community transformation with community capitals framework. *Community Development, 37*(1), 19–35. https://doi.org10.1080/15575330609490152

Eweje, G. (2006). The role of MNEs in community development initiatives in developing countries: Corporate social responsibility at work in Nigeria and South Africa. *Business & Society, 45*(2), 93–129.

Iloka, N. G. (2016). Indigenous knowledge for disaster risk reduction: An African perspective. *Jàmbá: Journal of Disaster Risk Studies, 8*(1), a272. http://dx.doi.org/10.4102/jamba.v8i1.272

IvyPanda. (2022). *Challenges of community development problem solution essay.* https://ivypanda.com/essays/challenges-of-community-development/

Koen, M. (2021). Sustainable future for early childhood: Applying the African Ubuntu philosophy to contribute to the holistic development of young children. *Sustainable Development in Africa*, 131–146.

Lutz, D. W. (2009). African Ubuntu philosophy and global management. *Journal of Business Ethics, 84*(3), 313–328.

Mugumbate, J., Mupedziswa, R, Twikirize, J, Mthethwa, Desta, A., & Oyinlola, O. (2023) *Understanding Ubuntu and its contribution to social work education in Africa and other regions of the world.* Social Work Education, https://doi.org10.1080/02615479.2023.2168638

Mugumbate, J., & Nyanguru, A. (2013). Exploring African philosophy: The value of Ubuntu in social work. *African Journal of Social Work, 3*(1), 82–100.

Mugumbate, J. R., Tarusikirwa, M. C., Nyoni, C., Mtetwa, E., Nyikahadzoyi, K., Dhemba and Nyaruwata, L. T. (2022). People-centred development (PCD): Philosophies, key concepts and approaches to teaching, learning and practice. *People Centred—The Journal of Development Administration, 7*(1), 1–12.

Mungai, N. W. (2014). Ubuntu approaches to working with immigrant communities. In K. Goel, V. Pu Ila, & A. P. Francis (Eds.), *Community work: Theories, experiences, and challenges* (pp. 214–235). Niruta.

National Research Council. (2009). *Focusing on children's health: Community approaches to addressing health disparities: Workshop summary.* National Academies Press.

Shevellar, L., & Westoby, P. (Eds.). (2018). Wicked problems and community development: An introductory essay. In *The Routledge handbook of community development research* (pp. 3–19). Routledge.

Sindima, H. (1990). Community of life: Ecological theology in African perspective. In C. Birch & Willam Eakin (Eds.), *Liberating life: Contemporary approaches in ecological theology* (pp. 137–147).

Tuckman, B. W. (1965). Developmental sequence in small groups. *Psychological Bulletin, 63*(6), 384.

Tuckman, B. W. (2001). Developmental sequence in small groups. *Group Facilitation, 3*, 66.

Tutu, D. M. (2004). *God has a dream: A vision of hope for our time.* Rider.

CHAPTER 3

COMMUNITY DEVELOPMENT IN UGANDA

A Historical Inquiry in the Practice of Meeting Community Needs

Venesio Bwambale Bhangyi and Senkosi Moses Balyejjusa

ABSTRACT

Community development in Uganda is rooted in both historical collective indigenous ideals as well the transformational endeavors of the post-independence governments. In the past two decades, community development has gained heightened attention as the country seeks to transform its society from a peasant low-income state to a middle-income society. This is evidenced by social-economic transformation being the theme of the past and present national development plans in this period. This chapter, therefore, discusses community development in Uganda as a historical practice of meeting community needs. It explores the historical roots and contemporary influences on community development in Uganda. It then outlines the challenges and opportunities of community development in the country. Using the human needs thinking as its theoretical framework, the chapter is constructed using a qualitative approach to guide systematic literature review, the analysis of secondary data and the resultant comparative thematic analysis. Recommendations that challenge the temporariness, politicization and foreignness of community development practice are offered. These include, among others, technical professionals leading the design of sustainable policies, building shared interests that incorporate technical and political considerations, the integration into policies of local development experiences, and building internal development funding through domestic mobilization of resources

Community Development Practice in Africa: Putting Theory Into Practice, pp. 35–49
Copyright © 2024 by Information Age Publishing
www.infoagepub.com
All rights of reproduction in any form reserved.

and inputs. It then draws conclusions suggesting that Uganda's community development could yield more if linked with bottom-up processes, informed by local community experiences/voices, and integrated with agrarian livelihood practices in which a majority of both rural and urban communities derive wellbeing.

Keywords: community needs, community development, social development, social transformation, community practice, development politics, Uganda

Introduction

Community development in Uganda has gained heightened attention in the last two decades as the country seeks to transform its society from a peasant low-income state into middle income society. This is evidenced by its inclusion as the anchoring theme in the country's past and present development plans (Republic of Uganda, 2020). According to the Ministry of Gender, Labour, and Social Development (2016), this is aimed at providing a framework for mobilizing and empowering communities. This in turn is intended to facilitate communities to appreciate, participate, demand and uptake social services. In the end, it is anticipated to create community pathways and resources to improve their social-economic wellbeing. As such, community development has been viewed as the magic bullet to mobilize communities into collective action, galvanize them to engage in a productive income economy, and generate solutions to common social problems (Ministry of Local Government, 2021; Republic of Uganda, 2020).

In view of the above, this chapter engages with community development in Uganda. It explores the conceptual, historical, and contemporary debates that inform the country's community development policy. The historical factors in the early independence development euphoria are discussed. The contemporary factors such as efforts in the public and non-public sector actors are also presented. These factors provide an understanding of current community development policy and interventions that largely consider communities as receivers rather than providers of development. As such, the challenges to community development in Uganda, including excessive politicization of development and over reliance on externally generated development models that continue to undermine local development thinking are articulated. Available opportunities such as the existing institutional framework and historical experiences in community led initiatives are discussed. These should in part constitute the foundation on which further community development actions can be built. Proposal for action by policy makers, practitioners, and leaders are made including building grass-root support for development policy, strategies for the depoliticization of community development, and fostering meaningful collaborations between technocrats and communities.

Consequently, the chapter is structured beginning with an introduction to the ideals and conceptions of community development in Uganda. This is followed by placing community development in the human needs thinking, thereby theoretically framing it as a response to community needs. The history and evolution of community development in Uganda is then discussed, placing attention on the actions of the multiple actors. The chapter then explores the challenges and opportunities of community development in Uganda. It ends with a discussion of the recommendations and conclusions.

Methodology and Approach

The arguments in this chapter are constructed using a qualitative approach to guide a systematic literature review and secondary data analysis. Data is sourced from government and non-profit sector documents. Historical (archival) and contemporary documents, reports, journal articles and other web-based sources were engaged. Such documents were purposively selected for referencing community development, social development, and or community interventions. In addition, data sources and documents on the Uganda country context were of primary interest to the authors and were also purposively selected for inclusion. These were supported by documents referencing community development in other contexts and from a variety of disciplines including social work, social welfare, social development, development economics, and political economy. Overall, 39 sources from the 91 exploratory list were selected for detailed analysis. Comparative thematic analysis of the literature and documents was then conducted. The resultant themes and sub-themes constitute the building blocks of the arguments in the various sections of this chapter.

Conceptualization of Community Development in Uganda

In Uganda, a community is defined as a group of people living in a geographical area or who share a common culture (including interests) and an organized social structure that exhibits some awareness of their common identity (Ministry of Gender, Labour, and Social Development [MOGLSD], 2016). Community development also refers to frameworks for the mobilization and empowerment of communities to appreciate, participate, demand, and uptake social services with the aim of improving their socioeconomic indicators of wellbeing (MOGLSD, 2016). This development is expected to address human progress that is equitable and empowers vulnerable and marginalized groups to participate fully in development initiatives. When linked with social transformation, community development is a process of enabling change and development of society through empowering communities to harness their potential (MOGLSD, 2016).

The National Development Plan (NDP III) refers to community development as interventions that enhance the productivity and social wellbeing of the population through empowering families, communities, and citizens to embrace national values and actively participate in sustainable development (Republic of Uganda, 2020). On the other hand, the local economic development policy refers to community development as a process through which local governments, the private sector, and communities form partnerships to mobilize, manage, and invest resources effectively into socioeconomic ventures that stimulate locality growth and development (Ministry of Local Government, 2014).

From these conceptions, this chapter defines community development in Uganda as the policies, programs, and interventions that promote improved living conditions of local places, peoples, and communities through collaborative actions of public and non-public local and national actors through leveraging public, private, philanthropic, and community resources to meet human needs at both individual and community levels.

From this conceptualization, community development: (1) is a process of change and development through social transformation; (2) focuses on local geographical places or communities; (3) involves synergies of multiple actors through collaborations; (4) is intended to enhance wellbeing and living standards of local communities by adequately meeting needs; (5) comprises combinations of informal, indigenous, and formal interventions; (6) operates in awareness of indigenous cultures, knowledges, and aspirations; (7) promotes equity and empowerment of communities, including vulnerable and marginalized members; and (8) utilizes community resources, skills, and assets to spur transformation.

Community Development as a Response to Human Needs

There are diverse concepts presented in the literature as the focus of community development. These include human rights, livelihoods, assets, capabilities, poverty eradication, wellbeing, empowerments, and so forth (Haines, 2009; Ife, 2009). Despite this diversity, community development is essentially a response to human needs, both individual and community ones to promote wellbeing. The above concepts, presented as the focus of community development when critically analyzed in relation to human needs theories and lists of human needs, are either resources required to satisfy the human needs, or they are human needs themselves. For instance, assets, livelihood, and empowerment are resources (both physical and non-physical) that are required to satisfy human needs, while human rights and capabilities are human needs (Balyejjusa, 2019; Gough, 2014). Gough (2014) compares their (Doyal & Gough 1991) list of human needs to Nussbaum's (2011) human capabilities, and he argues that there is a great similarity in the two lists. The listed items of community assets by Haines (2009) are resources required to satisfy human needs. The assets are not an end in themselves but a means to an end, which is, meeting human needs to promote wellbeing.

The use of other terms rather than human needs is because human needs are perceived by these scholars as negative (e.g., Haines, 2009). For instance, Haines (2009) perceives human needs as problems or what is missing in the community, while Alkire (2006) perceives human needs as commodities. However, Balyejjusa (2022) argues that the concept of human needs has four meanings, that is, social problem, social solution, social resources, and social ends. Viewed that way, the concept of human needs is not entirely negative. In fact, it is more positive than negative, since it has three elements that are positive and one which is negative. Furthermore, the human needs concept is a familiar concept to the community members (Balyejjusa, 2022). It is therefore likely to enlist community participation in community development efforts and programs, which is a key prerequisite for sustainable community development. The needs that community development focuses on are diverse. They are biological, social, economic, psychological, and political in nature (Gasper, 2004; McLeod, 2014). However, this categorisation is not cast in stone, it is fluid in some instances. Some of the needs can fall under more than one category. For instance, education is both a social and an economic need. Unlike in the 1970s, when the focus was on the basic needs (survival needs), currently the focus is on needs that ensure that communities are sustainable and flourishing (Gasper, 2004; Mission for Community Development, 2022; Network for Community Development, 2022; Streeten et al., 1981).

Contemporary Community Development Practices in Uganda

This chapter analyses the processes of contemporary community development in Uganda by both public and non-public sector interventions since the country's independence in 1962. These actions are shaped by several forces, including public expansion of social services, humanitarian assistance, development assistance, growth in private capital, continuity of cultural institutions, and the formalization of self-help associations (Obote, 1962; Twikirize et al., 2019).

Public Sector Community Development

Community development in the early years (1962 to 1985) of independence was characterized by high expectations, regressions, and conflict. At independence in 1962, the Dr. Apollo Milton Obote government sought to build Uganda as a community of hope in which communities worked selflessly to meet personal, community, and national needs (Obote, 1962). A backbone for the expansion of public services in health, education, housing, agriculture, and road infrastructure was initiated. Unfortunately, the 1972 Asian expulsion ruined the national economy for the period 1972 to 1986, and the country descended into war and despair, with the successive governments unable to fathom a credible community services system (Makubuya, 2018).

In the 1980s to 1990s, public sector community development comprised of peace and recovery efforts to stabilize the country from the effects of the 1978–1986 war period (Republic of Uganda, 2015). Poverty reduction, establishment of community order, protection of fundamental human rights, and peace recovery-oriented developments were the key drivers of public community development policy (Mufumba, 2023). In the 1990s through the 2000s, public development resources were focused on improving human development indicators, thereby focusing on expanding education, health, water and sanitation, nutrition, and incomes (Republic of Uganda, 2020). From the middle 2000s, a shift was made toward building "hard community infrastructures"—physical construction projects that would, in turn, facilitate and support the delivery of social-economic services (Republic of Uganda, 2015). Power dams, national and community roads, water, and education infrastructures were setup across the country. From 2010 to 2022, public resources were more focused on developing programs that directly promote the welfare of communities, families, and vulnerable groups such as the women empowerment program and the youth livelihood program (Ministry of Finance, Planning and Economic Development, 2022; Republic of Uganda, 2020).

Non-Public Sector Community Development

In this sector, Non-Governmental Organizations (NGOs) have occupied a central place in meeting community development needs in the country

(Ministry of Internal Affairs, 2010). These comprise of multilateral humanitarian organizations such as the United Nations agencies, international non-profit organizations, national non-profit organizations, foundations, and faith-based organizations. Their influence started to grow in the 1980s and 1990s due to the huge community needs that resulted from years of civil war, the HIV/AIDS pandemic, extreme poverty, and weak capacities in government's community services (Ministry of Internal Affairs, 2010; Twikirize, 2014). Starting with humanitarian assistance, many have since evolved to provide developmental assistance. In recent times, some NGOs that emphasize human rights and democratic governance have stirred direct confrontation with government and the ruling class (NTV News, 2022). Despite such setbacks, national policy mandates them to work with government in enhancing social wellbeing of communities (Ministry of Gender, Labour, and Social Development, 2015, p. 38).

In addition, traditional cultural institutions have been actively engaged in Uganda's contemporary community development. The kingdoms of Buganda, Bunyoro, Tooro and Busoga traditionally implemented development programs through their prime Ministers' offices (Makubuya, 2018) and still do so. The *bataka* (residents) groups and *bulungi bwasi* (community service) models are examples of interventions built through Buganda kingdom programs, although communities also implement similar interventions on their own initiatives (Twikirize et al., 2019). It is also common for government interventions to confer duties and responsibilities to such entities (Ministry of Gender, Labour, and Social Development, 2015, p. 39). Tribal pride, responsibility, conformity, and identity are the cohesive forces that bind these communities into collective "communities of action."

Furthermore, community development is provided by Community-Based Organizations (CBOs) and informal actors. Thus CBOs, family helping systems, self-help associations, and other informal systems are drivers of community services (Twikirize et al., 2019). They are organized informally and voluntarily by communities, by local government community actors, or non-profit organizations change makers. Some of them, such as the burial societies, operate based on century-old traditions in meeting community needs. Others are formed to imitate the operations of formal entities such as village saving and loans associations that model micro-finance philosophies (Twikirize et al., 2019). Government has co-opted them as active agents of community change in some government interventions as well (Ministry of Local Government, 2021).

Challenges to Uganda's Community Development

Efforts and progress in Uganda's community development spectrum are riddled with numerous obstacles, both internal and external. While a number of these were articulated during the design of the second and third national development plans (Republic of Uganda, 2015, p. 8; Republic of Uganda, 2020, p. 2), others remained invisible to the country's top planners.

One such a challenge is that current community development is to a large extent externally driven. It is influenced by the sustainable development goals, the international civil society operations, and international donor community (NTV News, 2022; Republic of Uganda, 2020). These have impacted the ideology, design, and financing mechanisms of the local development policies. Despite the good intentions of such efforts, they remain in conflict and many times contradictory to local contexts, philosophies, development aspiration, and capacities. An example are interventions that build the social economy of women and exclude men. Yet men hold authority in majority households, which in many cases leads to family instabilities. Noyoo (2022) has argued, for example, that many development interventions for Africa that are externally initiated are incompatible with local realities and therefore do not work. For example, Western economic development models do not augur well with Uganda's mourning culture. While these economic models require workers to dedicate substantial hours to work, these same workers in Uganda are expected to mourn or support those in mourning for days or even weeks.

Another challenge arises from the over politicization of the community development landscape in the country. Public community development initiatives have been strongly tied to presidential and elective politics (Onyango-Obbo, 2022, 2023). Thus, old interventions are discarded for new ones every election period, leading to a temporariness of interventions. An example is when the Uganda women's empowerment program and the youth livelihood program were replaced by the parish development model (Ministry of Finance, Planning, and Economic Development, 2022). This logic underlying Uganda's political economy has become so flawed to the extent that even political support in many communities has not translated into positive development indicators (Kalinaki, 2022a). Such a politics has made it impossible for popular grass root socioeconomic demands to flow through the corridors of politics to reach the decision-making table. It has also led to a greater mismatch between resource allocation and development demands.

Furthermore, there is a growing recognition that indigenous voices, philosophies, and approaches to community development are getting crowded out of the country's development agenda (Tusasiirwe, 2022). While these philosophies and knowledge systems are tested, trusted, and ingrained in community cultures, and are relevant to local contexts (Twikirize & Spitzer, 2019), they are overlooked. At most, formal government efforts of learning from these indigenous initiatives are half-hearted and cannot inspire meaningful development interventions.

A final challenge to mention here is that community development interventions in the country are scattered across a range of ministries, departments, and non-profits (Republic of Uganda, 2014, 2015). In principle, the Office of the Prime Minister [OPM] is the coordination agency of all community development programs in the country. However, the national development plans (NDP II & III) have noted limited integration of development interventions as a challenge in development initiatives (Republic of Uganda, 2015, 2020). This has led to duplicated and isolation of community development actions. Thus, priorities get lost in these chaotic and "scatter-gun" pluralistic actions.

Opportunities in Uganda's Community Development

Despite these challenges, there are numerous opportunities in Uganda upon which a strong, sustained, and impactful community development practice can be built. The first opportunity is that community development now has its place in a central government ministry. The Department of Community Development was created in 2007 in the Ministry of Gender, Labour, and Social Development (MOGLSD, 2022). This department is envisioned as critical for service delivery in all social economic sectors. It has the mandate to mobilize communities to demand for services and uptake those services offered in various government sectors. It is operated through a chain of community development officers in districts, cities, municipalities, sub-counties, town councils, and parishes across the country. These ensure that communities are mobilized to uptake services, engage in income generation, attain literacy and numeracy (through formal schooling and adult literacy), and access other services to meet community development needs (MOGLSD, 2022).

A second opportunity is the integration of community development into national and local government planning. This is evidenced by explicit reference to community development strategies in the current national development plan III (Republic of Uganda, 2020). There is also strong emphasis on strategies that impact communities in the recently launched Parish Development Model (Ministry of Local Government, 2021). The parish development model is a government development intervention that is delivered through cooperatives formed at parish levels in communities. In addition, the national social protection policy references both public and community-based social protection approaches (MOGLSD, 2015). Third, there is strong political will at national level for community development. The current government led by the National Resistance Movement

(NRM) has outlined priorities for the social-economic transformation of the masses through addressing poverty, improving incomes and wellbeing (NRM, 2021).

Fourth, there are proposals to focus on mass transformation of communities and groups rather than individuals at both local, national, and international levels (Ministry of Local Government, 2021; Republic of Uganda, 2015; United Nations, 2015). The sustainable development goals are premised on leaving no one behind, while the national development plan of Uganda is themed on the transformation of the entire society. These promises provide opportunities to expand community development practice to reach all societies. As such, community development can contribute to meeting the unmet promise and potential in many Uganda villages to ignite a leap forward (Kalinaki, 2022b).

Fifth, there is a long and proud history of indigenous and informal self-help community development efforts to build upon (Ministry of Local Government, 2021; Twikirize et al., 2019; Twikirize & Spitzer, 2019). The potential of these experiences to Uganda's community development practice has been discussed at length in the recommendations section of this chapter. A final opportunity is the international social development efforts from which Uganda can benefit. The sustainable development goals (SDGs) provide the overall international policy direction for community development efforts in Uganda, while the community development interventions of international civil society agencies within Uganda can be enhanced to render relevance to local efforts. Learning from Balyejjusa (2019), when these SDGs are viewed through a human needs' language, they become universal and well known in daily community lives. This then extends possibilities for communities to participate in achieving the SDGs since they become relatable to the everyday needs that Uganda communities strive to address through community development.

Recommendations for Policy and Practice

This chapter makes four proposals toward building strong and impactful community development interventions in the country. These include: (1) a mix of technical and politicized approaches; (2) developing shared internal funding systems; (3) blending informal-indigenous-formal approaches; (4) and building collaborations between technocrats and communities.

Depoliticization of Community Development

Community development in Uganda should be depoliticized by placing the development processes in the technical hands of professionals. This will require a mixing of technical and politicized approaches to community development (Onyango-Obbo, 2023). This means that when politicians propose a development policy, the professionals in government departments and ministries should then take the lead in the design, development, and implementation of the policy. This will enable technical and community development practitioners to spearhead the community development agenda. This approach will then enable politicians to advance policies that are well researched, well prepared, and that have passed technical scrutiny. This may require restrain on the part of the political actors and their acceptance that the technical professionals can build their political wishes into solid community development interventions. In this way, the focus of development policy should be on technocratic indicators of development (Kalinaki, 2022a) such as improvements in poverty reduction, health, incomes, rural development, and family agricultural production.

Building Sustainable Internal Funding Capacities

Building in-country funding capacities is critical to the sustainability of the community development interventions. Thus, enhancing domestic resource mobilization for onward allocations to community development policy is important. This will require the transfer of more development resources to district local governments (Kalinaki, 2022a). In addition, legislative and administrative reforms that transfer development policy authority and resources to district governments and other dedicated community development agencies (Onyango-Obbo, 2023) are necessary. This is necessary because districts are located closer to communities than central government agencies. Attaching local district's development efforts for funding to development indicators in areas such as health, education, social service, and income economy of residents is also essential. Utilization of local community resources in self-help and lower local government development efforts is also critical (Republic of Uganda, 2014). To ensure equitable regional development, national level resources can be shared with districts through population and development-based indicators (Kalinaki, 2022a).

Integration of Indigenous, Informal, and Formal Approaches

There should be a strong acceleration of the integration of indigenous and informal self-help community development approaches into formal government community development interventions. This will require identification and understanding of the indigenous and informal community development approaches. Examples of such models include the *Bataka* groups and traditional child fostering systems (Twikirize & Spitzer, 2019). Other examples in Uganda are *Bulungi bwasi*, mutual aid groups, *Akabando* groups, and village saving groups (Twikirize et al., 2019). Their integration may require activism on the part of technocrats to ensure that they are integrated into formal policies. It could also be achieved through an active documentation of the potential of these models to inform their integration processes through a synthesis of community developmental aspirations for inclusion in higher-level planning (Republic of Uganda, 2014, p. 49).

Collaborations With Communities

There should be collaboration between technocrats and communities in the promotion of community development policy (Ministry of Local Government, 2021; Onyango-Obbo, 2023). This collaboration should be meaningful, and purposeful, to unleash a unique culture and a special sense of community, which is a great creative resource (Onyango-Obbo, 2022). The overall motivation of such collaborations should be to build a bottom-up community development policy that incorporates the wishes, experiences, and resources of local communities (Republic of Uganda, 2020). Listening to communities and strengthening existing community development initiatives is a good starting point. Working with community members as resource persons, policy advisors, or leaders is another important avenue for building this collaboration. This collaborative approach could help to build mass grass-root support and active engagement in development interventions by communities (Ministry of Local Government, 2021). Genuine collaborations should be built on the extent that communities must see action based on their input and leadership.

Conclusion

Discourses on community development in Uganda are prevalent in both political, professional, and community spaces intensified by current demands to transform communities toward high income status. This chapter has discussed the thought of community development in Uganda, approaching it from the conceptual, historical, and contemporary perspectives. Through this analysis, the challenges and opportunities in community development theory and practice have been distilled, setting forth recommendations that could enhance the impact of present and future community wellbeing improvement interventions. In agreement with Kalinaki (2022a), the chapter has argued vigorously that the negative outcomes of the country's flawed political economy have emerged from the wrong inputs at the macro-policy level, both in design and execution.

To remedy this scenario, the chapter suggests that Uganda's community development efforts could yield more if linked with bottom-up processes, informed by local community experiences/voices, and integrated with agrarian livelihood practices in which a majority of both rural and urban communities derive wellbeing. Furthermore, the temporariness of interventions due to vagaries in the political cycle could be controlled if politicians and professionals in community development build shared interests and mutual respect in working toward local communities' prosperity. Leaders, policy makers, practitioners, and researchers are called upon to act and implement the recommendations proposed in this chapter. Similarly, readers must task leaders and authorities in their localities to act on these proposals.

REFERENCES

Alkire, S. (2006). Needs and capabilities. In S. Reader (Ed.), *The philosophy of need* (pp. 229–252). Cambridge University Press.

Balyejjusa, M. S. (2019). Sustainable development practice: the central role of the human needs language. *Social Change*, *49*(2), 293–309.

Balyejjusa, M. S. (2022). Social needs framework: an alternative framework to analysing and addressing social problems. In R. Baikady, S. Sajid, J. Przeperski, V. Nadesan, M. R. Islam, & J. Gao (Eds.), *The Palgrave handbook of global social problems*. Palgrave MacMillan. https://doi.org/10.1007/978-3-030-68127-2_122-1#DOI

Doyal, L., & Gough, I. (1991). A *theory of human needs*. Macmillan.

Gasper, D. (2004). *The ethics of development*. Edinburgh University Press.

Gough, I. (2014). Lists and thresholds: comparing the Doyal-Gough theory of human need with Nussbaum's capability approach. In F. Comin & M. C. Nussbaum (Eds.), *Capabilities, gender, equality: Towards fundamental entitlements* (pp. 357–381). Cambridge University Press.

Haines, A. (2009). Asset-based community development. In R. Phillips, & R. H. Pittman (eds.), *An introduction to community development* (pp. 38–48). Routledge.

Ife, J. (2009). *Human rights from below: achieving rights through community development*. Cambridge University Press.

Kalinaki, K. D. (2022a). *The hybrid 'despotic democracy' is not working. Time to choose one*. Monitor. https://www.monitor.co.ug/uganda/oped/columnists/daniel-kalinaki/the-hybrid-despotic-democracy-isn-t-working-time-to-choose-one-3999176

Kalinaki, K. D. (2022b). *Forgotten voters and the empty promise of our politics-part II*. Monitor. https://www.monitor.co.ug/uganda/oped/columnists/daniel-kalinaki/forgotten-voters-and-the-empty-promise-of-our-politics-part-ii-3991388

Makubuya, N. A. (2018). *Protection, patronage, or plunder? British mechanisations and (B)uganda's struggle for independence*. Cambridge Scholars Publishing. https://www.cambridgescholars.com/resources/pdfs/978-1-5275-1345-7-sample.pdf

McLeod, S. (2014). Absolute biological needs. *Bioethics, 28*(6), 293–301.

Mission for Community Development. (2022). *Our programs*. https://www.mcodeuganda.org/our-programs/

Ministry of Internal Affairs. (2010). *The National NGO Policy: Strengthening partnership for development*. Retrieved July 4, 2023, from https://www.ngobureau.go.ug/sites/default/files/laws_regulations/2021/04/National%20NGO%20Policy%2C%202010.pdf

Ministry of Finance, Planning, and Economic Development. (2022). *Background to the budget 2022/2023 fiscal year*. Retrieved October 7, 2022, from https://www.finance.go.ug/sites/default/files/Publications/Background%20to%20the%20Budget%20FY%202022-23.pdf

Ministry of Gender, Labour, and Social Development. (2015). *National social protection policy*. Retrieved October 8, 2022, from https://mglsd.go.ug/wp-content/uploads/2021/05/National-Social-Protection-Policy-uganda.pdf

Ministry of Gender, Labour, and Social Development. (2016). *Social development sector plan (SDSP) 2015/16–2019/20*. Retrieved October 7, 2022, from https://mglsd.go.ug/wp-content/uploads/2019/05/SOCIAL-DEVELOPMENT-SECTOR-PLAN.pdf

Ministry of Gender, Labour, and Social Development. (2022). *Department of community development*. Retrieved October 7, 2022, frin https://mglsd.go.ug/community-development/

Ministry of Local Government. (2014). *Local economic development policy*. Retrieved October 6 2022, from https://molg.go.ug/wp-content/uploads/2021/08/National-LED-Policy.Final-Feb-2014-ver2signed.pdf

Ministry of Local Government. (2021). *Implementation guidelines for parish development model*. Retrieved October 15, 2022, from https://www.masindi.go.ug/sites/default/files/Implementation_Guidelines_for_FOR__PARISH_MODEL_OPERATION%5B1%5D.pdf

Mufumba, I. (2023, February 04). *Scorecard of NRM's 10-point programme*. Monitor. Retrieved July 4. 2023, from https://www.monitor.co.ug/uganda/special-reports/scorecard-of-nrm-s-10-point-programme-4111132

National Resistance Movement. (2021). *2021–2026 National Resistance Movement (NRM) manifesto: Securing your future*. NRM Secretariate. Retrieved October 5, 2022, from https://www.mediacentre.go.ug/sites/default/files/media/NRM%20Manifesto%202021-2026.pdf

Network for Community Development. (2022). *What we do*. Retrieved October 5, 2022, from https://ncduganda.org/category/whatwedo/

Noyoo, N. (2022). Critiquing western development paradigms and theories in the age of the Coronavirus (COVID-19): An African perspective. In M. C. S. Gonçalves, R. Gutwald, T. Kleibl, R. Lutz, N. Noyoo, & J. Twikirize (Eds.), *The coronavirus and challenges to social development: Global perspectives* (pp. 399–408). Springer.

NTV News. (2022, October 2). *Panorama: DGF ends support in Uganda*. Retrieved October 8, 2022, from https://www.youtube.com/watch?v=02cfpL_b9Ys

Nussbaum C. M. (2011). *Creating capabilities: The human development approach*. Harvard University Press.

Obote, M. A. (1962, October 9). *Prime minister Obote's speech on eve of Uganda's independence in 1962*. [Speech]. The Independent. Retrieved October 8, 2022, from https://www.independent.co.ug/obote-speech-on-eve-of-ugandas-independence-1962/

Onyango-Obbo, C. (2022, December 21). *Even Amin wouldn't take Uganda to World Cup*. Monitor. Retrieved July 4, 2023, from https://www.monitor.co.ug/uganda/oped/columnists/charles-onyango-obbo/even-amin-wouldn-t-take-uganda-to-world-cup--4062268

Onyango-Obbo, C. (2023, June 28). *A madman's solution to Kampala's rot*. Monitor. Retrieved July 4, 2023, from https://www.monitor.co.ug/uganda/oped/columnists/charles-onyango-obbo/a-madman-s-solution-to-kampala-s-rot-4286444

Republic of Uganda. (2014). *Local government development planning guidelines*. Retrieved October 9, 2022, from, http://npa.go.ug/wp-content/uploads/LG-PLANNING-GUIDELINES.pdf

Republic of Uganda. (2015). *The national development plan (NDPII) 2015/16–2019/20*. National Planning Authority. Retrieved October 9, 2022, from http://npa.go.ug/wp-content/uploads/NDPII-Final.pdf

Republic of Uganda. (2020). *The national development plan (NDPIII) 2020/21–2024/25*. National Planning Authority. Retrieved October 9, 2022, from http://www.npa.go.ug/wp-content/uploads/2020/08/NDPIII-Finale_Compressed.pdf

Streeten, P., Burki, J. S., Haq, U. M., Hicks, N & Stewart, F. (1981). *First things first: meeting basic human needs in developing countries*. Oxford University Press.

Tusasiirwe, S. (2022). Is it indigenisation or decolonisation of social work in Africa? A focus on Uganda. *African Journal of Social Work*, *12*(1), 1–11.

Twikirize, M. J. (2014). Social work education and practice in Uganda: A historical perspective. In H. Spitzer, J. M. Twikirize, & G. G. Wairire (Eds.), *Professional social work in East Africa: Towards social development, poverty reduction, and gender equity* (pp. 136–148). Fountain.

Twikirize M. J., Luwangula, R., & Twesigye, J. (2019). *Social work practice in Uganda: Learning from indigenous and innovative approaches*. Fountain.

Twikirize, M. J., & Spitzer, H. (Eds.). (2019). *Social work practice in Africa: Indigenous and innovative approaches*. Fountain.

United Nations. (2015). *Transforming our world: The 2030 agenda for sustainable development*. Retrieved October 10, 2022, from https://sustainabledevelopment.un.org/content/documents/21252030%20Agenda%20for%20Sustainable%20Development%20web.pdf

CHAPTER 4

ANALYSIS OF VILLAGIZATION MODEL OF RURAL COMMUNITY DEVELOPMENT IN TANZANIA MAINLAND THROUGH UBUNTU LENS

Meinrad Haule Lembuka

ABSTRACT

The chapter used documentary review method and Ubuntu theory to analyze a villagization model of rural community development practiced in Tanzania that entails socioeconomic and political development in a rural community in Tanzania. The development of post-colonial Tanzania is based on land-oriented and developing village communes with local available resources based on African cultural values (Ubuntu). Results have shown that Tanzania, through the villagization model, succeeded in restoring village communities, social services and improved the lives of Tanzanians. Also, apart from increased level of self-dependence, villagization facilitated the provision of education, health facilities, clean water, and other social welfare services and projects that aimed to capacitate Indigenous people to bring their own development through their local settings known as village communes (Vijiji vya Ujamaa). Conclusively, throughout history, Africans lived in commune villages and have had ways of knowing and understanding the physical, social, experience, and mystical meanings that reflected African development, villagization practice was a relevant model in post-colonial Tanzania and Africa as it entailed Indigenous culture and ecology. Africa and villages are inseparable, but the need to revisit village systems is inevitable for truly sustainable development in Tanzania and the rest of Africa.

Keywords: villagization, rural community development, self-dependence, sustainability, Ubuntu

Introduction

Tanzania mainland, formerly known as Tanganyika, before it became independent in 1961, was a very rural and poor country with more than 120 ethnic groups. The first president of the country, the late Dr. Julius Kambarage Nyerere, envisioned that rural development would take priority through a villagization model from the dawn of independence since Tanzania had land and not money. Its development programmes would have to be land oriented (Nyerere, 1976) and thus developing village communes with local available resources based on African cultural values (Ubuntu) were inevitable (Shivji, 2010).

The villagization model was influenced by the fact that at the dawn of independence, Tanzania was a typical rural nation hampered by colonial impacts, lack of social services and rural villages were inaccessible in delivering social services that would improve the lives of Tanzanians. Nyerere advocated for more aggregated settlements or villagization (Shivji, 2010, pp. 120–33). Through villagization practice in rural Tanzania, there was an improvement of the general welfare in the country with increased provision of education, health facilities, clean water, and other social welfare services (Shivji, 2010, pp. 120–33). Understanding this transition requires a review of pre-colonial Africa.

Pre-Colonial Africa

Traditionally, Africa was covered by communal villages with extraordinarily strong social ties known as Ubuntu/Obuntu and this was hampered by the intruders from outside the African continent (Mugumbate & Chereni, 2020). African peoples' survival depended, among others, on their ability to maintain their ways and means of interacting and interpreting their world(s) (Apusigah et al., 2006). African development was based on social ties and collective efforts in communities, which is referred to as Ubuntu, putting less emphasize on individual efforts (Mugumbate & Chereni, 2013). Regardless of how it was reported, Africa, south of Sahara, contained strong village systems that evolved over time in which indigenous Africans strived to master their environment and a true understanding of development. Africa was never a static continent but constantly searched for better/alternate ways of social improvement, including livelihoods (economically, socially, spiritually, physically, and politically). These African systems were connected and interconnected under family-hood and collective efforts under Ubuntu cultural values (Mugumbate & Nyanguru, 2013; Ndiege, 2019).

Tanzania became independent in 1961 from British colonial rule and like other African countries, moved with the tide of post-colonialism. It was important to reclaim the pre-colonial systems as a re-entry point (Shivji, 2009). Tanzania opted for villagization policy and practice as among vital components to restore and reclaim African ways. Tanzania saw the need to uncover or re/discover the ways that our forebears used to know, build knowledge(s) and other development components (Nyerere, 2011).

Ali Mazrui asserts, these form part of our heritage (Mazrui, 1986). Yet, these remain the intrusive elements of our heritage. Mazrui (1986) wrote that:

> While the West was going to the moon, Africans were going to the village. Africans needed to go to the village. For, it is in the village that Africans can find their true selves as Africans. Africaness started in the village and African roots will remain in the village. Laid buried there is the umbilical cord, Africans maternal connection sustaining the dyad! While Africans understand that their worlds connect with other worlds, Africans also need to realize that they cannot trade off Africa for alien ones, in which Africans remain disoriented, alienated, and colonized. (p. 23)

Thus, returning to the village becomes an existential imperative and relevance for sustainable development in Tanzania and the rest of Africa (Mazrui, 2005; Nyerere, 2011).

Post-colonial African countries were full of decolonization and some African countries like Ethiopia, Mozambique and Tanzania took the practical path to villagization (Nyerere, 1967, 2011). According to Apusigah et al. (2006):

> As we return to the village, we need to understand that our village is, was and has not been a perfect place. As we look back with nostalgia to our past and reclaim our ways, we need to understand that our forebears had produced some knowledge but had not completed the process. We need to understand that our forebears were constantly searching for meanings and even welcomed intruders as part of that search. (p. 11)

Villagization model was practiced under Ujamaa policy (African socialism), The introduction of the Ujamaa policy was regarded as a step forward to the socio-political and economic changes in the post-independent period

54   M. H. LEMBUKA

in Tanzania. Nyerere, as the founder of the Ujamaa policy in his side, stood firm to ensure the Ujamaa policy restored the personal dignity and the socio-economic welfare of Tanzanians which were lost during the colonial period (Nyerere, 2011).

Methodology

The chapter used documentary review method or desk research to analyse the villagization model in Tanzania mainland setting. The chapter has drawn on secondary data and the author's observations to present the findings in a systematic manner where online searching of secondary data through google scholar was conducted. Ubuntu theory was used to guide this review and was thought to be relevant to villagization practice in Tanzania. African Ubuntu values are directly reflected in a villagization model in terms of African ecology, people's experiences, and cultural values (Mugumbate & Nyanguru, 2013; Van Breda, 2019).

Ubuntu Theory

According to Mugumbate and Nyanguru (2013):

> [Ubuntu refers to] a collection of values and practices that Black people of Africa or of African origin view as making people authentic human beings. While the nuances of these values and practices vary across different ethnic groups, they all point to one thing – an authentic individual human being is part of a larger and more significant relational, communal, societal, environmental, and spiritual world. (p. 1)

As a concept, Ubuntu denotes *humanism* or *humanness*; Ubuntu is one of several related African cultural values and practice that recently gained a worldview in understanding and solving social, economic, and political phenomenon. There are commonalities of ubuntu values across societies in the African continent and these commonalities are found in areas such as value systems, beliefs, practices, and others (Mugumbate & Chereni, 2020).

Ujamaa Policy

Ujamaa, the Swahili word for extended family, was a social and economic policy developed and implemented in Tanzania by late president Dr. Julius Kambarage Nyerere (1922–1999) between 1964 and 1985 based on the idea of collective farming and the "villagization" of the countryside,

Ujamaa (Boddy-Evans, 2019). According to Dr. Nyerere (1967), development cannot come from outsiders and that people can only develop themselves from within. Villagization intended to empower Indigenous people and their available resources. Both Ubuntu and Ujamaa will guide the following understanding of the villagization model.

Background to the Villagization Model

The above scholars added logical reasoning to African scholars and leaders who opted for villagization policy and practice across Africa, including Tanzania as a case study. Tanzania, through the Ujamaa policy, opted villagization practice as the right path for African sustainable development and this model commenced in 1973, which resulted in an experiment of developmental villages between 1973 and 1982 in rural parts of Tanzania (Hartmann, 1983; Nyerere, 2011). This was a remarkable example of large-scale state planning with favorable economic and ecological consequences for peasants (Scott, 1998; Shivji, 1995).

The country envisioned that "True Development is Development of the People, Not Things" (Nyerere, 1967, p. 7). Since independence, the country envisioned and implemented community development policies, strategies, programs, and projects that aimed to empower people to control their own development through their local settings known as village communes (Vijiji vya Ujamaa). The villagization model adopted African Ubuntu values and practice in support of African socialism and self-reliance policy (Nyerere, 2011; Scott, 1998).

African Socialism and Self-Reliance (Ujamaa na Kujitegemea)

The Ujamaa village was not a new concept, but a colonial distorted African practice and based on the post-Arusha Declaration of 1967 that Tanzania envisioned for developing its people (Nyerere, 1967). Nyerere (1967) states, "Develop people not things, and that people can only develop themselves. No-one can be forced into an Ujamaa village" (p. 8). The Ujamaa village was built on the values of African Ubuntu through voluntary spirit and people centered activities (Coulson, 1975; Mugumbate & Chereni, 2013).

Tanzania's expressions of self-reliance and its elaboration of the policy of Ujamaa Vijijini (rural socialism) stressed the need for a type of development that was rural-based and derived its dynamism from internal sources and communal production by villagers. The country invested in the villagization model that spearheaded changes in the rural areas, the most impoverished sector of the country (Hartmann, 1985; Shivji, 2010). Tanzania's own attempt was not a practical impossibility; indeed, it was the logical solution for a poor country to adopt this model given extreme shortages of capital, technology, and trained workforce (Hartmann, 1991). Post-colonial Tanganyika was completely rural and poor, people were in favour of Nyerere's regime in seeking for alternative solutions for existed socioeconomic problems (Shivji, 2010).

The Ujamaa policy became a national agenda to fast track socioeconomic and political development where several approaches were imposed in lieu of national policies, strategies, and other guidelines (Mwongozo) that embraced African ecology, dignity, and cultural values (Ubuntu). These approaches facilitated operations of rural villages, and later familyhood agriculture (Kilimo cha Ujamaa) was replaced by a policy of villagization in 1974. As a result, around 5 and a half million people were physically resettled in the space of three years (Coulson, 1982; Nyerere, 1976, p. 42).

Villagization Model in Tanzania

Villagization has been defined as "the grouping of a population into centralized planned settlements" (Survival International, 1988, p. 16). It is frequently confused with "resettlement" as the two policies often occur at the same time and may overlap. The basic notion of villagization is regrooming into villages, which usually does not involve moving significant distances. The houses in the villages may be laid out in straight lines, in a grid pattern, but this is not always the case (Sanga, 2019). Villagization refers simply to the agglomeration of rural living units to facilitate state administration. However, these government-planned villages in Tanzania in the 1970s (termed as developmental or registered villages) involved more than the concentration of rural populations. These villages introduced state capacity at the local level by introducing village councils responsible for taxation, enforcement of property rights, and provision of public goods (Osafo-Kwaako & Nyerere, 2011).

The Arusha Declaration (1967) was an initial step for the villagization approach since it emphasized agricultural development, social equality, stressing self-sufficiency in food, and socialist rural development (Nyerere, 2011). Between 1969 and 1973, more radical policies were passed which appeared to extend the "rural agriculture revolution." In the agricultural sector, the policy of promoting voluntary Ujamaa villages were replaced by the collectivist principles of Ujamaa established by the Presidential Circular 1/69 (Nyerere, 1967) that transferred power to the poor peasants to give them a chance to organise and develop themselves under communal production in villages (Shivji, 2010).

In 1971, the policy of Mwongozo (National Guidelines) was passed which gave workers powers to control their production processes and gave them security of employment (Nyerere, 2011). In addition, various redistributive measures were passed to alleviate the poverty of the masses. A vast campaign of mobilization was undertaken by Party leaders in the regions, in the districts and in the villages to implement the policy of Ujamaa Vijijini (Hartmann, 1991).

The idea for collective rural agriculture seemed like a sound idea that Nyerere's government could afford, providing equipment, facilities, and material to a rural population if they were brought together in the so-called nucleated settlements, each of around 250 families. Establishing new groups of rural populations also made the distribution of fertilizer and seed easier, and it would be possible to provide a good level of education to the population as well (Hartmann, 1991). The process started slowly and was voluntary at first. By the end of the 1960s, there were only 800 or so collective settlements. In the 1970s, people left the cities and urban areas, moved to the established collective villages and by the end of the 1970s, there were over 2,500 of these villages across Tanzania (Hartmann, 1991).

Villagization as an African Ubuntu

According to Dr. Julius Nyerere (1967) who pioneered villagization in Tanzania, "In our traditional African society we were individuals within a community. We took care of the community, and the community took care of us. We neither needed nor wished to exploit our fellow men" (p. 3). He argued that these core African ubuntu values just needed to be strengthened and built in a natural context of African commune villages (Nyerere, 1967). Both villagization and Ubuntu promote teamwork and collaboration, group cohesiveness and group support. The cornerstone of African development is a deep sense of belonging to a group, be it the extended family, the clan, or the community. They both work on the premise that everyone must contribute towards community initiatives and aspirations and, by implication, toward national development (Mugumbate & Chereni, 2020).

Peace and harmony were the key ideals in the realization of villagization model under the pillars of Ubuntu thus it was necessary to embrace modality of African democracy through collective voluntary association. Villagization became democratic in nature and granted the opportunity of a voluntary association of people who decided on their own free will to live together and work together for their common good toward national development (Nyerere, 2011). This type of development under Nyerere is what Tanzania needed (Ashly, 2020). Dr. Nyerere's villagization policy was able to unite a large country of more than 100 ethnicities into a cohesive postcolonial state (Ashly, 2020).

Discussion

Post-colonial Africa needed a villagization policy and practice to restore African views and practice. Tanzania is among the countries that thought going back to the village was inevitable to restore African dignity and relevant development. After independence in 1961, Tanzania, like the rest of Africa, was reclaiming itself by returning to its roots, to its traditions and cultures. Seeking its past to understand the present with the view of shaping its future, Tanzania developed a villagization policy to restore the African social structure of commune villages to foster true and sustainable development (Hartmann, 1991). Other scholars have highlighted the precaution of the process of decolonization and restoration of the African practice of villagization which became one of the restored indigenous models (Apusigah et al., 2006).

With the reference to Arusha Declaration (1967), Tanzania, under President Dr. Nyerere and TANU (the Tanganyika African National Union), set a path for Tanzania towards socialism and self-reliance, with villagization as an important component. Nyerere (1968) expanded on the objective of building socialism in Tanzania based on the traditional family values of mutual respect, sharing of basic goods and services held in common, and the obligation of everybody to work (Komba, 1995).

Villagization began as a voluntary program in Tanzania, although government officials took advantage of unseasonal floods in 1969 to persuade people to move. The lure of social services attracted people to villages (Coulson, 1982). However, the tune eventually changed. Nyerere and his government felt that villagization was proceeding too slowly; their promise to transform rural areas might lose credibility. According to one expert, "the original aim of villagisation was to provide a happier life for people by living together and to increase production by working together. But many peasants were hesitant about the first, and the second did not work because of both internal and external resistance" (Coulson, 1975, p. 57). However, in one frequently cited case, "working together" was successful but seen as a threat by Tanganyika National Union (TANU) (Maghimbi, 1995).

In the March Presidential Circular No. 1 (Government of Tanzania, 1969b) the Government of Tanzania directed that "All Government policies, and the activities and decisions of all Government officials, must therefore be geared towards emphasizing the advantages of living together and working together for the good of all" (p. 2). This policy change was fully reflected in the Second Five Year Plan for Tanzania which started in

July 1969 (Government of Tanzania, 1969a). From this time on all Government Departments started placing as many of their projects as they could in Ujamaa villages (Coulsin, 1975).

In November 1973, the President was quoted in the Daily News as saying, "To live in villages is an order" (Havnevik, 1993, p. 205). It has been argued that compulsory villagization was meant to reverse the process of the peasantry slipping away from government control (Hyden, 1980, p. 129). Forced villagization in Tanzania happened through "'operations," and several writers emphasise the appropriateness of the military terminology (Havnevik 1993; Raikes, 1986; Shivji, 2009). Operations were aimed at the massive villagization of people in a short time; in 1973, Nyerere made it compulsory to live in villages in three years (Raikes, 1978).

The campaign had spectacular results, although the numbers are disputed and the government claims that 13 million Tanzanians, or 90% of the rural population, had moved into villages by 1976 (Lappé & Beccar-Varela, 1980, p. 99). More conservative estimates posit that villagization involved around 5 million Tanzanians (Hyden, 1980) and some officials competed to produce impressive figures (Raikes, 1986; Scott, 1998). Yet there were some benefits from villagization, and they include considerable gains in the supply of social services and education (Havnevik, 1993; Hyden, 1980). Many people saw advantages to being nearer to roads and schools (Coulson, 1977, p. 93). Quality of life was seen to improve considerably in many rural areas (Legum, 1988).

Villagization affected pastoralists in Tanzania. A recent study of its impact (Lane, 1998) argues that whatever the potential merit of providing improved services to rural populations, the settlement of pastoralists poses serious challenges to common property resources management. The Barabaig herders who settled did so out of poverty and had no choice but to limit their migration to the distance their herds could travel to and from the homestead in one day. The concentration of animals in villages had a negative ecological impact and led to a further decline in levels of production (Kikula, 1997).

Ironically, urbanisation in Tanzania increased faster than anywhere else in the world in the 1970s (O'Connor, 1988). People's dissatisfaction with the villagization program led them to continue to the towns. Villagization reduced people's freedom and concentrated power and control in the hands of local party leaders, which may have been an incentive for others to move to town (Shivji, 2009). Also, people were wrenched from the land where they had always lived; once they were on the road, they often decided to move further to the city (Mazrui, 1986 & 2005).

Although the classes were open air with poorly trained teachers, these drawbacks "do not overshadow the fact of a great effort in the establishment of such facilities, of a great dynamic in their growth, and particularly that these were perhaps, beyond political mobilisation, the most important arguments capable of attracting people into the villages" (Coelho, 1993, p. 363). A study of the environmental impact of villagization in Tanzania (Kikula, 1997) argues that even with long-term negative aspects for the environment, there were many positive things from a social perspective, especially social service infrastructure, such that the success or failure of villagization depends on the angle from which it is examined (Kikula, 1997, p. 214). Tanzania made very impressive achievements in literacy and primary education in the 1970s (Coulson, 1982; Lorgen, 1999).

Lessons Learned

Overall, this chapter has shown that most of the major success and challenges during villagization model in Tanzania have impacted both rural and urban development, yet there is more to learn that can be applied in the national and global development agenda. The following are the lessons learned from villagization model.

- Villagization was seen to overcome the problems of tribalization, a plague which beset other newly independent African countries that drove people to separate into ethnic groups based on ancient identities (Nyerere, 2011);
- Tanzania's expressions of self-reliance and its elaboration in the policy of Ujamaa Vijijini (rural socialism) have influenced the national development agenda (Mazrui, 2005);
- The rationale behind villagization is social, political, environmental, agricultural, militaristic, administrative, or a mix of several of these. In terms of security, it can be considered safer to live together in a village than alone in a homestead (Boddy-Evans, 2019);
- Ujamaa had a strong element of welfarism, which no doubt was instrumental in improving social indicators such as health, education, water, and so forth, among most of the people (Shivji, 2010).

Conclusion

Villagization in Africa is inevitable, but it only requires relevant and comprehensive assessment and planning in relation to other factors. Despite some shortfalls that the villagization model of Tanzania demonstrated, it remains to be a practical and brave decision that Tanzania took on returning to the village and it should be taken as an evidence-based practice and success story toward decolonization. There is much to learn from the villagization model of Tanzania, including fixing its shortfalls, since it has succeeded in proving the strengths of Ubuntu values in the decolonization process regardless of the external influence and post-colonial syndromes.

Africa should never feel ashamed of going back to the village and fixing the past. Ubuntu values should be used to guide Africans in the process. While Africa returns to the village the need to rethink Indigenous social systems and socialization processes could be drawn from African Ubuntu champions like the Late Dr. Julius Nyerere, Madiba Mandela, Kenneth Kaunda, Samora Machel, Patrick Lumumba, Kwame Nkrumah, and Desmond Tutu, and so forth. These African Ubuntu champions laid the foundations for the decolonization process and back to Africa movements, including villagization. They inspired Africans to return to their origins in search of reconstructing African cultural values and ecology (Ubuntu).

REFERENCES

Apusigah, A. Issaka, F., & Afegra, D. (2006). African Knowledges and sciences: Africans return to the village: Reconstructing identities and engendering praxis. In D. Millar, S. B. Kendie, A.A. Apudigah, & B. Haverdort (Eds.), *African knowledges and science: Understanding and supporting the ways of knowing in Sub-Sharan Africa* (pp. 86–97). Compas.

Ashly, J. (2020, December 17). *Tanzania: Remembering Ujamaa, the good, the bad and the buried.* African Arguments. https://africanarguments.org/2020/12/tanzania-remembering-Ujamaa-the-goodthe-bad-and-the-buried/

Boddy-Evans, A. (2019). *What was Ujamaa and how did it affect Tanzania? Nyerere's social and economic policy in 1960s and 1970s Tanzania.* https://www.thoughtco.com/what-was-ujamaa-44589

Coelho, J. P. B. (1993). *Protected villages and communal villages in the Mozambican Province of Tete (1968–1982).* [PhD thesis, University of Bradford].

Coulson, A. (1975). Peasants and Bureaucrats. *Review of African Political Economy, 2*(3), 53–58. https://www.jstor.org/stable/3997823

Coulson, A. (1977). Agricultural policies in mainland Tanzania. *The Review of African Political Economy 4*(10), 74–100.

Coulson, A. (1982). *Tanzania: A political economy.* Clarendon Press.

Government of Tanzania. (1967). *The Arusha Declaration.*

Government of Tanzania (1969a). *Tanzania Second five-year plan for economic and social development, 1st July, 1969–30th June, 1974.*

Government of Tanzania. (1969b). *Government Circular No 1.*

Hartmann, J. (1983). *Development policymaking in Tanzania 1962–1982: A critique of sociological interpretations* [Doctoral dissertation, University of Hull].

Hartmann, J. (1985). The Arusha Declaration Revisited. *African Review, 12*(1), 1–11.

Hartmann, J. (1991). The search for autonomy and independence: Foreign policy and the Arusha Declaration. In J. Hartmann (Ed.), *Re-thinking the Arusha Declaration* (pp. 151–159). Nielsen and Son.

Havnevik, K. (1993). *Tanzania: The limits to development from above.* Nordiska Afrikain Institutet.

Hyden, G. (1980). *Beyond Ujamaa in Tanzania: Underdevelopment and an uncaptured peasantly.* University of California Press.

Kikula, I. (1997). *Policy implications on environment: The case of villagisation in Tanzania.* The Nordic Africa Institute.

Komba, D. (1995). Contribution to rural development: Ujamaa and villagisation. *Mwalimu: The Influence of Nyerere*, 32–45.

Lane, C. (1998). Introduction. In C. Lane (Ed.), *Custodians of the commons: Pastoral land tenure in East and West Africa* (pp. 1–25). Earthscan.

Lappé, F. M., & Beccar-Varela, A. (1980). *Mozambique and Tanzania: Asking the right questions.* Institute for Food and Development Policy.

Legum, C. (1988). The Nyerere Years. In M. Hodd (Ed.), *Tanzania after Nyerere* (pp. 3–11). Pinter.

Lorgen C. C. (1999). *The experience of villagization: Lessons from Ethiopia, Mozambique, and Tanzania.* Oxfam-GB.

Maghimbi, S. (1995). The conflict between the state and grassroots-based institutions in Tanzania's rural development. In P. G. Foster (Ed.), *The Tanzanian peasantry: Further studies* (pp. 37–50). Avebury.

Mazrui, A. (1986). *The Africans: A triple heritage.* BBC Publications.

Mazrui, A. (2005). The re-invention of Africa: Edward Said, V. Y. Mudimbe, and Beyond. *Research in African Literatures, 36*(3), 68–82.

Mazrui, A. (2005). *Julius Kambarage Nyerere, African politics and myself.* http://www.afroarticles.com/article-dashboard

Mugumbate, J., & Chereni, A. (2020). Now the theory of Ubuntu has its space in social work. *African Journal of Social Work, 10*(1), 5–17.

Mugumbate, J., & Nyanguru, A. (2013). Exploring African philosophy: The value of ubuntu in social work. *African Journal of Social Work, 3*(1), 82–100.

Ndiege, B. P. (2019). Community development practices in Tanzania: Issues and challenges. *Revue Internationale Animation, Territoires et Pratiques Socioculturelles, 16*, 13–20.

Nyerere, J. K. (1967). *The Arusha Declaration and TANU's policy on socialism and social-ism and self-reliance.* Tanganyika African National Union (TANU).

Nyerere, J. K. (1968). *The Arusha Declaration: Freedom and socialism.* Oxford University Press.

Nyerere, J. K. (1976). *Freedom and socialism/Uhuru na Umoja, A selection from writings and speeches, 1965–1967.* Oxford University Press.

Nyerere, J. K. (2011). *Freedom, non-alignment and south-south co-operation: A selection from speeches, 1974–1999.* Oxford University Press.

O'Connor, A. (1988). The rate of urbanisation in Tanzania in the 1970s. Tanzania after Nyerere. In M. Hodd (Ed.), *Tanzania after Nyerere* (pp. 136–142). Pinter.

Osafo-Kwaako, P., & Nyerere, J. (2011). *Long-run effects of villagization in Tanzania.* https://hanibalhamidi.files.wordpress.com/2014/12/studi-ujamaa.pdf

Raikes, P. (1978). Rural differentiation and class formation in Tanzania. *The Journal of Peasant Studies, 5*(3), 285–325.

Raikes, P. L. (1986). Eating the carrot and wielding the stick: The agricultural sector in Tanzania. In J Boesen, Kjell J. Havnevik, J. Koponen, & R. Odgaard (Eds.), *Tanzania: crisis and struggle for survival* (pp. 105–141). Scandinavian Institute of African Studies. https://eurekamag.com/research/001/568/001568503.php

Sanga, S. A. (2019). Practitioners' perspectives on land resource conflicts and resolution in Tanzania. *The Journal of Rural and Community Development, 14*(2), 87–106.

Scott, J. (1998). *Seeing like the state: how certain schemes to improve the human condition have failed.* Yale University Press.

Shivji, I. G., (1995). The rule of law and Ujamaa in the ideological formation of Tanzania, Social *and Legal Studies, 4*(2), 147–174.

Shivji, I. G. (2009). Land tenure problems and reforms in Tanzania. In G. R. Murunga (Ed.), *Where is Uhuru? Reflections on the struggle for democracy in Africa* (pp. 106–123). Fahamu Books.

Shivji, I. G. (2010). The village in Mwalimu's thought and political practice. In C. Chachage & A. Cassam (Eds.), *Africa's liberation: The legacy of Julius Nyerere* (pp. 120–133). Pambazuka.

Survival International, (1988). *For their own good: Ethiopia's villagisation programme.*

Van Breda, A. D. (2019). Developing the notion of Ubuntu as African theory for social work practice. *Social Work, 55*(4), 439–450.

SECTION II

MODELS AND APPROACHES TO COMMUNITY

CHAPTER 5

ASSET-BASED COMMUNITY-DRIVEN DEVELOPMENT (ABCD) AS AN APPROACH AND MODEL TO ADDRESS THE CHALLENGES OF AFRICA

Hanna Nel

ABSTRACT

Asset-based community-driven development (ABCD) has gained momentum in South Africa on different levels by government, corporate sector, civil society, and academia. ABCD values the capacity, skills, knowledge, and connections in individuals and communities, focusing on what is strong and what they have and not on what is wrong and does not have. It enables communities to lead their own development by co-investing their own assets, taking advantage of opportunities, and leveraging their own resources with resources of government, businesses, and other organizations. Based on many years of applying and experiencing ABCD, this chapter attempts to establish a practice model in terms of principles, phases, methods, and techniques. The phases consist of connecting and discovering, dreaming/visioning, designing, delivery, disconnecting, and departing. Methods and techniques imbedded in the phases are, for example, storytelling, asset mappings, leaky bucket technique, and participatory monitoring and evaluation techniques. Ubuntu, an African philosophy that puts high value on connectedness, relationships, trust, engagement, and social networks, emphasizes social assets, and which forms the basis of ABCD. The potential of ABCD in South Africa is that it puts in place all the building blocks for real and meaningful sustainability of

Community Development Practice in Africa: Putting Theory Into Practice, pp. 67–83
Copyright © 2024 by Information Age Publishing
www.infoagepub.com
All rights of reproduction in any form reserved.

community interventions and the organizations that manage and lead these interventions. The outcome of ABCD is that it builds resilient, self-reliant, confident communities.

Keywords: Ubuntu, asset-based community development, resilience, engagement, asset mapping

Introduction

The Asset-Based Community-Driven Development (ABCD) approach and method have gained momentum in Africa over the last 20 years, with an overwhelming response and interest by government (national, provincial, and local), corporate sector, civil society, and academia (Mansvelt, 2018; Mathie & Cunningham, 2003, 2005; Nel, 2018a, 2018b). To address South Africa's unique history of oppression, colonialization, and the violation of human rights, studies show that the ABCD approach provides the building blocks for real and meaningful sustainability of communities (Emmett, 2000; Landry & Peters, 2018; Nel, 2018a 2018b; Pretorius & Nel, 2012). The ABCD approach aims to bring about social and economic improvements in the lives of primarily the most vulnerable, enhance their human capabilities, opportunities, and choices about the lives that they wish to lead (Frediani, 2010; Nel et al., 2021; Patel, 2015). Furthermore, this approach addresses unemployment, poverty and inequality and embraces indigenous knowledge systems and culture and enhances the decoloniality practice (Mathie & Cunningham, 2003, 2005). The ABCD is not only an approach but also a practice model involving community-led, participatory phases, methods, and techniques, and embraces principles such as self-reliance, dialogue, co-ownership, and sustainability.

The chapter will provide an overview of ABCD as an approach and give specific attention to the ABCD as a practice model including principles, phases, steps, and techniques for practice specifically relevant within the context of South Africa. The role of government and external stakeholders play will be highlighted. The building of relationships and trust, components on which ABCD is built, is closely linked with the African worldview and Ubuntu, a philosophy that is central to African life.

African World View and Ubuntu

An African worldview refers to the "culture, beliefs, values, practices, and knowledge of people of African origin" (Nel et al., 2021, p. 30). It is an oversimplification to refer to an African worldview in a single way and understanding. However, there is an underlying unity in the diversity of African culture which dates to before its shared experience of suppression, colonization, and acculturation. The African worldview includes the aspects of being person/human centered (humanist and community based), holistic (the interconnectedness of everything), and it manifests culturally in orientations to possessions, time, nature, human activity, religion, and ethics (Mugumbate & Chereni, 2019; Mugumbate et al., 2023; Nel et al., 2021; Simba, 2021). These commonalities in sub-Saharan Africa are included in Ubuntu (Nguni) Botho (Sesotho) Bunhu (Xitsonga) Vhuntu (Tshivenda). Ubuntu is translated into English as African humanism, humanity, and humanness (Mugumbate & Chereni, 2019; Mugumbate et al., 2023). Ubuntu is a philosophy that is central to African life. The core of Ubuntu is "I am, because we are," which means I cannot be if you are not. High value is placed on sharing, generosity, hospitality, brother and sisterhood, empathy, and humaneness. Ubuntu places high value on connectedness, which equals relationships, trust, engagement, and social networks (Brons, 2015; Gade, 2012; Maphosa & Keasley, 2015). Connectedness moves communities, which is the equivalent of community building. Ubuntu is thus the soul and spirit of community in Africa and the mechanism that drives ABCD (Brons, 2015; Gade, 2012). Ubuntu is a core of the survival of African families to building sustainable communities. Persons are understood in the context of their collective identity and not separate and individual, because personhood is expressed in terms of relationship, caring, sharing, and group solidarity. Ubuntu is thus the foundation of partnerships and networks, a collective benefit rather than self-interest. It is thus important to strengthen the wholeness and interconnectedness in communities, as it equals both Ubuntu and ABCD (Gade, 2012; Nel et al., 2021).

There is, however, criticism of Ubuntu, of which a few reasons are mentioned. First, it values the collective above the individual, and thus appears to force a feeling of community at the expense of an individual's wellbeing. Second, there is a huge disconnect between the ideals of Ubuntu and the lived reality of most South Africans. People question the existence of Ubuntu or its power as a social value by the occurrence in Africa of autocratic leadership, corruption and nepotism, sexism, the incidence of rape and child rape, violent acts of xenophobia, and the degradation of the environment. Third, Ubuntu does not offer a solution as a foundation for a unique African form of democracy and question its value in citizenship education. Four, it is argued that Ubuntu is inherently patriarchal and conservative. Five, its usefulness as a guiding principle for South African society is also diminished by its vagueness and ability to accommodate a range of meanings. Six, the meaning Ubuntu once had as a social value, has lost its relevance (Brons, 2015; Mugumbate & Chereni, 2019; Mugumbate et al., 2023; Maphosa & Keasley, 2015; Simba, 2021). However, within the context of ABCD, Ubuntu is still relevant as relationships, respect for each other and humanness is the essence of human beings. How one interacts with other human beings, nature, or the Creator, Ubuntu was and still is the guiding principle and forms the foundation of ABCD (Nel et al., 2021).

ABCD as an Approach

The ABCD is an approach that focuses on the strengths, capabilities, resources, and creativity of people and not on their problems and needs. The ABCD approach was coined and applied by Kretzmann and McKnight (1993) in the United States of America, as a way of counteracting the problem-based approach to community development. However, the approach is widely applied globally, with huge successes in Africa specifically (Demeshane & Nel, 2018; Mansvelt, 2018; Nel & Pretorius, 2012; Nel, 2018a, 2018b, 2020; Pretorius & Nel, 2012). Its foundation is that communities can drive the development process themselves by identifying and mobilizing existing, but often untapped or "under-tapped" assets. This approach values the capacity, skills, knowledge and connections in individuals and communities, focusing on what is strong and what they have and not on what is wrong and does not have (Homan, 2011; Ife & Tesoriero, 2006; Kretzmann & McKnight, 1993; Mathie & Cunningham, 2003, 2005, 2008). The approach assists community members in developing "new eyes about themselves and their surroundings," and for professionals "it shifts the conversation from thinking of citizens as objects to fix, to assets to tap" (Morse, 2011, p. 11). The ABCD approach represents a shift toward encouraging and affirming community agency, self-determination, and ownership, and sets a foundation for active citizenship (Kramer et al., 2012).

In reaching community agency, self-determination, and ownership, ABCD encourages an appreciation and mobilization of assets in communities. Assets are more than just resources. Awareness of assets facilitates engagement with resources (Mathie & Cunningham, 2003). The following assets are emphasized by the literature on ABCD, namely human, physical, financial, natural, and social assets (Green & Haines, 2008; Ife & Tesoriero, 2006; Kretzmann & McKnight, 1993; Mathie & Cunningham, 2003; McKnight & Block, 2010; Pretorius & Nel, 2012). Human assets include skills, talents, knowledge, experience, and the creative capabilities of people. Physical assets include, amongst others, man-made assets such as buildings, tools, livestock, and machinery. Financial assets refer to money earned through working in the formal or informal sector, savings in the bank, or benefiting from state social grants. Natural assets refer to God-made assets, such as access to land, water, agriculture, and minerals. Finally, social assets refer to networks, social bonds, voluntary associations, and the quality of relations among people within communities (Green &

Haines, 2008; Kretzmann & McKnight, 1993; Nel & Pretorius, 2012; Pretorius & Nel, 2012). Social assets refer to Ubuntu, which is related to the networks, connectedness and relationships of trust and reciprocity. Social assets are inherent in associations where members work together in collaborative action (Green & Haines, 2008; Ife & Tesoriero, 2006). Social assets are the assets that enable access to other assets (Mathie & Cunningham, 2003). No single asset area can sufficiently increase livelihood outcomes, but a range of assets is needed for people to move toward greater economic sustainability. Assets are also the basis on which people act.

ABCD enables communities to lead their own development by co-investing their own assets, taking advantage of opportunities, and leveraging their own resources with resources of government, businesses, and other organizations. ABCD is seen as a shift that accentuates the notion of civic duty in relation to rights, developing consciousness of people toward taking greater control of their future, leverages local assets and reinforces local, organic leadership (Nel & Pretorius, 2012; Nel, 2018a, 2018b).

ABCD Principles

The principles of ABCD could be understood best by a comparison between the deficit and the asset-based approach (see Table 5.1). The deficit-based approach is seen as a glass half empty and the asset-based approach as a glass half full (Eliasov, 2013; Homan, 2011; Kretzmann & McKnight, 1993; Mathie et al., 2017; Nel & Pretorius, 2012; Nel, 2018a 2018b; Nel et al., 2021; Preece, 2017).

Table 5.1

Deficit-Based Approach Versus the Asset-Based Approach

DEFICIT BASED APPROACH	ASSET-BASED APPROACH
Glass half empty	Glass half full
Focuses on problems, deficits, weaknesses, and past failures	Focuses on opportunities, strengths, and future possibilities and successes
Sees local people as customers, clients, beneficiaries, or service users	Sees local people as active citizens, co-owners, learning partners
Provides services to people	Develops and co-produces services and interventions with people

(Table continued on next page)

Table 5.1 (Continued)

Deficit-Based Approach Versus the Asset-Based Approach

DEFICIT BASED APPROACH	ASSET-BASED APPROACH
Glass half empty	Glass half full
Relies on outside experts and bureaucratic systems	Is non-bureaucratic, focuses of people's strength and knowledge, prioritizes by the community
Sees programmes as the answer	People are the answer
External funds drive the process	Funds do not drive the process. It is an internal relationship and trust driven process (Ubuntu)
Is driven by colonial, external culture, and practices	Is rooted in indigenous culture and practices

ABCD Practice Model

The ABCD model has been applied in various communities, locally and globally, toward building empowered, self-reliant communities. It is a transformative process, slow, unpredictable, and often the greatest impacts are not visible, such as the development of trust, relationships, confidence, and local informal leadership. By following the process, community members become aware of the power situated in themselves and thus potentially reverse internalized powerlessness, engage in real democracy through strengthening opportunities for collective efforts and helping to build local capacity for action (Landry & Peters, 2018; Nel et al., 2021). Figure 5.1 outlines five phases, with participatory monitoring and evaluation as an ongoing process during all the phases. The five phases of the process are connecting and discovery, dream, design, delivery and disconnecting, and departing phase. Each phase is further described below, along with examples of methods and techniques that can be used to implement it. The process requires flexible, long-term involvement from community development practitioners in reaching sustainable, empowered, and self-reliant communities (Nel et al., 2021; Swanepoel & De Beer, 2011; Weyers, 2016). Eliasov (2013, p. 29), is of the opinion that it is the process that "holds the magic," and if the process is facilitated in an effective way, people could change their mindsets from poverty-stricken to a mindset of belief that they (the community members) have the power and ability to become independent owners of their own lives. It is a consciousness-building process and the engagement in all the phases and steps can change people's lives from the beginning because of the way the process is designed and managed.

Figure 5.1

The ABCD Process

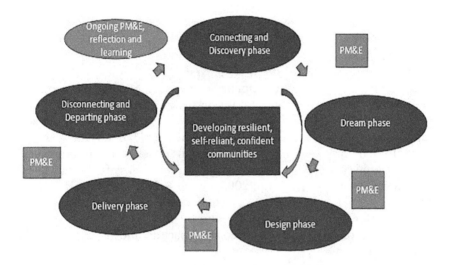

Phase 1: Connecting and Discovery

The process begins with a period to connect and build relationships with community members and different stakeholders in the community, and to discover in collaboration with the community, "what worked well," their assets, strengths, opportunities, future aspirations and to determine how "what worked well" can be galvanized and used as a stepping-stone toward the desired future. To connect and engage with community members is to spark Ubuntu, reminding community members of the meaning of Ubuntu, namely "I am because of you." This phase is time consuming and community practitioners tend to rush through this phase with the result that many projects fail. This is a conscientization process and needs to be done intensively as people need to be actively involved in the steps below (Homan, 2011; Nel & Pretorius, 2012; Nel et al., 2021).

During this phase of connecting and discovery, the community development practitioner usually makes use of storytelling to discover positive stories about the best of their past, which helps to uncover assets and strengths that communities can use to address their challenges and to build on to sustain their livelihoods. Storytelling is about interaction and the building of relationships, which is strongly associated with the African culture and Ubuntu (Nel & Pretorius, 2012; Nel et al., 2021; Pretorius & Nel, 2012). Through storytelling people discover what their strengths and capabilities are as well as what they care about and their motivation to act on what they care about. They also discover the networks of relationships inside the community (Block, 2009; Eliasov, 2013; Nel, 2011; Ssewamala, et al., 2010).

Trusting relationships are formed as people share their stories. Storytelling is based on the *appreciative inquiry approach*, developed by Cooperrider and Srivastva in the 1980s, appropriate and widely applied in an African context (Cooperrider & Whitney, 1999; Nel, 2011; Whitney et al., 2010).

An extensive time is usually spent on mapping of assets, looking for achievements in the past and what is working and strong (Nel, 2011; Nel et al., 2021). The five types of assets discussed under the ABCD approach mapped are namely physical, social, natural, personal/human, and financial assets. To maximize the discovery of strengths, assets, and opportunities, the communities are viewed as diverse and capable webs of gifts and assets (Ashford & Patkar, 2001; Braun, 2005; Green & Haines, 2008; Nel et al., 2021). The community practitioner connects different role players with each other and encourages the building of new relationships and the strengthening of existing ones, based on capacities and strengths (Block, 2009; Nel et al., 2021).

Mapping is done with the purpose of developing an awareness of assets, skills, strengths, and capabilities. Becoming aware of strengths and assets energies and stimulates a vision of the future and begins to leverage internal and external resources to support the vision. Mapping also fosters participation, the forming of new relationships, and the strengthening of existing relationships.

The human assets, which are often overlooked, are located inside the community, and controlled internally by the community. The "head, heart, hands" tool could be used for mapping of personal human skills, gifts, and talents. The head skills refer to knowledge people have, for example, strategic planning and knowledge of gardening. Assets of the heart refer to the passion people have, for example, old people, children, and animals, and hands skills refer to skills a person has gained at home, work, in the community, for example, hair-cutting, carpentry, sewing, beadwork and baking (Nel & Pretorius, 2012; Pretorius & Nel, 2012; Nel, 2015; Nel, 2018a, 2018b, 2020). Mapping of physical and natural assets is a tool that is usually done in one exercise. These are usually followed by a transact walk through the community. Community members are usually surprised to discover the various physical and natural assets in the community (Nel, 2015; Nel, 2018a, 2018b; Nel et al., 2021). The physical man-made assets are, for example, buildings, roads, electricity, and institutions, such as higher education institution, public schools, health care services, police, banks, and parks (Nel, 2015; Nel, 2018a, 2018b; Nel et al., 2021). Natural assets refer to assets such as vacant land, rivers, and mountains.

Economic assets refer to assets such as wages, salaries, grants, and savings groups (called "stokvels"). A useful tool for the mapping of the community's economic assets is the leaky bucket. This tool helps community members to understand how the local economy works and how people exist in economic terms (for example, sources of income, what people spend their income on, and how well local resources are maximized for local benefit). The leaky bucket is a useful tool for demystifying community economics (Mathie & Cunningham, 2008).

The fifth kind of asset, namely the social assets, includes relationships, care for each other, networks, trust, and reciprocity on which people rely to make a living. Mapping of associations and community-based organizations indicate then relationships in the community and are the engines of community action (Green & Haines, 2008; Ife & Tesoriero, 2006). These are associations and organizations formed and controlled by community members, such as citizen associations and community-based organizations. Venn diagrams are usually used as a tool to enable citizens to discover their associations and community-based organizations (Mathie & Cunningham, 2005; Nel & Pretorius, 2012).

Phase 2: Dream/Vision

Through the connecting and discovery phase, people find a focus and create a vision. Based on the connecting and discovery phase where assets, strengths and capabilities were discovered the group discuss how they can build on their strengths to better their community based on the discoveries made in the discovery phase. Community visioning is a collaborative process of giving the people who live, work, and play in a place the opportunity to have a say about what they want their community to be like in the future. They construct a vision of "what their community might be like if they build on and improve the best of what is and strengths they have become aware of" (Nel et al., 2021, p. 173). The facilitation of the process of a participatory visioning usually takes place through a couple of sessions. Tools that are successfully used in the vision phase are the "goal or vision tree," drawings, collages, logos, poems and songs, a story without a middle and to write provocative propositions or slogans (Nel et al., 2021). These tools energize people and enable them to develop dreams for the future. It is important to develop realistic dreams that are based on the assets discovered in the connecting and discovery phase. This phase stretches people in looking beyond their assets and build a vision based on their assets.

Phase 3: Design

Designing or planning is a pro-active process where the participants take control by making decisions about the design. It is the beginning of the transformation process from stories, ideas, visions and feelings to actions and projects. Designing is a collective learning process and the task of the whole action group. The steps taken in this phase are to revisit the vision, decide on the long-term goal/s and short-term objectives. For a vision to become a reality, goals and actions must be planned. The Planning Evaluation and Review Technique (PERT) and Gannt planning models are usually used by community members in this phase. The PERT model is used for the long-term plan and the Gannt for short term planning purposes (Nel et al., 2021).

Through the discovery and vision phases, people show leadership and interest in forming a core group to be able to find a focus and develop a plan. The connecting and discovery and visioning phases usually excite a few people who want to see their community driving the development process in the present and future (Preece, 2017). The core group leads the design of a plan based on the assets and vision the community has discovered. The members of the core group who have discovered and mobilized their own assets and dreams start realizing their power and gain confidence; and have a commitment toward a unifying and strengthening outcome (Block, 2009; Emmet, 2000; Johar, 2017). It is evident in South Africa that the ABCD model and approach instill a kind of leadership which moves communities from focusing on a reactive orientation which dwells on the past, and which focuses on lack and needs, to an orientation where people use their assets and take ownership of their future in collaboration with external resources (Nel, 2018a, 2018b; Nel et al., 2021).

Phase 4: Delivery of the Design

At the delivery stage of the ABCD process, the emphasis is on gathering and activating assets to reach the goal and objectives set out in the design phase in achieving desired community outcomes. Research shows that, if the process has been implemented according to the above process and steps, the community decides how to mobilize their own assets (Eliasov, 2013; Eliasov & Peters, 2013; Weyers, 2016; Yeneabat & Butterfield,

2012). The practitioner constantly assisting community members becomes aware of incremental successes and when mistakes are made, to have an attitude that mistakes are learning opportunities to learn and grow (Nel et al., 2021).

When the community becomes self-reliant and takes ownership of their own development using their own assets, they leverage activities, resources, and investments from outside the community to support locally defined development while retaining control over the process. Decision making is situated in local community members and the institutions and organizations who initiated and mobilized the activities lead by "stepping back" into a supporting and helping role (Homan, 2011; Landry & Peters, 2018; Preece, 2017). External resources can be more effectively utilized if the community has already mobilized its own resources and knows what is needed from external resources. This potentially transforms the community into active participants in development, leading toward sustainability (Demeshane & Nel, 2018; Nel, 2018a, 2018b). These transformative efforts lead to local social and economic development, which have a ripple effect on the wider community (Brooks et al., 2021; Nel, 2018a).

Phase 5: Disconnecting and Departing

When sustainability is reached the community practitioner could disconnect and depart. This phase is not a once-off event but a process which consists of preparation for disconnecting and departing, evaluation, disconnecting, the stabilization of achievements and building sustainability and departing. Factors contributing to sustainability are where people assert their rights and recognize, develop and/or enhance the potential of their assets to achieve their socioeconomic well-being. The core group moves toward a stage where the autonomy lies fully with the team members (Nel, 2018a, 2018b; Nel et al., 2021; Whitney et al., 2010). The leadership of the team members is value-driven, shared, transformative, appreciative, and service-orientated (Green & Haines, 2002; Nel, 2019; Nel et al., 2021). The team members are relationship-driven, inclusive, positive in nature, and enable community members turning creative potential into positive power. Team members of the core group are equipped to envision and shape plans, develop their aptitude and potential, confront social injustices, and establish a culture of collective sharing and action (Nel, 2018a, 2018b; Nel et al., 2021; Whitney et al., 2010).

People who are participating in the community interventions are introduced to participatory monitoring and evaluation (PM&E) from the initiation of the community interventions. PM&E is to track implementation and outputs systematically and to see to which degree the intervention is achieving its objectives and where changes may be needed. The importance is that the community members must be involved so that they can recognize the progress made by the community members and strengthen the sustainability of activities. The community practitioner gradually reduces their involvement in the activities of the group and encourages the active participation of the group to take the lead in tracking and analyzing progress and deciding on corrective action (Nel et al., 2021). Monitoring and evaluation are regular, routine processes of short-term reflection to improve the effectiveness of ongoing activities and progress, which must be done in all the phases from the connection and discovery phase until the disconnecting and departing phase, but especially in the delivery phase. All involved must design the evaluation process and questions to be asked. The main aim of participatory monitoring and evaluation is a time for reflection on the learning that takes place and where to improve. Methods and techniques that can be utilized for monitoring and evaluation are written questionnaires, structured and informal oral interviews, group discussion method, observations, drawings, slides, photos before and after, drama and stories (Nel et al., 2021).

Examples From Practice

ABCD projects are expanding as communities become familiar with the ABCD model.

Example One

A popular kind of project in South Africa is the establishment of vegetable gardens. Unemployed people become aware through the discovering of their assets that they could start their own vegetable gardens instead of relying on food parcels from the government and other organizations. These vegetable gardens usually start when practitioners introduce training to community members on how to start vegetable gardens. Community members combine their assets, noticing that they have different assets and by pulling them together, they could start their vegetable gardens. They usually start with vegetable gardens in their yards. As more people join the project, they look for bigger land, work collaboratively on the land and start selling vegetables to the community and even supermarkets. People build relationships in the process, realize the strength of collective efforts, and expand their effort to the bigger community.

Example Two

A community realized the problem of young unemployed youth with drug addiction problem. These drug addicts gathered daily in a park where they used drugs and made drug deals with drug dealers. The park became a dumping ground for rubbish as well. As it became too dangerous to visit the park, nobody could visit the park. A group of young unemployed out-of-school people started cleaning the park and the drug addicts became threatened by them and did not gather there anymore. The young out-of-school youth decided to go from house to house to collect money (R5 per household) and started cleaning the community. Later, they borrowed a truck from a resident in the community to take the rubbish to the municipality landfill. After six months, the municipality started involving them in the cleaning up of the park and bigger community by providing them with trucks and bins for cleaning up.

Limitations of the Model

There are, however, limitations of the ABCD model. First, ABCD over emphasizes the contributions of community members and associations in terms of community building initiatives. This could distract attention from the role and responsibilities of external stakeholders such as government and businesses in the development of communities and put these stakeholders "off the hook" so to speak (Foot, 2012; Friedli, 2011; MacLeod & Emejulu, 2014). This scenario is changing in South Africa as external stakeholders are, on various levels such as local government level, deliberately engaged and involved in development endeavors. Second, ABCD is seen as "neoliberalism with a community face," meaning that the model encourages a free-market system and a hostility toward government-sponsored social welfare (MacLeod & Emejulu, 2014). On this note, Ennis and West (2010) are of the opinion that ABCD practitioners train communities to survive within Western societies that are driven by neoliberal models instead of challenging, for example, the economic system. This situation is changing in South Africa as ABCD practitioners are consciously enhancing township economies, which are embedded in decolonized African culture and practices, challenging the economic system. Third, while ABCD has some opportunity for creating dialogue with the macro-level structures that impact communities, for example, government, municipality and businesses, the approach has been criticized because it tends to ignore issues related to power and oppression (Mathie & Cunningham, 2003). For professionals and, most importantly, the communities they serve, the ideological foundations of the unjust macro issues might be difficult to accept but also difficult to challenge. However, in South Africa, attempts are made to address power issues and oppression by establishing dialogues between government officials and residents of communities. Last, in addition to above, a major criticism of ABCD is that written descriptive reports primarily written by the agency that undertook ABCD initiatives mainly focus on reporting about the capacity building of community members and associations (internal-looking) without reporting on structural changes (external-looking) brought about by the approach (Mathie et al., 2017). However, ABCD makes progress in enabling communities to work closely with local stakeholders, such as the government.

Conclusion

In South Africa, the ABCD approach and practice model put in place are the building blocks for real and meaningful sustainability of community interventions and the organizations that manage and lead these projects. ABCD provides the foundation for independence and sustainability. The five assets are the core of the process with the social asset, and thus Ubuntu as the glue that drives the process. Ubuntu, which is embedded in the African culture, enables communities to lead their own development by co-investing their own assets, taking advantage of opportunities, and leveraging their own resources with resources of government, businesses, and other organizations. ABCD provides the basis for real ownership and self-determination with the purpose of becoming independent citizens of the country.

REFERENCES

Ashford, G., & Patkar, S. (2001). *The positive path, using appreciative inquiry in rural Indian communities*. Department for International Development (DFID), International Institute for Sustainable Development (IISD).

Block, P. (2009). *Community, the structure of belonging*. Berrett Koehler.

Braun, A.R. (2005). Beyond the problem-solving approach to sustainable rural development. In J. Gonsalves, T. Becker, A. R. Braun, D. Campilan, H. De Chaves, J. Rivaca-Caminade, & R. Vernooy (Eds.), *Participatory research and development for sustainable agricultural and natural resource management a sourcebook volume 1: Understanding participatory research and development* (pp. 129–135). Canada. International Potato Center-Users' Perspectives with Agricultural Research and Development and International Development Research Centre.

Brooks, D., Miller, F., & Dunscombe, M. (2021). *Asset-based community development (ABCD): An emerging practice for the future of local government*. IACD Virtual world community development conference, Nairobi, Kenya.

Brons, L. L. (2015). Othering, an analysis. *Transcience, a Journal of Global Studies*, 6, 69–90.

Cooperrider, D. L., & Whitney, D. (1999). Appreciative inquiry: A positive revolution in change. In P. Holman & T. Devane (Eds.), *The Change handbook: Group methods for shaping the future*. Berrett-Koehle.

Demeshane, J., & Nel, H. (2018). An application of the process of appreciative inquiry in community development: an example from Soweto, South Africa. *Southern African Journal of Social Work and Social Development, 30*(3), 1–17. https://doi.org/10.25159/2415- 5829/3599

Eliasov, N. (2013). *Asset based and citizen led development (ABCD): ABCD training of trainers' toolkit*. Zanolele Insipiritual Creations.

Eliasov, N., & Peters, B. (2013). *Voices in harmony, stories of community-driven development in South Africa*. Coady International Institute.

Emmett, T. (2000). Beyond community participation? Alternative routes to civil engagement and development in South Africa. *Development Southern Africa, 17*(4), 501–518.

Ennis, G. & West, D. (2010). Exploring the potential of social network analysis in asset-based community development practice and research. *Australian Social Work, 63*(4), 404–417.

Frediani, A.A. (2010). Sen's capability approach as a framework to the practice of development. *Development in Practice Journal, 20*(2), 173–187.

Foot, J. (2012). *What makes us healthy? The asset approach in action: Evidence, action, evaluation*. https://www.scdc.org.uk/media/resources/assets-alliance/What%20us%20healthy.pdf

Friedli, L. (2011). *Always look on the bright side of life: The rise of asset approaches in Scotland*. Scottish Anti-Poverty Review. The Poverty Alliance.

Gade, C. B. N. (2012). What is Ubuntu? Different interpretations among South Africans of African descent. *South African Journal of Philosophy, 31*(3), 484–503. https://doi.org/10.1080/02580136.2012.10751789

Green, G. P., & Haines, A. (2008). *Asset building and community development*. SAGE.

Homan, M. S. (2011). *Promoting community change, making it happen in the real world*. Brooks/Cole, Cengage Learning.

Ife, J., & Tesoriero, F. (2006). *Community development, community-based alternatives in an age of globalization* (3rd ed). Pearson.

Johar, N. (2017). Community participation: A cementing process, theorising various dimensions and approaches. *Journal of Construction in Developing Countries, 22*(Supp. 1), 47–61.

Kramer, S., Amos, T., Lazarus, S., & Seedat, M. (2012). The philosophical assumptions, utility and challenges of asset mapping approaches to community engagement. *Journal of Psychology in Africa, 22*(4), 537–546.

Kretzmann, J. P., & McKnight, J. L. (1993). *Building communities from the inside out, a path toward finding and mobilizing a community's assets*. Center for urban Affairs and Policy Research.

Landry, J., & Peters, B. (2018). *Assets on the right(s) track? Reflections at the intersection of human rights-based approaches and asset-based and citizen-led development* (Innovation Series No. 19). Antigonish: Coady International Institute.

MacLeod, M. A., & Emejulu, A. (2014). Neoliberalism with a community face? A critical analysis of asset-based community development in Scotland. *Journal of Community Practice, 22*(4), 430–450. https://doi.org/10.1080/10705422.2014.959147

Mansvelt, N. (2018). Implementing ABCD tools and processes in the context of social work student practice. *Social Work/Maatskaplike Werk, 54*(1), 132–143.

Maphosa, S. B., & Keasley, A. (2015). Disrupting the interruptions: Re-considering Ubuntu, reconciliation and rehumanization. *African Renaissance, 12*(2), 16–47.

Mugumbate, J. R., & Chereni, A. (2019). Using African Ubuntu theory in social work with children in Zimbabwe. *African Journal of Social Work, 9*(1).

Mugumbate, J. R., Mupedziswa, R., Twikirize, J. M., Mthethwa, E., Desta, A. A., & Oyinlola, O. (2023). Understanding Ubuntu and its contribution to social work education in Africa and other regions of the world. *Social Work Education*, 1–17.

Mathie, A., & Cunningham, G. (2003). From clients to citizens: asset-based community development as a strategy for community-driven development. *Development in Practice, 13*(5), 474–486.

Mathie, A., & Cunningham, G. (2005). Who is driving development? Reflections on the transformative potential of asset-based community development. *Canadian Journal of Development Studies, 26*(1), 175–186.

Mathie, A., & Cunningham, G. (Eds.). (2008). *From clients to citizens, communities changing the course of their own development.* Practical Action Publishing.

Mathie, A., Cameron, J., & Gibson, K. (2017, January 1). *Asset-based and citizen-led development: Using a diffracted power lens to analyze the possibilities and challenges,* https://doi.org/10.1177/1464993416674302

McKnight, J., & Block, P. (2010). *The abundant community.* Koehler.

Morse, S. (2011). Communities revisited: The best ideas of the last hundred years. *National Civic Review, 100*(1), 8-14.

Nel, J. B. S. (2011). An application of appreciative inquiry in community development in South Africa. *The Social Work Practitioner-Researcher, Die Maatskaplikewerk Navorser-Praktisyn, 23*(3), 343–362.

Nel, H. (2018a). A comparison between the asset-oriented and needs-based community development approaches in terms of systems changes. *Practice: Social Work in Action, 30*(1), 33–52. https://doi.org/10.1080/09503153.2017.1360474

Nel, H. (2018b). Community leadership: a comparison between asset-based community-led development (ABCD) versus the traditional needs-based approach. *Development Southern Africa, 35*(6), 839–851. https://doi.org/10.1080/0376835X.2018.1502075

Nel, H. (2019). Management functions. In L. K. Engelbrecht (Ed.), *Management and supervision of social workers: Issues and challenges within a social development paradigm* (2nd ed.). Cengage.

Nel, H. (2020). Stakeholder engagement: Asset-based community-led development (ABCD) versus the traditional needs-based approach to community development. *Social Work/Maatskaplike Werk, 56*(3), 264–278. http://socialwork.journals.ac.za/pub; http://dx.doi.org/10.15270/52-2-857

Nel, H., Louw, H., Schenck, R., & Skhosana, R. (2021). *Introduction to participatory community practice.* Unisa Press.

Nel, H., & Pretorius, E. (2012). Applying appreciative inquiry in building capacity in a non-governmental organisation for youth: An example from Soweto, Gauteng, South Africa. *Social Development Issues, 34*(1), 37–55.

Patel, L. (2015). *Social welfare and social development in South Africa* (2nd ed.). Oxford University Press.

Preece, J. (2017). *Community engagement and lifelong learning; the porous university*. Palgrave/Macmillan.

Pretorius, E., & Nel, H. (2012). Reflections on the problem-based approach and the asset-based approach to community development. *The Social Work Practitioner-Researcher/Die Maatskaplikewerk Navorser-Praktisyn, 24*(2), 266–287.

Ssewamala, F. M., Sperber, E., Zimmerman, J. M., & Karimli, L. (2010). The potential of asset-based development strategies for poverty alleviation in Sub-Saharan Africa. *International Journal of Social Welfare, 19*, 433–443.

Simba, P. (2021, March 2021). *A feminist critique of Ubuntu: Implications for citizenship education in Zimbabwe* [PhD thesis in Education Policy Studies, Faculty of Education, Stellenbosch University].

Swanepoel, H., & De Beer, F. (2011). *Community development: Breaking the cycle of poverty* (5th ed.). Juta.

Weyers, M. L. (2016). *The theory and practice of community work: A South African perspective* (2nd ed.). Keurkopie.

Whitney, D., Trosten-Bloom, A., & Rader, K. (2010). *Appreciative leadership*. McGraw Hill.

Yeneabat, M., & Butterfield, A. K. (2012). Part 3: Practice; "We can't eat a road:" Asset-based community development and the Gedam Sefer community partnership in Ethiopia. *Journal of Community Practice, 20*, 134–153.

CHAPTER 6

SELF-HELP GROUP AS A COMMUNITY DEVELOPMENT PLATFORM FOR RURAL HOUSEHOLDS IN KENYA

Atieno Paul Okello, Oino Gutwa Peter, and Atieno Obara Rebeccah Chawiyah

ABSTRACT

Globally, governments and other development practitioners have over the past four decades advocated for grassroots community development in reducing poverty. This drive has led to the emergence of different policy interventions that encourage human-centered approaches, such as self-help groups' (SHGs) empowerment. In rural areas, poverty and marginalized groups have forced populations to pool their resources to achieve both individual and community development. Whereas participation in SHGs has been documented to improve the livelihood of members, the contribution of these groups to community development has not been adequately documented. Moreover, even when SHG movements have been expanding annually, the poverty level is also rising in equal volume. This chapter uses *collective action* theory to guide documentation on how SHGs contribute to the development of the communities at large through impacting household members' livelihoods. The chapter also delves into the impact of intra- and inter-group conflicts, including group finance-related factors. The approach which development partners, including the government, should adopt to integrate the formation of SHGs in their poverty alleviation and gender empowerment interventions is also discussed. In addition, the chapter discusses how such interventions should be acceptable socially, economically, politically, and culturally for the general community development. This would ensure that the resulting community development is environmentally sustainable and generationally stable for the people.

Keywords: household members, community development, livelihoods; self-help group; SHG intra-inter group conflicts

Introduction

Kenya has an economy with a lower-middle income. Despite having the biggest and most developed economy in Eastern and Central Africa, 16.1% of Kenya's population (as of 2022/2023) falls below the global poverty line (World Bank, 2023). Furthermore, the bulk of Kenya's 7.8 million people living in severe poverty were in rural regions in 2022. A total of 7.8 million persons in rural areas lived on less than $1.90 USD per day, while 1.2 million urban residents were among the very poor. The major causes of this extreme poverty are health issues, political corruption, and economic inequality. Poverty makes these things worse. The Kenyan government has received assistance from foreign organizations in its attempts to combat poverty. Over the last 40 years, governments and other development professionals have promoted grassroot development as a means of eradicating poverty.

Self-Help Groups (SHGs)

In light of constraints on financial inclusion experienced by poor and marginalized populations, their financial needs and community development must be addressed only in unique ways. One such innovative approach to include the previously excluded and marginalized population into the mainstream financial services and support community development is participation in self-help groups (SHGs).

Often comprising 8–20 members, SHG members engage in saving and lending activities, dominating the development landscape in the last three decades, particularly in South Asia and Africa (Brody et al., 2017). In such countries, women have gained knowledge in monetary handling and independence as well as networks in the society through SHG participation. This highlights the existence of empowerment arising from participation in SHGs for women, hence developing their communities (Yunus, 2003). Similarly, in developing their communities, participants of these groups also engage in educative messaging such as healthcare. SHGs are formed for a variety of reasons, yet the primary documented purpose has been economic empowerment of poor women and other marginalized segments and hence socioeconomic development of the communities (Gugerty et al., 2019).

Significance and Purpose

Understanding the importance of SHGs in community development is significant in highlighting conventional platforms where the poor and vulnerable families can access critical services. Such services are not only limited to financial inclusion and economic empowerment but also include fora where important information such as reproductive health information is conveyed to people, especially women. SHGs also form critical platforms through which government services such as agricultural support are channeled. Non-state actors have also found SHGs to be important platforms for channeling support to poor families at the grassroots level. For the alleviation of poverty, especially at the grassroots level of the family unit, all players have found SHGs to be important platforms. SHGs are therefore pivotal to achievement of several targets of the sustainable development goals (SDGs) (World Bank, 2023).

Literature Review

The origin of the contemporary self-help group movement can be traced to the Grameen Bank of Bangladesh, which was founded by Mohamed Yunus in 1975 (Yunus, 2003). According to Atieno et al. (2021), the concept of SHG gained traction during the 1970s when Mohammad Yunus launched Grameen Bank in Bangladesh to implement a lending scheme for the poor. Seibold (2012) offers a succinct description of how Yunus drove his microcredit agenda through SHGs for the poor. When Yunus knew his target group—the poor people of Bangladesh—and what he needed to make different, he implemented his findings in a practical way. Yunus "wanted to understand the village" (Siebold, 2021, p. 61) of Jobra, which he had selected to be the starting point of his project to eradicate poverty in Bangladesh (Yunus & Yusus, 1998). As he was a professor at the University of Chittagong, he had a pool of students to use as manpower for his project. Yunus sent his students out to gather information about the inhabitants of Jobra village—close to the University of Chittagong. They asked questions to determine the inhabitants' financial situation. Questions included whether they owned land, if yes, how much, what crops they grew, how long those crops could sustain their families, and so forth. Yunus tried to understand Bangladesh by understanding Jobra. Jobra was "his"

Bangladesh. He then approached those categorized as poor and offered membership in Islamic Banking (Yunus, 2004).

Yunus' next move was to put his new clients, or borrowers as he called them, into groups of five to ten people. These groups, which were about 97% female, gave security to the borrowers. They could give each other support as well as a sense of responsibility to their fellow borrowers in the group. The group played a major role in the disbursement of the loans as it decides which two group members will get the first payments. First, the Grameen Bank extends loans only to two group members. If these two repay regularly for the next six weeks, two more members can become borrowers. The chairman of the group is the last borrower of the five. Also, the control function in the Islamic Banking system was not performed by the bank but was fulfilled from within the group. Everybody in the group wanted their fellow borrowers, and thus the group, to succeed. This was a natural means of accountability within the group as opposed to an external means of control (Yunus, 2004).

Though the model was rare and considered revolutionary in the 1970s, when there were only a handful of fledgling enterprises in Asia and Latin America, the popularity and acceptance of microfinance has become manifest in the vast numbers of microfinance institutions, recently estimated at more than 7,000 by the World Bank, serving more than 20 million poor people in developing countries (World Bank, 2023). In fact, the true numbers are difficult to estimate, because institutions are community-based, informal, and in many countries relatively unregulated. But where there were virtually none 35 years ago, there are undeniably many today. This acceptance has culminated in the awarding of the 2006 Nobel Peace Prize to Muhammad Yunus and the Grameen Bank of Bangladesh, and the United Nations declared 2005 the International Year of Microcredit (Yunus, 2004).

Existing literature focusing on SHGs and its contribution to community development through empowerment continuum concentrates in Asia (India in particular) as well as Sub-Saharan Africa (SSA). For instance, Brody et al. (2017) used a mixed-methods systematic review to explore the impact of women's SHGs on women's socioeconomic and political empowerment for community development in South Asia and other developing countries. They found that women's economic SHGs have positive effects on economic and political empowerment and the general development of their communities. Nichols (2021) investigated the efficacy and equity of SHGs as platforms for development programs using 64 interviews and 6 focus group discussions collected from an agriculture and behavior change intervention delivered through SHGs in eastern India. Results revealed that, while SHGs are a promising platform for health messaging, this is largely dependent on norms of attendance, socioeconomic conditions, and social capital. Social capital is important both within SHGs as well as between SHGs and the implementing organization. Areas with more mature SHGs had greater economic security, allowing more active participation in the intervention than those with more poverty and young SHGs.

In Uttar Pradesh (India), Anand et al. (2020) assessed whether women's SHGs can contribute to sustainable community development. Findings showed that sustainable community development was enhanced through various socioeconomic programs for the group members. In Africa, Meehan and Mengistu (2016) assessed the impact of Tearfund SHG intervention following El Nino disasters in Ethiopia, emphasizing the importance of technical support and advice to the success of these groups. The facilitators played a crucial role in a group's performance and all groups received advice on conservation, management of resources and avoidance of waste, savings culture, and diversification of income generation through loans for business activity. Groups that received training on conservation agriculture and disaster risk reduction showed greater mitigation and adaptive behaviors than those that did not. Another study by Aikaruwa et al. (2014) investigated the social functionality of SHGs in two wards of Shinyanga District in Tanzania. Data was collected from 120 respondents and revealed that the groups were purely informal yet accelerated community development through offering credit and saving facilities to its members, offering social support, and technical support. These groups have been beneficial to members both socially and economically.

Similarly, van Hulst-Mooibroek's (2017) mixed-methods study analyzed the extent to which the SHGs program implemented by five local partners increased the food security of marginalized groups and their resilience to crisis in a sustainable way. Their findings show that SHGs have an even stronger potential in fostering community development through disaster risk prevention, business development, and conservation agriculture.

The Concept of SHG

As explained above, a SHG is a voluntary autonomous association of between 10 and 20 persons from the homogeneous weaker and supposedly marginalized section of the society with a common interest, formed and managed democratically without any political affiliation (Baishya et al., 2020). The core aim of SHGs is to pool efforts for the purpose of solving a community problem. Previously, SHGs were groups formed by people who could not access formal financial services from banking systems, hence were relying on savings and lending from group membership (Chitere, 2018).

India's National Bank for Agriculture and Rural Development (NABARD) launched its savings group linkage program in 1992 and developed a policy framework and capacity building program for NGOs and SHGs to facilitate these linkages. By 2000, savings groups had become a central part of the Indian government's efforts to mitigate poverty and promote rural livelihoods. As of 2006, NABARD estimated that over 1,500,000 savings groups were in existence. In India, SHGs are categorized and monitored in three different arrangements based on how these are linked with their supporting organizations. They are commonly referred to as Bank-promoted, Government-promoted model and NGOs-promoted. Today, financing through SHGs has become the best medium to include the rural poor in the formal financial sector (Bharamappanavara & Jose, 2015). In sub-Saharan Africa (SSA), SHGs build on longstanding forms of collective savings and labor, including rotating savings and credit associations (ROSCAs) that were widespread prior to NGO-led initiatives (Gugerty et al., 2019).

In recent years, many NGOs have created and disseminated similar collective savings models, such as village savings and loan associations (VSLAs) that build on the ROSCA foundation (Odell, 2012). CARE, an international NGO, launched its first formal savings group program in Niger in 1991, and several large NGOs, including Catholic Relief Services, Plan International, Oxfam, the Aga Khan Foundation, World Vision, and Pact have since introduced savings group promotion programs across the continent (Odell, 2012). According to a 2011 report, the number of savings groups in Africa reported by seven NGOs across 35 countries estimated to be around 200,000, reaching over 3.8 million people, however it is likely that this estimate considerably understates the true number of such groups (Odell, 2012). Some governments in sub-Saharan Africa seek to provide some support to SHGs through government extension agents. But, unlike the situation in India, most governments in the SSA have not created explicit policy frameworks designed to link SHGs to financial institutions or public institutions.

In Kenya, the government through the Ministry of Planning and National Development has strengthened SHGs by rolling out various funding programs such as Uwezo Fund, Women Enterprise Development Fund, and Youth Enterprise Development Fund among others since the year 2008 (Atieno et al., 2021) This has been purposely undertaken so that the poor and vulnerable groups including women and youth can also make decisions in their economic welfare as well as contribute to the country's economic growth and realization of rural development (Seibold, 2012). SHGs have therefore formed a milestone in enhancing household livelihood among the poor, especially in the rural parts of Kenya and in SSA (United Nations Development Programme, 2020). In the contemporary situation, SHGs take three prominent forms: (1) savings groups; (2) women's health groups; and (3) farmer groups. The following sections provide brief descriptions of these groups, as presented by Anderson et al. (2014).

Savings Groups

Rotating Savings and Credit Associations (ROSCA), popularly known as merry-go-round, Accumulating Savings and Credit Associations (ASCAs), and Village Savings and Loan Associations (VSLAs), may be initially formed by individuals, and are later often promoted by NGOs or government agencies. Savings groups often have multiple aims of fostering community development through providing reliable mechanisms for savings and expanding access to credit; these include promoting opportunities for income-generating activities, providing alternative forms of insurance, and increasing the social capital of participants. In countries such as India, Bangladesh and other Asian Nations, savings groups are often linked to financial institutions to secure funds and gain access to external loans. Some savings groups have a set savings cycle, often a year long, at the end of which funds are dispersed and members are free to leave without penalty; other groups are intended to have more permanent membership. Savings groups are commonly used as a platform to deliver health and empowerment interventions. Unlike many group-based microfinance programs, savings SHGs focus primarily on savings and mobilizing internal funds, rather than taking out loans from outside sources.

Women's Health Groups

These are typically formed and facilitated by local women who have been selected and trained by an intervening NGO. Women's health groups are formed to increase knowledge about maternal and community health issues and to mobilize community responses, often through a "Participatory Learning and Action" model. They are usually made up exclusively of women of reproductive age or women who are pregnant, though meetings are often open to any who wish to participate. This type of SHG is almost always time-bound, lasting one to three years.

Farmers' Groups

Farmers' groups are typically larger than other SHGs, ranging from 12 to 40 members, and most often include both women and men. Goals include increasing access to credit and inputs, risk-pooling, accessing high-value markets to sell goods, and facilitating knowledge exchange and, in the long run, the communities of the group members are developed. Farmer group members may also participate in savings groups or collective agricultural activities. They are usually formed and supported by NGOs and are typically intended to be ongoing.

Theory of Collective Action for Understanding SHGs Participation

Participation in SHGs is sufficiently discussed under the lenses of Mancur Olson's Collective Action theory (Olson, 1965). In 1965, Mancur Olson published *The Logic of Collective Action*, a highly prized contribution to the body of literature explaining successes and failures of collective action (Desai & Joshi, 2014). According to Czech (2016), Olson's (1965) book continues to provide scholars with cardinal insights into one of the theories mostly associated with social movement activities, thanks to its universal method of individualistic perspective and economic calculus. Methodological individualism was the reason for its success as it allowed for closer scrutiny of former theories. A collective action situation exists "when a number of individuals have a common or collective interest, when they share a single purpose or objective, and when individual, unorganized action, will either not be able to advance that common interest at all, or will not be able to advance that interest adequately" (Olson, 1965, p. 7). The theory articulates that people who share common traits are more likely to share social networks, affecting subsequent interaction and cooperation. Like-minded people may have preferences for working with each other; they may also have better knowledge on how to sanction and reward each other, which is important for establishing cooperation.

In collective action theory, a group should be treated as an assembly of rational individuals, not as an entity itself. Olson's (1965) main assumptions in deriving the theory were thus methodological individualism and rational behavior of individuals. Thus, Olson assumed that group behavior should be explained by economic calculus, determined by the incentives and costs that each member of a group faces. In other words, Olson applied economic methods into social phenomenon, whose understanding was at best vague. In Olson's view, even if individuals do share a common goal and even if the transaction costs of organizing a group are nil, this is not enough for a collective action to take place. We should consider the relation of benefits to costs on an individual, not group, level. First, even if collective benefits are large, the benefit gained by a single individual will probably be much smaller and may not cover the costs borne. And second, if all members of a group will benefit from the collective action, then there is no incentive for an individual to engage in these activities.

Small groups provide collective goods only through the voluntary action of their members. The incentives to free-ride or shirk are limited here by social control or by transparent effects of group action. However, a small group can take up a successful collective action even if only one member of the group will cover all the costs—on the condition that the benefits will outweigh the costs borne by this individual. In this situation, shirking and free riding do not matter, because the group will obtain benefits, anyway. For all these reasons, Olson (1965) names these groups privileged ones and points to the fact that these groups are most successful in gaining privileges and providing collective goods. He also notices that many successful large groups work in subgroups: committees, councils, and boards, because this is efficient. Similarly, business lobbies often gain privileges because they are organized not as the whole business class, but as oligopolistic branches which pursue their own particular interests. According to Tembo (2015), this occurs because having a common interest or concern among members of a group (community, region, country) or any other grouping does not mean they will act to maximize gains for the whole group.

The theory of collective action befits SHG discussions in three critical ways as follows:

First, group membership of SHGs is always small (between 8 and 20 members). This implies that the collective action problem or free-rider problem will be closely checked and promptly addressed. The collective action problem emerges in group settings where all individuals can materially profit by not contributing to the group (Olson, 1965). However, when all individuals withhold contribution, collective action fails, and all are worse off. If individuals all act in their own material self-interest in these situations, it would seem impossible for public goods to be produced. According to Willer (2009), conflicts exist in a collective action between individual and group level rationality because low level of contribution among members in a bigger group like community level outfits leave the entire body worse off. The tension existing between individual and collective interests in groups with large membership therefore results in collective action being regarded as a *social problem* where what is rational, in the narrow economic sense, at the individual level is irrational for the group.

Second, rationality issues experienced in the collective action problem are one of the conditions behind SHG formation: the small voluntary groups have common interests in group formation. Types of groups: savings groups, women's health groups, and farmers' groups each have a common goal. In savings groups, members purely desire to save and obtain credit. In women's health groups, members are trained and enrolled in specific healthcare problems. On the other hand, members in farmers' groups are interested in obtaining farm inputs and getting good markets for their products. In SHGs, conflicts of interests are adequately minimized.

Third, the fact that in SHG arrangements, group meetings are held weekly, hence addressing the collective action problem or free-rider problem. The face-to-face weekly meetings (Weingärtner et al., 2017) can pick free-riders and understand their motives hence capable of addressing this problem. This chapter therefore provides some highlights to, among others, some of the challenges facing SHGs in the continuum of livelihood development for rural households.

Obstacles Confronting SHG Participation

Despite documented benefits attributed to SHGs and the huge growth in the number of such groups, there are challenges to SHG participation:

1. There are considerable cases of eligible families who are yet to join SHGs and also many SHG members who have dropped out of their groups, willingly or unwillingly. This is a pointer that there are serious obstacles confronting participation in SHGs in different contexts.
2. Lack of training on economic activities to support members through income-generating activities (IGAs), dominance (and sometimes dictatorship) by the group leader, members who often fail in their monthly savings, members who fail to attend regular meetings, lack of economic activity other than micro lending and less profit from income-generating activities engaged in from SHG microcredit form major obstacles in participation continuously in the group activities (Baishya et al., 2020).
3. Weakness in financial management, defaults in micro-credit repayment and mode of recoveries, and governance by group management are also challenges that confront participation in SHGs.
4. Lack of discipline to conduct regular meetings, regular savings and record keeping; rigidity of the banks on the withdrawal of savings; erosion of mutual trust; non-rotation of leaders; disbursement of bank loans equally among the members; and lack of a long-term view are also some of the issues inhibiting participation in SHGs.
5. Issues that may confront smooth operations of SHGs revolve around the conducting of face-to-face meeting, loans and repayments, and group cohesion, among others.

According to Ballem et al. (2012), for every 2,490 groups registered at the beginning of each year, an estimated 144 groups become defunct at the end of the same year in India.

Recommendations

Recommendations for addressing the issues concerning SHGs are as follows: It is observable that the intent of SHGs is to provide a pathway for various socioeconomic engagements that would foster general community development. This is possible when groups of between 8 and 20, with homogenous characteristics formed with such intentions, pool their savings for the purpose of loaning each other and engaging in various activities. With each member being the guarantor of the other members, and the collateral being one's savings, it becomes easier even for rural household members to access credit and engage in economic activities that would hence develop the communities. The coming into play of development agencies such as NGOs has provided linkages for these SHGs, connecting them further to financial institutions. In addition, most governmental agencies have found a suitable mechanism for channeling development programs to the grassroots in SHGs, hence enabling critical support to reach the very poor in society. Thus, previously unbanked poor households without collateral have found themselves as being one of the serious customers of formal financial institutions across South Asia and sub-Saharan Africa.

Conclusion

This chapter also concludes that participation in SHGs has experienced numerous challenges. Migration from one place to another due to various factors, such as unemployment, marriage (for women), and drought or poverty, is a significant obstacle constraining participation in SHGs. Default in loan repayment implies that other members, being guarantors, will be obliged to pay for the defaulter, a situation which constraints participation in SHGs to a large extent. Similarly, poor bookkeeping due to fraudulent officials or lack of knowledge in financial record-keeping makes members lose track of their savings and hence fail to have faith in the group. Another significant obstacle is the inconvenience that weekly meeting attendance and group activities cause to members since most of these people are in the informal sector and work seven days a week. Group conflicts are also another obstacle confronting participation in SHGs. Conflicts occur due to partiality practices by some group officials or the area officer in charge of social development. These obstacles can lead to mass dropout leading to defunct groups.

The implications of the conclusions are that a people-structured platform has been put in place in the form of SHGs upon which development interventions to grassroots can be channeled. Similarly, due to linkages to financial institutions and development opportunities opened up by the existence of SHGs, workable solutions to overcome challenges noted should be crafted continuously. Moreover, efforts to create conducive contexts within which SHGs thrive should be a concern of all stakeholders and scholars, requiring further research.

To help in streamlining SHGs, government departments responsible for social development should appoint qualified bookkeepers to maintain the books of SHGs. Similarly, the relevant government department should also appoint a qualified person to act as an arbitrator in charge of conflicts within various SHGs. Finally, the relevant government department should conduct annual assessments in the sector (SHG movement) to reveal progress and shortcomings which are experienced by various players.

REFERENCES

Aikaruwa, D. B., Sumari, G. A., & Maleko, G. N. (2014). Social functionality of self-help groups in Tanzania. *Journal of Business Administration and Education*, 5(2), 99–136.

Anand, P., Saxena, S., Martinez, R. O., & Dang, H.-A. H. (2020). *Can women's self-help groups contribute to sustainable development? Evidence of capability changes from Northern India*. IZA Discussion Papers, IZA DP No. 12940.

Anderson, C. L., Gugerty, M. K., Biscaye, P., True, Z., Clark, C., & Harris, K. P. (2014). Self- help groups in development: A review of evidence from South Asia and sub-Saharan Africa. *EPAR Technical Report #283*. Evans School of Public Policy & Governance, University of Washington. https://epar.evans.uw.edu/sites/default/files/epar_283_shg_evidence_review_brief_10.23.20.Pdf.

Atieno, P. O., Moseh, G., & Ombachi, N. K. (2021). The role of self-help groups' structures in uplifting the livelihoods of households in Nyakach Sub County of Kisumu County, Kenya. *International Journal of Research and Innovation in Social Science*, V(VI), 239—246.

Baishya, M., Sarkar, A., & Argade, S. (2020). Problems concerning women's participation and dropout from self-help groups in Koraput District of Odisha, India. *International Journal of Current Microbiology and Applied Sciences*, 9(6), 3180–3186.

Ballem, A., Mohammad, G. A., & Venkata N. A. (2012). *Why do people not join or drop out of SHGs?* MicroSave—Market-led Solutions for Financial Services.

Bharamappanavara, S. C., & Jose, M. (2015). Group dynamics and collective performance of self-help groups under different microcredit delivery models in Karnataka. *Agricultural Economics Research Review*, 28(1), 1–13.

Brody, C., Hoop, T. D., Vojtkova, M., Warnock, R., Dunbar, M., Murthy, P., & Dworkin, S. L. (2017). Can self-help group programs improve women's empowerment? A systematic review. *Journal of Development Effectiveness*, 9(1), 15–40.

Chitere, P. O. (2018). Self-help groups as a means for development and welfare: Their characteristics, membership, and performance in Kenya. *International Journal of Social Work and Human Services Practice, 6*(2), 30–45.

Czech S. (2016). Mancur Olson's collective action theory 50 years later. A view from the institutionalist perspective. *Journal of International Studies, 9*(3), 114–123. https://doi.org/10.14254/2071-8330.2016/9-3/9

Desai, R. M., & Joshi, S. (2014). Collective action and community development: Evidence from self-help groups in rural India. *The World Bank Economic Review, 28*(3), 492–524.

Gugerty, M. K., Biscaye, P., & Leigh Anderson, C. (2019). Delivering development? Evidence on self-help groups as development intermediaries in South Asia and Africa. *Development Policy Review, 37*(1), 129–151.

Meehan, F., & Mengistu, E. (2016). *Drought, resilience, and self help in Ethiopia: A review of Tearfund Self Help Groups following El Nino*. Tufts University. https://www.agri-learning-ethiopia.org/wp-content/uploads/2015/10/SHG-Report-FINAL.pdf

Nichols, C. (2021). Self-help groups as platforms for development: The role of social capital. *World Development, 146*(2021), 1–12.

Odell, M. (2012). *Micro-finance in Africa: State-of-the-Sector Report 2011. Closing the gap*. Retrieved from the CARE website: https://www.care.org/sites/default/files/documents/MF-2011-CARE-Access-Africa-Closing-the-Gap.pdf

Olson, M. (1965). *The logic of collective action: Public goods and the theory of groups* (Harvard Economic Studies, Vol. 124). Harvard University Press.

Seibold, G. (2012). *Mohammad Yunus and the Grameen Bank—How Muhammad Yunus shows at the example of the Grameen Bank how even in a Muslim setting micro-finance banking can be implemented on a secular base*. Unpublished paper submitted to ZamZam University, Mogadishu, Somalia.

Tembo, F. (2015). *Improving service provision: Drawing on collective action theory to fix incentives*. A governance practitioner's notebook: Alternative ideas and approaches. Organisation for Economic Cooperation and Development (OECD), pp. 281–300.

The United Nations Development Programme. (2020). *Human development report, accelerating gender equality and women empowerment*.

Van Hulst-Mooibroek, H. (2017). *Final evaluation of the self-help group/food security programme, Horn of Africa*. Tear Netherlands/Tearfund UK Protracted Crisis Programme.

Weingärtner, L., Pichon, F., & Simonet, C. (2017). *How self-help groups strengthen resilience: A study of Tearfund's approach to tackling food security in protracted crises in Ethiopia*. Overseas Development Institute. https://www.odi.org/sites/odi.org.uk/files/resource-documents/11625.pdf

Willer, R. (2009). *A status theory of collective action*. Emerald. https://sociology.stanford.edu/publications/status-theory-collective-action

World Bank. (2023, May 4th). *Measuring development: Mitigating the risks and impacts of climate change*.

Yunus, M., (2003). *Banker to the Poor: Micro-lending and the battle against world poverty*. PublicAffairs.

Yunus, M. (2004). Grameen Bank, microcredit and millennium development goals. *Economic and Political Weekly*, 4077–4080.

Yunus, M., & Yusus, A. J. M. (1998). *Banker to the poor*. Penguin Books India.

CHAPTER 7

AFRICAN CENTERED COMMUNITY DEVELOPMENT IN SOCIAL WORK

Exploring Imbewu Youth Empowerment Centre as an Asset-Based Community Informed Project

Thembelihle Brenda Makhanya

ABSTRACT

The global adoption of Western and European principles only in community development prevents engagement and maximal use of unique African assets and realities. There is a need for expanding the community development terrain by engaging with African forms of development. Although adopting scholarship from the global north in developing African communities can bear minimal benefits, the unique realities of the African continent, calls for the African scholarship that is sensitive, value-driven and has an interest in the wellbeing of African communities. Based on the narrative literature review and Afrocentric framework, this chapter engages with African community development perspectives in social work interventions. Imbewu Youth Empowerment Centre (IYEC) is illustrated as an example in the call for assets-based community informed development. The call is for people at the grassroots level to be actively involved and to have perspectives in their own development. The chapter argues for community development projects to serve as a strategy for social justice and effective service delivery. Hence, the emphasis is on development in African societies that is based on maximizing the use of resources for the community to be served. For a decolonial transformation in social work practice, there is thus a need for national and global development projects to be the collaborative efforts that resonate and be rooted on the assets and perspectives of people at the grassroots level. The call is for advancement of bottom-up rather than top-down approaches only in sustaining development.

Keywords: community development, Afrocentric, IYEC, transformation and social work

Introduction

Social work focuses on three methods of interventions, namely, case, group, and community work (Sesoko, 2015). Intervention at a community level is influenced by the shared needs of the majority population in a community (Nel, 2018). This is one of the crucial interventions based on its target on a larger and broader scale. Community development is thus the intervention at a community level. The brief definition of community development will foreground the discussions. Community refers to people who share and interact in a space (Goel, 2014). Chauya (2015) views community as a group of people who share common perspectives and joint actions. Development focuses on advancements, which is a transition from a state of need to a state of improvements (Chauya, 2015). The focus of community development is therefore on coordinating local people to work together to improve not only individual needs but also that of the community. Indeed, Nel (2020) argues that "Community development aims to enhance sustainable development in a way that engages community members, who take ownership of their own development and become self-reliant" (p. 264). Several stakeholders coordinate this kind of intervention. Thus, community development initiatives are run by different organizations, such as non-profit and faith-based organizations, community-based initiatives, and government institutions.

Community development is one of the important interventions of social workers, since the focus is on a person within the environment. Through engaging with global and local literature, this chapter explores community participation as a tool for development in Africa. Meaningful community development allows for exploration of local voices and experiences to be incorporated in advancements for change and sustainability (Makhanya, 2021; Nel, 2020). The discussions in this book chapter refer to Imbewu Youth Empowerment Centre (IYEC) as an example of an asset-based community informed intervention. This, in turn, serves as a tool for community empowerment since it encourages a grassroots/bottom-up approach for community development to reflect the society it serves (Nel, 2020). African centered approaches play a crucial role in the outcomes of community development that aim to improve the lives of African people (Makhanya & Zibane, 2020).

The chapter takes into consideration the impact of global pandemics, such as colonialism and apartheid, on the underdevelopment of South African rural communities. Social work is conceptualized and its role in community development is discussed. African centeredness as a framework for decolonization in community development with the focus on valuing community views and perspectives is explored. Imbewu Youth Empowerment Centre as a form of community development is discussed and the conclusions highlight lessons for African centered, asset-based community development.

Uncovering the Role of Colonialism and Apartheid in African Communities

COVID-19 (the coronavirus) in Africa (He et al., 2020) came during the period where the continent was struggling to reverse the injustices of the past caused by colonialism and apartheid. Colonialism was the policy of acquiring full or partial political control over another country, occupying it with settlers, and exploiting it economically (Ndlovu-Gatsheni, 2020). Colonialism was the invention of asymmetrical and colonial intersubjective relations between colonizers and the colonized (Gray & Mazibuko, 2003). It economically institutes dispossession and transfers of economic resources from indigenous to those who are colonizing. It claims to be a civilizing project, as it hides its sinister motives (Makhanya, 2021). The project also creates institutions and structures of power that sustain colonizer-colonized relations of exploitation, domination, and repression (Ndlovu-Gatsheni, 2020). For instance, Western/European countries oppressed the African continent in different ways. The late 15th century marked the arrival of European and Western powers in Africa (Birmingham, 1995). The arrival brought changes in the African indigenous system, wars, and slave trades disrupting African spaces (Ndlovu-Gatsheni, 2020). Such power imposition and control were proclaimed as "white people burden of developing African countries" (Birmingham, 1995, p. 1). It thus altered forever African culture, indigenous knowledge systems, and natural resources that African communities had relied on for sustaining livelihood in communities.

Colonial racism also demonstrated how Europeans ruled over Africans for the advancement of European and Western colonizers (Tsotsi, 2000, p. 6). For example, the Europeans hierarchically arranged the people of the world, with Caucasians at the top (the dominants), and indigenous peoples at the bottom (Tsotsi, 2000). Africans were placed at the bottom because they were regarded as having inadequate physical abilities and qualities as humans to independently advance their development (Zibane, 2018). Hence, the assets, land, and resources of African indigenous communities were confiscated, and some demolished, while the Western norms were elevated (Tamburro & Tamburro, 2014). This process brought not only a massacre of resisting African people but also massive underdevelopment of the African countries and communities. Although in South Africa, colonialism dismantled around 1902, apartheid resuscitated the discrimination and oppression (Makhanya, 2021).

Apartheid was a policy or system of segregation or discrimination on the grounds of race. Apartheid was a racial segregation system in South Africa that was enforced through legislation by the National Party from 1948 to 1994 (Masuku & Makhanya, 2023; Okoth, 2006). It is interesting to mention that, although there were already many trained South African social workers during apartheid, they were consumed by the apartheid government (Smith, 2010). Thus, they could not respond to African societal needs and brutality. This suggests that, although social work was meant to alleviate human suffering (Smith, 2013), it could not rescue Africans from oppression. The social workers at that time were used as a state instrument, thus not supporting any movement struggle of the Africans (Smith, 2014). Some African social workers were, however, not happy with the setting; as a result, they went behind the apartheid government and supported African movements that were advancing development of African societies (Makhanya, 2020).

According to Patel (2005), community work led by social workers, such as political movements, did have a transformative character in challenging apartheid social welfare. For instance, a South African Black Social Workers Association participated in a two-day first protest action against apartheid in Cape Town in 1980 (Smith, 2014). Another example of social workers resisting apartheid is found in the activities of Build a Better Society, where social workers were working in the Cape flats and beyond in mobilizing and conscientizing African people about fundamental human rights and community advancements (Smith, 2014). These activities and others contributed to the South African transition to democracy. Although the democratic liberations and engagements are in place, decolonial and African-centered engagements are continuing debates (Smith, 2010) due to the continuous suffering and underdevelopment of African communities (Makhanya, 2022). Hence, scholars argue that colonialism and apartheid have ended in the ideal rather than in the material sense (Smith, 2010).

Community Development in Social Work

International Federation of Social Workers (IFSW) general meeting and International Association of Schools of Social Work (IASSW, 2014) general assembly defined social work as a practice-based profession and academic discipline that focuses on the collaborative efforts for empowerment and advancement of human life. This locates the responsibilities of a social worker within a critical, interactive, and socially engaged paradigm (Ornellas et al., 2018). Social workers are change agents in individuals, groups, and communities (Nel, 2020). Thus, community development is fundamental to this focus.

Developing a community includes interest-based, place-based, and other forms of community interest (Nel, 2018; Phillips & Pittman, 2009). In this sense, community can be theoretically understood as the combination of three dimensions, namely human ecology, systems, and field theory (Goel, 2014). Human ecology refers to interrelationships where local people interact to meet their requirements and the relationships of caring (Goel, 2014; Sesoko, 2015). Systems theory perceives the community as a combination of different sub-systems for achieving common goals (Trotter, 2021). It is the combination of individuals holding certain status for community objectives. The focus is on social interaction (Goel, 2014; Hustedde, 2009). Relationships in the community can emanate from shared identities, such as culture, place, and ideology (Nel, 2020). It is the responsibility of the community to function, assist, and support its members (Nel, 2015). Use and sharing of resources is central to community development (Vincent, 2009). Communities hold a central role to their members' social, economic, spiritual, and political factors as they provide a sense of belonging to their individual members (Goel, 2014; Nel, 2018). From the brief descriptions, one can attest that community development focuses on inclusiveness (Vincent, 2009) and participation, with social workers coordinating such community interaction for empowerment and advancement (Kreitzer, 2012; Nel, 2020).

From the above, community development is the intervention approach in social work that focuses on people united for common interest (Goel, 2014). The community development approach can be adopted when dealing with marginalized communities that face social issues (Hearn & Tanner, 2009). Most of such issues emanate from unjust broader policies and failure of the state. Goel (2014) argued that,

> The failure of neo-liberal policies and the social democratic welfare state in meeting human needs has become evident in the last four decades and the current 21st century where widening gaps between the rich and poor, an increase in hunger, poverty, crime, and social unrest is evident in most of the world. (p. 6)

There is thus a need for processes that ensure resilience in communities. Empowerment is thus a central human dignity in principles of community development (Chawane, 2000; Nel, 2020). As argued by Goel (2014), for progressive change in the social structures, social policy must change to advance the lives of the disadvantaged. This is a call for collective responsibility in addressing unjust policies (Makhanya, 2021). There is a need for people to participate and be engaged in all levels of societal intervention for sustainability, which is crucial in community development (Nel, 2020).

The Community Development Process

The process of community development includes establishing the organizing group, creating a mission statement, identifying community stakeholders, collecting, and analyzing information, developing effective communication processes, expanding the organization, and creating the vision statement (Vincent, 2009, p. 64). It is crucial for the process of creating a comprehensive strategic plan to have a leadership and plan management team. Plan implementation needs to be followed by an evaluation of the outcomes. That is, to examine if the project achieved its intended outcome. After the process, it is important to create new goals and objectives for sustainable development (Nel, 2015; Vincent, 2009).

In the process of developing the community, planning, designing, and deciding who will be at the decision table (Okubo, 2009) might not be simple. It is thus fundamental to recruit the stakeholders for support (Nel, 2020; Okubo, 2009). West (2009) emphasizes the importance of establishing community-based organizations that are critical in the developing of leadership skills (Kolzow, 2009). It is also important for community developers to acknowledge that skills do not emanate from birthright, but they are learned and developed (Kolzow, 2009). There is thus a need for collaboration to mentor local leadership. The focus should also be on community assessment and human infrastructure. The process of community development needs to be based on fundamental professional values. In developing communities, social work professional values include honesty, loyalty, fairness, courage, caring, respect, tolerance, duty, and lifelong learning (Vincent, 2009). This is for improving the quality of life for all citizens through building shared values, goals, objectives, and vision (Nel, 2020).

This discussion presents community development in social work as the solidarity building strategy that includes relationships, structure, power, shared meaning, communication, and decision making (Hustedde, 2009, p. 20). One of the community development approaches that social work has embraced is asset-based community development (Kretzmann &

McKnight). Asset-based community development is defined as an approach that focuses on assets, capabilities, and strengths in facilitating community advancement through collaboration with different stakeholders (Nel, 2020). The focus is on capacity building: "The main focus of the community development approach is on instituting those interactive processes that help communities to take autonomous decisions on meeting their needs and addressing issues that affect their life the most" (Goel, 2014, p. 6). The focus is also on collective action instead of individual approach. For example, IYEC can be regarded as a form of asset-based community development. The NGO focuses on what is existing in the community rather than what is missing, a form of social capital in building a community (Mattessich, 2009). Phillips and Pittman (2009, p. 7) also argued that development is a form of "social capital or capacity" that uses the abilities of the community members to mobilize resources for community development (Nel, 2018). Thus, despite challenges such as being time consuming, costly, and other difficulties (Haines, 2009), the IYEC NGO as a form of community development focuses on working together. The emphasis is on the need for "social capital building or capacity building," which is a comprehensive effort to and support in solving community problems (Phillips & Pittman, 2009, p. 7).

African Centeredness as a Form Of Decolonisation in Community Development

Afrocentricity, Afrocentric worldview, or African-centered worldview are terms used interchangeably. Afrocentricity merged back in 1954, and Marcus Garvey was one of the activists of ideology (Chawane, 2000). Molefe Asante then popularized the term in the 1980s (Chawane, 2000). Afrocentricity suggests that Africans must look at knowledge and experiences and understand them based on African perspectives (Kreitzer, 2012). The focus is on African viewpoints. Asante (2003) defines Afrocentricity to mean "placing African culture at the centre of any analysis that involves studying African people" (p. 6). It is a mode of thought and action in which the centrality of African interests, values, and perspectives predominates (Asante, 2003). Theoretically, it is placing the African people at the center of any analysis of African phenomena. It is an intellectual movement and a political view of simple re-discovery of "African Centeredness" (Chawane 2000, p. 79). Decoloniality is central to this focus.

Decoloniality is a school of thought used principally by an emerging Latin American movement that focuses on untangling the production of knowledge from a primarily Eurocentric episteme (Makhanya, 2021). It critiques the perceived universality of Western knowledge and the superiority of Western culture. Decoloniality is the practice of decolonization by critically examining dominant practices and knowledge in modern society (Ndlovu-Gatsheni, 2015). Asante (2003) proposes five Afrocentric methods for decolonial and Afrocentric community engagement. Such methods are also crucial for asset-based community development interventions.

- The phenomenon needs to be explored within its location. The phenomenon needs to be analyzed against the psychological relationship of its time and space. This means that phenomenon exploration must always be located. This allows for the exploration of complex interrelations of different phenomena based on diverse locations (Asante, 2003). Thus, the needs that are addressed by community intervention must be identified by those affected based on their experiences.
- The Afrocentric paradigm view phenomenon as made of diversity and dynamics; thus, the phenomenon's location is accurately recorded amid fluctuations (Asante, 2003). This means that the explorer/investigator must be aware of his/her standpoint in critical analysis. These dimensions include but are not limited to culture, history, location, and politics. For example, this method conscientizes social workers in communities to be critical of their role and position during community development interventions.
- Afrocentrism views culture from an etymological perspective (Asante, 2003), a word that is used to acknowledge the importance of knowing the author and his/her locational/ origin before analysis. Asante emphasizes the importance of considering the background and location of the author, who has produced specific knowledge. Knowledge can only be applied to different contexts with the conscious mind of its source of origin. This is to allow context-specific applications. Thus, the strategies used for community development interventions need critical engagement before application.
- The masks behind the rhetoric of power, privilege, and position are uncovered in Afrocentrism to understand places created by principal myths (Asante, 2003).
- Asante (2009) further argues that "the Afrocentric method locates the imaginative structure of a system of economics, bureau of politics, the policy of the government, expression of cultural form in the attitude, direction, and language of the phenomenon, be it text, institution, personality, interaction or event" (p. 4). This means that nothing is taken for granted in Afrocentric methods, but all existence is subject to critical

analysis. Afrocentric theory encourages people to be empowered in community intervention process by including their cultures and interests (Makhanya, 2021; Nel, 2020).

The above discussion suggests Afrocentricity as a perspective that allows Africans to be subjects rather than objects on Europe's fringes. Gray and Mazibuko (2003) also viewed Afrocentric as referring to an idea and a perspective which holds that African people can and should see, study, interpret, and interact with people, life, and reality from the vantage point of African people rather than from the vantage point of European people, or Asian, or other non-African people. Such an attitude allows for mobilization of assets within the community for development that relates to the realities of community members (Nel, 2015). It is a philosophical perspective associated with the discovery, location, and actualization of African agency within the context of history and culture. For instance, the South African history of colonialism and apartheid suggests certain legacies that cannot be overlooked in community development processes of the country. This suggests that Afrocentric is concerned with discovering the African's central place in every case to determine interventions, engagements and development based on their experiences for context-specific relevance (Asante, 2003; Ramose, 1998). It is with this understanding that community assets can be mobilized and used effectively for community development.

Imbewu Youth Empowerment Center as a Form of Asset-Based Community Development

Imbewu Youth Empowerment Centre (IYEC) NPO no: 254-023, is a non-profit organization located on the southern side of KwaZulu-Natal, Port Shepstone, South Africa. The organization is in the rural and underdeveloped part of the area. It was founded by seven young people, who are university graduates but reside in the community. Founders come from diverse fields such as Social Work, Psychology, Education, Economics and Community Development and were able to use their educational careers as assets for developing their community. Due to high issues of poverty, teenage pregnancy, drug and alcohol abuse and other social ills, the NGO works with local schools for academic guidance and offers psychosocial support to young people in the community through workshops and awareness campaigns. The focus is on inclusiveness and welfare of the disadvantaged community members. Several issues contributed to the collaboration and establishment of the NGO. For instance, several students (from social work, education, and management) noticed the vulnerability of young people in rural areas of KwaZulu Natal (KZN) during their university practice. They noticed how institutions such as day care, primary and high schools located in such communities suffer with issues such as career guidance, learning materials and an appropriate learning environment without exposure for other institutions to offer support. This vulnerability leads to school dropouts, teenage pregnancy, and drug abuse (Makhanya, 2021). Hence, the NGO founders shared an idea with others, which was to locate the Centre in one of the rural areas to focus on coordinating support for young people. Thus, Imbewu Youth Empowerment Centre was born in January 2019 and registered with the Department of Social Development in November 2020.

Programs offered by IYEC include subject-career awareness with Grade 9 and Grade 12 learners. The NGO also works with matric learners regarding post school orientation through the program called *umhlahlandlela* (crafting the way). Support and collaboration are encouraged and from the month of May 2021, the NGO managed to start to work with a day care center and three high schools in the rural community. Lateef (2021) argued for an African centered community framework when working with young people for development and IYEC focused on the needs of African young people.

Although the office bearers of IYEC reside out of the community due to work and education, in contemporary society, relationships are not limited to space and known people, but extend to unknown spaces and people (Goel, 2014). Hence, the program also sources support from other people out of the community due to their expertise, which adds value to the community needs and intervention. Kenny (2011) calls for a kind of development which moves beyond the comfort of home in practice. Hence, community development is practiced through NGOs such as Imbewu Youth Empowerment Centre to encourage active citizenship where community member's strategies are used to improve the community well-being. For sustainability and active participation, the IYEC programmes adopted principles of engagement, such as starting where the community members are to address their concerns. This makes people act on their concerns. The focus is on empowering and sharing resources (Chauya, 2015) to ensure community participation and empowerment (Nel, 2020).

Society has a responsibility to make people achieve their full potential. But equal opportunities for growth need to be presented to all for just distribution of resources (Goel, 2014). That is the fundamental focus of IYEC. The focus is on forming stakeholder's involvement, participation, and understanding community resources (Barreteau et al., 2013) and mobilizing different approaches, allowing participation from the community and development.

Lessons for Asset-Based Community Development

Asset-based community development programs need to be people centered. As argued by Nel (2015), community assets and strengths need to be mobilized for sustainable development. Due to searching for employment and education, community relocation of skills possessed by young people is inevitable. Hence, IYEC took the direction of mobilizing already existing skills in the community for development. Although the NGO founders were in different cities due to employment and education, effective use of technology for communication allowed progress in organizational activities. Indeed, Goel (2014) agrees that contemporary society is advanced in technological connections which locate people together despite the distance to advance the interest of the community.

It is the responsibility of the community to take care of its members by building awareness of the needs and assets of the community and advocate for development that resonates with people's voices (Nel, 2020). The Afrocentric approach also appreciates development that is centered on people's perspective (Makhanya, 2022). The Afrocentric social work in community development adopts a holistic intervention that embraces a wide range of perspectives in advancing the wellbeing of community members (Goel, 2014). The call is on embracing local knowledge and encouraging the integrated development approach (George, 2000), centering the interest of community and their participation as adopted by IYEC. The focus is also on the participatory approach which demands community participation.

Since community development is "elusive and esoteric" Afrocentric community work needs to focus on local needs, assets, and local organizations (Fairfax, 2016, p. 5). Cultural practices need to center on Afrocentric community development (Fairfax, 2016). This is also true for the local economy, which needs to be developed by its members (Hearn & Tanner, 2009) and deals with unemployment and workforce issues collectively at a community level. The focus also is to attract new investors in the community through marketing a united and visionary collective identity (Phillips & Pittman, 2009), as per the strategy adopted by IYEC.

The development of the project is influenced by finance (Hamer & Farr, 2009) and due to limited funding support, local people are used for affordability, sustainability, and local participation (Wheeler, 2009). The focus is on centering the needs of African people in development. This is a call for recovering together in development after the colonial historical context of rule and divide (Trotter, 2021). Having local people as collective decision makers in development (Trotter, 2021) is the basis of advancements in Africa. For example, IYEC engages with local authorities such as Inkosi (King), Induna (Head men) and the municipal council in the programs that are implemented in the community. The focus is to show respect and appreciation of local people's values and cultures and engaging with people who suffered the historical exclusion in fundamentals of the society (Trotter, 2021). Justice recovering starts by acknowledging the sufferings of African people (Scott, 2021) in the past and in the present and appreciate their struggles, norms, and cultures. This call is for a collective agenda, working together and African people centeredness for community development.

Conclusion

The focus in this chapter has been on practically advancing African centered, asset-based community development. The unique realities of the African communities suggest a need for development that is sensitive to culture and diversity. Imbewu Youth Empowerment Centre is highlighted as one of the examples of an intervention strategy based on mobilization of community assets and strength for advancement. What is important to note is that due to a history of colonialism and discrimination, some grassroots interventions might be perceived as irrelevant, minor, or barbaric by the global north but critical to African context and realities. The local voice is thus key to grassroots development. This is a form of African-centered community development which values community connection, participation, and supportive relationships. The discussion in this chapter suggests that adoption of projects that are meaningful and encouraging community participation at grassroots level is the basis of collective action in African community development, that allows for sustainable and collective enhancement.

ACKNOWLEDGMENT

This work is based on the research supported by the National Institute for the Humanities and Social Sciences (NIHSS)

REFERENCES

Asante, M. K. (2003). *Afrocentricity: The theory of social change* [Online]. Retrieved May 19, 2020, from https://multiversityindia.org/wp-content/uploads/2010/05/Afrocentricity.pdf

Asante, M. K. (2009). *Afrocentricity*. University of New York Press.

Barreteau, O., Bots, P., Daniell, K., Etienne, M., Perez, P., Barnaud, C., Bazile, D., Becu, N., Castella, J., Dare., W., & Trebuil, G. (2013). Participatory approaches. In B. Edmonds & R. Meyer (Eds.), *Simulating social complexity* (2nd ed., pp. 253–292). Springer.

Birmingham, D. (1995). *The decolonization of Africa* [Online]. Retrieved February 26, 2017, from https://www.saylor.org/site/wp-content/uploads/2011/04/Decolonization-of-Africa.pdf

Chauya, I. V. (2015). *The effectiveness of community development groups in poverty reduction with regards to individual community members: The case Of Likasi area development programme in Mchinji District, Malawi* [Unpublished master's thesis, University of South Africa].

Chawane, M. (2000). The development of Afrocentricity: A historical survey. *The Western Journal of Black Studies, 24*(4), 78–99.

Fairfax, C. N. (2016). Community practice and the Afrocentric paradigm. *Journal of Human Behavior in the Social Environment, 27*(1–2), 73–80. http://dx.doi.org/10.1080/10911359.2016.1263090

George, V. (2000). *Community development: Through external aid in rural South Africa, Welverdiend Village—A case study* [Unpublished master's thesis, University of Stellenbosch].

Goel, K. (2014). Understanding community and community development in the concept of community. In K. Goel, V. Pulla, & P. Francis (Eds.), *Community work: Theories, experiences and challenges* (pp. 1–15). Niruta Publications.

Gray, M., & Mazibuko, F. (2003). Social work in South Africa at the dawn of the new millennium. *International Journal of Social Welfare, 11*(3), 191–200.

Haines, A. (2009). Asset-based community development. In R. Phillips & R. Pittman (Eds.), *An Introduction to community development* (pp. 67–78). Routledge.

Hamer, J., & Farr, J. (2009). Community development finance. In R. Phillips & R. Pittman (Eds.), *An introduction to community development* (pp. 301–3012). Routledge.

Hearn, W., & Tanner, T. (2009). Assessing your local economy: industry composition and economic impact analysis. In R. Phillips & R. Pittman (Eds.), *An introduction to community development* (pp. 166–180). Routledge.

He, F., Deng, Y., & Li, W. (2020). Coronavirus disease 2019: What we know? *Journal of Medical Virology, 92*(7), 719–725.

Hustedde, R. (2009). Seven theories for seven community developers. In R. Phillips & R. Pittman (Eds.), *An introduction to community development* (pp. 44–66). Routledge.

International Federation of Social Workers & International Association of Schools of Social Workers. (2014). *Global definition of social work* [Online]. Retrieved March 24, 2023, from https://www.ifsw.org/what-is-social-work/global-definition-of-social-work/

Kenny, S. (2011). Towards unsettling community development. *Community Development Journal, 46*(1), 7–19.

Kolzow, D. R. (2009). Developing community leadership skills. In R. Phillips & R. Pittman (Eds.), *An introduction to community development* (pp. 119–132). Routledge.

Kreitzer, L. (2012). *Social Work in Africa: Exploring culturally relevant education and practice in Ghana.* University of Calgary Press.

Kretzmann, J. P., & McKnight, J. L. (1993). *Buildings communities from the inside out: A path toward finding and mobilizing a community's assets.* Center for Urban Affairs and Policy Research.

Lateef, H. (2021). What is African-centred youth development? A content analysis of Bantu perspectives. *Journal of Ethnic and Cultural Diversity in Social Work, 32*(1), 12–22. https://doi.org/10.1080/15313204.2020.1870600

Makhanya, T. (2022). Azibuyele Emasisweni: Exploring the discourse of Ubuntu philosophy in social work education and practice. *African Journal of Social Work, 12*(6), 136–143.

Makhanya, T. B. (2020). Exploring the students' experiences of (De) coloniality: A case study of social work programme at a South African university in the province of Kwazulu-Natal. [Unpublished PhD thesis, University of KwaZulu-Natal].

Makhanya, T. B. (2021). The phenomenology of colonialism: Exploring perspectives of social work graduates in the African university. *Journal of Critical studies in Teaching and Learning, 9*(1), 38–57.

Makhanya T. B., & Zibane, S. (2020). Disfavoured by the system: African student voices on the absence of indigenous languages in the South African higher education institutions. *Language Matters, 51*(1), 22–37.

Masuku, M., & T. Makhanya. (2023). Ubuntu philosophy and decolonisation: interpretation of inclusivity in higher education. In M. O. Maguvhe & M. M. Masuku (Eds.), *Using African epistemologies in shaping inclusive education knowledge* (pp. 395–410). Palgrave Macmillan. https://doi.org/10.1007/978-3-031-31115-4_21

Mattessich, P. W. (2009). Social capital and community building. In R. Phillips & R. Pittman (Eds.), *An introduction to community development* (pp. 79–93). Routledge.

Ndlovu-Gatsheni, S. J. (2015). Decoloniality as the future of Africa. *History Compass, 13*(10), 485–496.

Ndlovu-Gatsheni, S. J. (2020). *Decolonization, decoloniality, and the future of African Studies: A conversation with Dr. Sabelo Ndlovu-Gatsheni* [Online]. Retrieved July 9, 2020, from https://items.ssrc.org/from-our-programs/decolonization-decoloniality-and-the-future-of-african-studies-a-conversation-with-dr-sabelo-ndlovu-gatsheni/

Nel, H. (2015). An integration of the livelihoods and asset-based community development approaches: A South African case study. *Development Southern Africa, 32*(4), 511–525.

Nel, H. (2018). Comparison between the asset-oriented and needs-based community development approaches in terms of systems changes. *Practice, 20*(1), 33–52.

Nel, H. (2020). Stakeholder engagement: Asset-based community led development (ABCD) versus the traditional needs-based approach to community development. *Social Work/Maatskaplike Werk, 56*(3), 264–278.

Okoth, A. (2006). *A History of Africa: African nationalism and the de-colonisation process.* East African Publishers.

Okubo, D. (2009). Community visioning and strategic planning. In R. Phillips & R. Pittman (Eds.), *An introduction to community development* (p. 77). Routledge.

Ornellas, A., Spolander, G., & Engelbrecht, L. K. (2018). The global social work definition: Ontology, implications, and challenges. *Journal of Social Work, 18*(2), 222–240. https://doi.org/10.1177/1468017316654606

Patel, L. (2005). *Social welfare and social development in South Africa*. Oxford.
Phillips, R., & Pittman, R. (2009). A framework for community and economic development. In R. Phillips & R. Pittman (Eds.), *An introduction to community development* (pp. 3–19). Routledge.
Ramose, M. B. (1998). Foreword. In S. Seepe (Ed.), *Black perspectives on tertiary institutional transformation*. Vivlia.
Scott, S. (2021). Thoughts on centering blackness and employment equity in Detroit [Online]. Retrieved September 20, 2023, from https://centerforcommunityinvestment.org/news/thoughts-on-centering-blackness-and-employment-equity-in-detroit/
Sesoko, M. (2015). Community work: A social work method. In P. Mbedzi, L. Qalinge, P. Schultz, J. Sekudu, & M. Sesoko (Eds.). *Introduction to social work in the South African context*. Oxford University Press.
Smith, H. L. (2013). *Social work education: Critical imperatives for social change* [Unpublished Ph.D. thesis, University of the Witwatersrand].
Smith, H. L. (2014). Historiography of South African social work: Challenging dominant discourses. *Social Work/Maatskaplike Werk, 50*(3), 305–331.
Smith, L. (2010). Pursuing a vision for social justice: Ethical dilemmas and critical imperatives in the South African context. In D. Zaviršek, B. Rommelspacher, & S. Staub-Bernasconi (Eds.), *Ethical dilemmas in social work: International perspective*. University of Ljubljana.
Tamburro, A., & Tamburro, P. (2014). Social services and indigenous peoples of North America: Pre-colonial to contemporary times. In H. N. Weaver (Ed.), *Social issues in contemporary native America: Reflections from Turtle Island* (pp. 45–58). Ashgate.
Trotter, J. (2021). *Recovery together: Developing a collective and equitable approach to economic recovery*. Retrieved September 20, 2023, from https://centerforcommunityinvestment.org/news/recovery-together-developing-a-collective-and-equitable-approach-to-economic-recovery/
Tsotsi, W. M. (2000). *From chattel to wage slavery*. W. M. Tsotsi.
Vincent, J. (2009). Community development practice. In R. Phillips & R. Pittman (Eds). *An introduction to community development* (pp. 124–144). Routledge.
West, M. (2009). Establishing community-based organizations. In R. Phillips & R. Pittman (Eds.), *An introduction to community development* (pp. 176–199). Routledge.
Wheeler, S. (2009). Sustainability in community development. In R. Phillips & R. Pittman (Eds.), *An introduction to community development* (pp. 94–110). Routledge.
Zibane. S. (2018). *Human behaviour and the social environment. Course Reader Social Work one—SOWK 102*. University of KwaZulu-Natal. https://www.studocu.com/en-za/document/university-of-kwazulu-natal/social-work/human-behaviour-and-social-environment-sowk-102/68782149

SECTION III
COMMUNITY ENGAGEMENT IN AFRICA

CHAPTER 8

COMMUNITY DEVELOPMENT PRACTICE IN AFRICA

An Autoethnographic Reflection of Development Through the Bikpakpaam (Konkomba) Example in Ghana

Matthew Gmalifo Mabefam

ABSTRACT

This chapter explores the conceptualization and practice of community development through the lens of Bikpakpaam, an indigenous ethnic group in Ghana. It invites community development practitioners to pay critical attention to local conceptualizations and understandings of community development. Through the author's own critique and reflections, this chapter argues that local community development approaches should be highlighted as development approaches alongside other external approaches that are used to instigate development within their contexts. This invitation provides an opportunity to value and appreciate multiple community development approaches that are not necessarily mainstream make sense for the target audience, thus providing room for development intervention that is more targeted to the needs of the community.

Keywords: community development, NGOs, community organizing, Nnoboa, Ubuntu

Introduction

What is development? What is community development? Who conceptualizes it? How is it approached? Whose interests are being met? These questions seem straightforward on the surface, but in responding to them, the author found them extremely difficult to answer, drawing on his experience as a development scholar and practitioner of over a decade. The author worked with local NGOs and government departments in Ghana as a volunteer between 2005–2010. These NGOs designed, planned, and implemented different programs to instigate community development in their catchment areas. Though the author played different key roles in the implementation of these programs, one of his key responsibilities was community organizing. He moved from one community to another to mobilize communities for meetings, workshops, and sensitization events, among others.

This chapter critiques the normative understanding and practice of community development, interweaving these ideas with the author's experience as a community worker in Ghana, using the Bikpakpaam ethnic group as an example. The author, drawing from his own experiences with this community, offers alternative ways for development approaches to be effective for African communities. In sum, this chapter argues that local community development approaches should be highlighted as development approaches alongside other external approaches that are used to instigate development within their contexts. By so doing, the chapter contributes to scholarly literature on wealth in people, place, and environment over wealth capital as an individual pursuit; the attainment of which has left many in a precarity, even though they are talented, hardworking, and skillful and yet are in a constant state of survival. What is an alternative like? Let's find out.

Community Development Scholarship, Practice, and Emerging Issues

The author starts by critiquing the misconception of the history of community development practice in Africa. Academic literature, when referring to the history of community development, states that it started with the colonial governments after the Second World War when they established the Department of Social Welfare and Community Development to deal with some of the development issues that emerged (Abloh & Ameyaw, 1997). This author views this history as an inaccurate representation of community development practice as it ignores the many efforts communities themselves have engaged in over many years to improve their well-being without external interventions.

The author's line of argument is also directly connected to the fact that local communities' strategies of community development either are intentionally ignored within community development discourse or even if such strategies and approaches are known, they are taken for granted and not considered as community development practice approaches. The consequential effects of such ways of theorizing and practising development deny the agencies of local people to community development and thus, require a rethink. Being cognizant of the above assertion expressed by the author, it is not to deny the positive outcomes that have emerged from international community development practice. The author's views are that examining community development practice from when external actors started intervening is limited in focus.

In addition to the above gap being identified, recent scholarship on community development further exposes some limitations on how community development is conceptualized and practiced. For example, Gyan and Baffoe (2014) found that some community stakeholders in Kenyase expressed a lack of involvement in community development decision-making. This is despite the point that most organizations would argue that participation or involvement of the communities in the design, plan, and implementation of their activities are shaped by community involvement. While these ideas may be captured in policy documents as principles, there seems to be a disconnection between such framing and applications. As Gyan and Baffoe highlighted in their study, many stakeholders were not involved in decision-making that influenced community development interventions in their communities. This was a serious concern, as they felt ignored in their communities due to such neglect. Perhaps it is one of the reasons why some development/community development projects fail. Specifically, Gyan and Mfoafo-M'Carthy (2022) spoke to the participation of women in community practice and noted that there was evidence of limited opportunity for women's participation. They identified this limitation as a lack of participation that stems from a multiplicity of factors, such as patriarchy, colonialism, and neoliberal ideologies. This is despite the currency of gender, and especially women's participation that has characterized development work for some time now.

Drawing from the author's experience as a community practitioner in Ghana, one of the things he noticed was that sometimes there would be representations from the different population groups in community meetings that were convened to engender development. However, not everyone present contributed to making decisions at such forums. This, therefore, leads to making a point that being present at a meeting does not necessarily mean participation. However, the author noticed that from the local community development approach perspective, authority was often devolved to the various population groups to engage their constituents on an issue and their contributions were channeled to the initiator of such an intervention. For example, at the community level, there is female leadership, youth leadership, and male leadership, among many others. When they need the voice of these groups, it might be difficult to elicit them at the central meeting that invites these people. However, if the issue was already devolved to their leader to consult them, people would be more willing to discuss and bring out issues of concern as the author learned and observed in the field. The leader then presents the views of their consultations at a central meeting convened for the purposes of discussion. It was interesting to note that this meeting was open to anyone to still contribute, and as a check of what their leader is putting across on their behalf. This gives rise to the highest level of accountability and responsibility on the part of the leaders and their constituents.

Community Development Approaches in Africa: The Missing Piece

There is no denying the fact that before colonization, different communities always had ways of engaging in community development. However, at the encounters between communities and the external *other*, for example, trade with the Arab world or the Western world through commodity trade, slave trade and colonization and post-colonization have had a profound influence on community identities, organizations, and approaches to development today (Hopkins, 1968; Klein, 2010; Lydon, 2009; Mamdani, 2018; Nunn, 2008; Rodney, 2018). To be clear, with or without any of the above influences, this author believes that there would still be changes in approaches to community development practice. This is because community development approaches are always dynamic. They are in constant adjustments which are influenced by time, events, and interactions, both internal and external.

Today, while there are relics or new forms of community development ideologies in different communities across Africa, there are some approaches that this author highlights as examples. Though the argument has always been made that African cultures are collective, this author is aware that there are also varied forms of individualism that are also inherent in some communities or individuals' lifestyles in Africa (Mabefam, 2019, 2022). However, the interesting part is that an individual can exhibit any of these approaches at different times, thus leading to what the author describes as somewhere *in-between* situations (Mabefam, 2022). Despite the many adjustments and changes that have influenced African reasoning, the idea of community is still quite strong.

Let us highlight some community development approaches in Africa as illustrations; the Nnoboa (Afriyie, 2015; Amoah-Mensah, 2021; Appiah-Mensah, 2021), Ujamaa (Collier et al., 1986; Hydén, 1980; Jennings, 2008), Dabo in Ethiopia (Bartel, 1975) and Ubuntu (Mabovula, 2011; Mugumbate & Nyanguru, 2013). Ujamaa was one of the development ideologies adopted by the Tanzanian government after it gained independence. It was a flagship program by Julius Nyerere, the first president of Tanzania. Ujamaa, according to Hunter (2008), is "translated variously as familyhood, community and socialism, and more generally as 'development', as idea and practice" (p. 473). The central idea of Ujamaa was that development was community-based and self-reliant. This would mean that it was a type of development approach that was intended not to leave anyone behind (Tanganyika African National Union (TANU), 1967); Nyerere, 1987). This was adopted as a national development approach captured in the Arusha Declaration of 1967 (Government of Tanzania, 1967). Although Ujamaa as a development framework became eminent in 1962, it was given a national impetus through the declaration as a response to exploitative models that were in practice in Tanzania at the time, plausibly the relics of colonial exploitation which Nyerere sought to break from (Nyerere, 1987).

Ubuntu is quite a popular philosophy that is said to underpin many African ways of life in Sub-Saharan Africa. Though Ubuntu is complex as it is different in different communities, it is often captured in academic literature as "I am because we are" (Battle, 2009; Hailey, 2008; Murove, 2012). This demonstrates the essence of connectedness and community and that the individual is part of the bigger society, and the well-being of that individual is linked to the well-being of the community. This, therefore, implies that any development that has no benefit for the community is not tolerated. Like Ubuntu or Ujamaa, there are many such approaches in other communities across Africa, including Nkpawiin among the Bikpakpaam of Ghana in West Africa, which will be discussed with fresh insights from the field. It is also important to note here that the author is not oblivious to some of the weaknesses of the above approaches to development, and hence he does not engage with these approaches in an uncritical way. The author takes a critical stance in critiquing the weaknesses of some of these approaches, as is captured elsewhere in his writings (Mabefam, 2022). The methodology for this research was autoethnography, in which the author's own critique and reflections drive this chapter.

Autoethnography Among Bikpakpaam

Butz and Besio (2009) define autoethnography as the "practice of consciously, or deliberately, wanting to understand or represent some worldly phenomenon that exceeds the self" (p. 1660). Furthermore, Reed-Danahay

(1997) defines autoethnography as "a form of self-narrative that places the self within a social context" (p. 9). As the above definition of autoethnography by Reed-Danahay and Butz and Besio highlight, the author is interested in a reflexive and reflective self-narrative understanding of community development practice among Bikpakpaam and linking his experience as a community worker with the traditional models of development. The author's engagement in community development practice started in 2005, with ongoing fieldwork in Ghana in 2009, 2012, 2016, and 2022. During these visits to the field, the author took notes and interviewed community members, leaders, NGO officials, and government departments and agencies. The qualitative data gathered from these interactions have been enormous and focuses on different aspects of people he works with, but for the purposes of this chapter, he focuses on community development aspects only. For the analysis and presentation of data, the author employed a thematic and sub-thematic approach, starting with Bikpakpaam conceptions of development, community development, and the various approaches that are used to instigate development. The analysis of the data was guided by Braun and Clark's (2006) six steps of thematic analysis including familiarizing oneself with the data, generating initial codes and labels in relation to the research questions, developing and reviewing the themes, naming the themes and finally, writing the report.

The Conceptualization of the Practice of Community Development Among Bikpakpaam

The Bikpakpaam ethnic group was colonially labeled as the "Konkomba" (Maasole, 2006; Rattray, 1932). Their history of migration is complex as identified by historians, but they are in large numbers in Ghana and Togo in West Africa (Kachim, 2019). The CIA World Factbook (2023) reports in the demographics of Ghana that Bikpakpaam is the eighth largest ethnic group in Ghana, representing 3.5% of the total population. Until recently, Bikpakpaam settled in small villages and engaged in farming, fishing, and hunting as their main economic livelihood. They are proud Yam farmers, and this is indicative of the establishment of Yam markets in important cities in Ghana named after them. For example, the Konkomba Yam market in Accra, Kumasi, and Chamba are just a few to mention.

When seeking to understand what development is among Bikpakpaam, the common terminology that comes up is M-muumuu (Mabefam, 2022, 2019). Though Bikpakpaam would often refer to development as m-mumuun, its direct translation is "growth." Growth may not be able to capture the exact meaning of the development as conceived and practised by Bikpakpaam, however, it is the closest term to the English terminology. Community development, therefore, is called kiting aa mumuun. During the author's interactions and observations in the communities, Bikpakpaam would emphasize to the author that m-mumuun or kiting aa mumuun is a collective endeavor. It is a type of development that every member of the community is required to be a part of. In the same way, the benefits of development that emerge from such a collective endeavor are also shared among members of the community. Thus, when efforts are made to embark on m-muumuu, it is the responsibility of every member to be a part of it. However, people are required to contribute according to their strength, capacity or what they have expertise in. To illustrate, the author draws from one of his encounters in Ghana with Utindaan (landowner) of a particular community who shared that it was his responsibility to mobilize people of the community to embark on m-mumuun. The very act of everyone contributing to bringing about m-mumuun brings about a sense of community ownership of the development and a sense of shared responsibility and accountability.

This author, based on the above, was keen to understand how they mobilize themselves to embark on community development or otherwise, what are the specific Bikpakpaam approach to kiting aa mumuun. Thus, he asked: "what approaches are used by Bikpakpaam to instigate kiting aa mumuun?" The author gathered that for Bikpakpaam, there are many approaches that they often use to bring about kiting aa mumuun. They have used such approaches to build houses, construct footpaths, engage in agricultural activities, and many more. Some of the approaches the author observed were Kimɔkbaan, Nkpawiin, and Totoo.

Approaches to Kiting aa Mumuun Among Bikpakpaam

Kimɔkbaan. Kimɔkbaan means unity, togetherness, or communal. Kimɔkbaan as a strategy of kiting aa mumuun is where the members of the community come together to embark on a development project that is mutually beneficial to the community and individuals that constitute the community. While living in some of the communities, the author observed that anytime one of the communities had done something that was thought to be a community's benefit, they often referred to that community as "binib gbaan kpa Kimɔkbaan pam." This translates as the people being very united or very communal. For example, in Bolni and its surrounding villages, it is the responsibility of everyone not to destroy the environment by cutting or burning trees but to also report anyone who has contributed to the destruction of the same. This responsibility makes every member of the community a "vigilante." And the sole purpose is for the benefit of the community. The author witnessed people who have defied this instruction who were fined heavily by Untidaan to serve as a deterrent to other people who might disobey such a directive as a sense of community development.

One of the issues the author also witnessed while doing fieldwork in Ghana was that some chainsaw operators from Bimbilla had come to the Bolni community to cut down trees to process them as timber for sale. This was a very controversial and sensitive issue, especially taking into consideration the fragile land ownership issue in the area, which had led to ethnic conflicts in the past. The chainsaw operators from Bimbilla had made the argument that the land and whatever was on it belonged to them and thus they did not need the permission of anyone to cut any tree they wanted. On the other hand, the community argued that the land was theirs and whatever was on it belonged to them, thus as part of their responsibility to keep the community protected as part of its development; it was their responsibility to protect the trees and the environment from any form of destruction. The community further argued that the very reason such trees were there was because their forefathers and foremothers protected them, and they have also taken the responsibility to protect them. While they did not permit residents to cut any tree without seeking permission, if need be, it was wrong for an external person who did not even live in the community to cut those trees for their individual or selfish purposes.

Despite threats and intimidations, Kimɔkbaan eventually won the case. While foreseeing that their continued resistance at the community level could result in conflicts due to experience, they reported the matter to government officials, such as the police and military services. The police called the two parties, the community on the one hand and chainsaw operators on the other hand and addressed the issue. The conclusion was that the chainsaw operators had no right to go to another community to cut down trees that were protected by the community for their selfish purposes. The above example to the community was a true sense of community development that was sustainable and beneficial to every member of the community, as opposed to an individual who wanted to cut down the trees and sell them off to make money. In this case, the sense of development was not wealth in money, but wealth in the environment, which could lead to their further well-being as a community. They were able to achieve this through Kimɔkbaan.

Tootoo. Bikpakpaam defines Totoo as a strategy of community development where each member of the community is tasked to contribute to a project in the community. This could be by kind or cash. Everyone contributes according to their ability or what they can afford. While, for example, people might be given a specific amount to contribute, there are also times when people are asked to bring whatever they can afford. Tootoo could also depend on age, gender, family, and family type. In one of the communities, there was a need to construct a footpath linking them to the main town, Bimbilla. Utindaan took responsibility for the construction of the footpath by calling for Nkpawiin (communal labor will be discussed in the next section).

A day was therefore set, and a town gong gong beater was asked to make an announcement. On the day of the Nkpawiin, some were allocated to the digging of the soil, others carried the soil and levelled the potholes on the path, and others cleared weeds and shrubs to make the pathway clear. Others were tasked with preparing food, while others sang, played the drums, and danced. It is also an expectation that anyone unable to make it due to a prior commitment must offer something else to compensate for their absence. In addition, permission needed to be sought, and the rationale was well explained for any absence to be accepted. Furthermore, anyone using the footpath that day contributed in-kind or cash before they were allowed to pass. This was regardless of whether they were from the community or not.

Nkpawiin. Nkpawiin is broadly translated as communal labour. It is used as a strategy for community development among Bikpakpaam. With regards to it being a strategy for community development, Utindaan (landowner/custodian) can make an announcement requiring every community member to offer their labor for a particular project they intend to initiate. The basic difference between Nkpawiin and other community development strategies among Bikpakpaam is that it strictly offers labour as a form of contribution. It can also be used by individuals in the community for their activities as well. For example, farmers (farming is one of the main economic activities of Bikpakpaam), can each use Nkpawiin as a strategy for helping one another in their farming activities. The lesson for using Nkpawiin either as a personal or community strategy for development is that it gives a sense of community ownership and support for one another. While working among Bikpakpaam, it was one of the most frequent strategies the author witnessed.

Discussion

There is no lack of development interventions in different communities, however, such interventions are externally framed and impact their effectiveness. Thus, Bikpakpaam example demonstrates a marginal approach that they felt was not often attended to by mainstream organizations that operate within their communities. This suggests that normative conceptualizing and the practice of development by mainstream organizations are sometimes at odds with what communities need. The fact that community development projects are tied to donor preferences, directions and sometimes the importance of a problem as defined by them may lead to exaggeration and dramatization of communities to attract sympathy and funding. This way of framing community development problems and addressing them is at times distant from community realities. This may suggest that some community members may feel neglected in participating and involvement in defining their problems and offering suggestions for mitigation (Gyan & Baffoe, 2014; Gyan, & Mfoafo-M'Carthy, 2022). To be precise, this chapter gathered that for Bikpakpaam, there are many approaches that they often use to bring about community development that are quite different from the picture painted. Some of the approaches the author observed were Kimɔkbaan, Nkpawiin, and Totoo.

The most important learning was the extent of shared responsibility in conceptualization and practicing community development as a scholar and practice contributor. From the definition of the meaning of development through to the approaches, Bikpakpaam notes the communal aspect of their being is the most important value. This is directly correlated with similar approaches from other African contexts, such as the Nnoboa Akans of Ghana (Afriyie, 2015; Amoah-Mensah, 2021; Appiah-Mensah, 2021), Ujamaa of Tanzania (Collier et al., 1986; Hydén; 1980; Jennings, 2008), Dabo in Ethiopia (Bartel, 1975), and Ubuntu (Mabovula, 2011; Mugumbate & Nyanguru, 2013).

Finally, Bikpakpaam's mode of development was not necessarily about the wealth of money but instead wealth in the environment, people, and place (Appau & Crockett, 2023). Though their article contributes to wealth in people and place, theirs was with migrant returnees to their homelands, communities and families and aspiring migrants. In their theorizing, money is central and directly linked to the significance of the migrant within their social milieu, and the gifts they can purchase with their money and the place of purchase. This leads to a hierarchy and importance attached to certain gifts from certain places. That was different for Bikpakpaam. As an illustration, Bikpakpaam resisted attempts by chainsaw operators to enrich themselves to the detriment of the community's ecological systems. That is Bikpakpaam's approach to development, if able to withstand the test of time, is sustainable, beneficial, and like Ubuntu, Ujamaa or others of a similar sort in Africa. Thus, they are worth underscoring and applied by mainstream development organizations and practitioners, especially at the time "sustainability" and living in harmony with nature and people have become a crucial component of development.

This is why the UN standardized framework for international development encapsulated in "Sustainable" Development Goals developed after the expiration of Millennium Development Goals is important to underscore (Sachs, 2012). By emphasizing "wealth in people, environment and place" rather than "wealth in money acquired by individuals" or capital in economic terms, this challenges "money" as the central logic of pursuing satisfaction in their community. There will never be enough for everyone, leading to a few being able to manage to leap to a financial level unimaginable. It is thus unsurprising as captured by Piketty (2013, 2021a) who, after decades of studying the Western world, found that although wealth had increased, it was only concentrated in the hands of a few. Based on this, it does not surprise the author when Piketty's (2021b) recent writings are calling for a redistribution of this wealth to benefit others in ways that even addresses not only current inequalities but also past inequalities that are triggered by the capitalist order, including that of colonization. Similar ideas are made by renowned anthropologist James Ferguson (2015) on his works in Southern Africa, which the author would like to link them to African cosmology of community development, which is present and benefits the wealth of people, places, and environment as key. This also contributes to knowledge of the place of social capital, people and connections that bind them (Adamtey & Frimpong (2018). The Bikpakpaam example was a close resemblance to social capital.

Conclusion

This chapter focused on community development practice through critiquing normative community development views on development, African views on development and his own experiences, reflections, and understanding of development. Interweaving these three views, an example of African community development was given through the lens of Bikpakpaam in Ghana. The author adopted an autoethnographic approach as a method for data collection. Findings were thematically analyzed and presented. The spur for this study was a constant questioning of the efficacy of external development actors' impact on community development in Ghana. The value of the chapter is in its invitation for consideration by mainstream development organizations to appreciate multiple community development approaches that are not necessarily mainstream but make sense for the target audience, thus providing room for development intervention that is more targeted to the needs of the community.

REFERENCES

Abloh, F., & Ameyaw, S. (1997). Ghana. In H. Campfen (Ed.), *Community development around the world: Practice, theory, research, training* (pp. 275–291). University of Toronto Press.

Adamtey, R., & Frimpong, J. (2018). Social capital as the missing link in community development planning process in Africa: Lessons from Ghana. *Ghana Journal of Development Studies*, *15*(1), 92–115.

Afriyie, A. O. (2015). Communal non-formal financial market system development: A model for nnoboa market system. *European Journal of Accounting Auditing and Finance Research*, 3(3), 48–60.

Amoah-Mensah, A. (2021). Nnoboa and Rotated Susu as agents of savings mobilization: Developing a theoretical model using grounded theory. *Qualitative Report*, 26(1), 140–175.

Appau, S., & Crockett, D. (2023). Wealth in people and places: Understanding Transnational gift obligations. *Journal of Consumer Research*, 49(6), 1053–1073.

Appiah-Mensah, S. (2021). *Re-imagining the pan-African security partnership: Towards a Nnoboa strategic culture in Africa* [Doctoral dissertation, University of Western Australia]. Perth.

Bartels, L. (1975). Dabo: A form of cooperation between farmers among the Macha Galla of Ethiopia. Social aspects, songs, and Ritual. *Anthropos, (H. 5./6)*, 883–925.

Battle, M. (2009). *Ubuntu: I in you and you in me*. Church Publishing.

Braun, V., & Clarke, V. (2006). Using thematic analysis in psychology. *Qualitative Research in Psychology*, 3(2), 77-101

Butz, D., & Besio, K. (2009). Autoethnography. *Geography Compass*, 3(5), 1660–1674.

Collier, P., Radwan, S., & Wangwe, S. (1986). *Labour and poverty in rural Tanzania: Ujamaa and rural development in the United Republic of Tanzania*. Clarendon Press.

CIA World Factbook Ghana. (2023). Retrieved April 13, 2023, from https://www.cia.gov/the-world-factbook/countries/ghana/

Ferguson, J. (2015). *Give a man a fish: Reflections on the new politics of distribution*. Duke University Press.

Gyan, C., & Baffoe, M. (2014). "I Feel Like I Don't Exist in This Community": Stakeholders' thought on their noninvolvement in community development initiatives in Kenyase. *Public Policy and Administration Research*, 4(12), 1–9.

Gyan, C., & Mfoafo-M'Carthy, M. (2022). Women's participation in community development in rural Ghana: The effects of colonialism, neoliberalism, and patriarchy. *Community Development*, 53(3), 295–308.

Hailey, J. (2008). *Ubuntu: A literature review*. Tutu Foundation.

Hopkins, A. G. (1968). Economic imperialism in West Africa: Lagos, 1880–92. *The Economic History Review*, 21(3), 580–606.

Hunter, E. (2008). Revisiting Ujamaa: Political legitimacy and the construction of community in post-colonial Tanzania. *Journal of Eastern African Studies*, 2(3), 471–485.

Hydén, G. (1980). *Beyond Ujamaa in Tanzania: underdevelopment and an uncaptured peasantry*. University of California Press.

Jennings, M. (2008). *Surrogates of the state: NGOs, development, and Ujamaa in Tanzania*. Kumarian Press.

Kachim, J. U. (2019). Origin, migration, and settlement history of the Konkomba of Northern Ghana, ca. 1400–1800. *Abibisem: Journal of African Culture and Civilization*, 8, 132–168.

Klein, H. S. (2010). *The Atlantic slave trade*. Cambridge University Press.

Lydon, G. (2009). *On Trans-Saharan Trails: Islamic law, trade networks, and cross-cultural exchange in nineteenth-century Western Africa*. Cambridge University Press.

Mamdani, M. (2018). Introduction: Trans-African slaveries thinking historically. *Comparative Studies of South Asia, Africa and the Middle East, 38*(2), 185–210.

Maasole, S. C. (2006). *The Konkomba and their neighbours from the pre-European period to 1914: A study in inter-ethnic relations in Northern Ghana*. Ghana Universities Press.

Mabefam, M. (2022). Limitless opportunities for wealth? Witchcraft as a strategy for (in)equality and economic (dis)empowerment. *Forum for Development Studies, 49*(2), 233–260.

Mabefam, M. G. (2019). *Witch camps in Northern Ghana: Contesting gender, development and culture* [Doctoral dissertation, University of Melbourne].

Mabovula, N. N. (2011). The erosion of African communal values: A reappraisal of the African Ubuntu philosophy. *Inkanyiso: Journal of Humanities and Social Sciences, 3*(1), 38–47.

Mugumbate, J., & Nyanguru, A. (2013). Exploring African philosophy: The value of ubuntu in social work. *African Journal of Social Work, 3*(1), 82–100.

Murove, M. F. (2012). Ubuntu. *Diogenes, 59*(3–4), 36–47.

Nunn, N. (2008). The long-term effects of Africa's slave trades. *The Quarterly Journal of Economics, 123*(1), 139–176.

Nyerere, J. K. (1987). Ujamaa: The basis of African socialism. *The Journal of Pan African Studies, 1*(1), 4–11.

Piketty, T. (2021a). *Capital and ideology*. Harvard University Press.

Piketty, T. (2021b). *Time for socialism: Dispatches from a world on fire, 2016–2021*. Yale University Press.

Piketty, T. (2013). *Capital in the 21st century*. President and Fellows, Harvard College.

Rattray, R. S. (1932). *The Tribes of the Ashanti Hinterlands, 1*. Clarendon Press.

Reed-Danahay, D. (1997). Introduction. In D. Reed-Danahay (Ed.), *Auto-ethnography: Rewriting the self and the social* (pp. 1–20). Berg.

Rodney, W. (2018). *How Europe underdeveloped Africa*. Verso Books.

Sachs, J. D. (2012). From millennium development goals to sustainable development goals. *The Lancet, 379*(9832), 2206–2211.

TANU. (1967). *The Arusha Declaration and TANU'S policy on socialism and self-reliance*. Publicity Section.

CHAPTER 9

COMMUNITY ENGAGEMENT IN IMPROVING AGRICULTURAL PRODUCTION

Lessons for Community Development Practice

Shamiso Mandioma and Abdulrazak Karriem

ABSTRACT

The chapter contributes to the literature on the practice of community development and how community engagement approaches impact the outcome of development projects in the Mazowe District of Zimbabwe. The authors investigate how a non-governmental agency, the Development Aid from People to People (DAPP), used participatory community engagement approaches in improving agricultural production of small farmers. The study adopted a qualitative case study methodology. Purposive sampling techniques were used to recruit and conduct semi-structured interviews with research respondents. The findings reveal that engagement strategies such as project meetings, topic days, demonstration plots, self-help group gardens, and exchange visits led to greater levels of interaction, transfer of knowledge and embracing of sustainable methods of farming. This improved small farmers' productivity and diversified their livelihoods. The findings also suggest that the adoption of bottom-up context specific strategies and the agency of small farmers positively contributed to the success of the project. Contrary to conventional narratives in the community development literature, communities are not passive beneficiaries of development; rather, as the findings of this study show, small farmers are active agents in their own development. Therefore, stakeholders interested in facilitating community development projects should promote participatory spaces where values such as reflective thinking, mutual understanding, and shared responsibility guide the conceptualization and implementation of development projects. This study recommends further research on the role of community engagement strategies in promoting community development in government and NGO supported agricultural projects in Zimbabwe and across the globe.

Keywords: community development, engagement, participation, capacity building, empowerment, bottom-up development approach, agricultural productivity, food security

Introduction

Agriculture plays a vital role in the livelihoods of small-scale farmers across the world. This is especially true for Zimbabwe, where it is the backbone of the country's economy and contributes to its food security. Approximately 68% of Zimbabweans reside in rural communities and their livelihoods are supported by small scale farming (International Fund for Agriculture Development [IFAD], 2021). The sector produces 70% of the country's staple crops such as maize, soyabeans, and groundnuts (Food and Agriculture Organisation [FAO], 2022). In addition, it provides employment opportunities for a significant population involved in producing, marketing, and transporting farm produce. Despite the significant role that small farmers play in the national economy, production levels have been deteriorating, resulting in food security and livelihoods being threatened (World Bank, 2020). Declining productivity levels is attributed to a range of macro-economic challenges, such as lack of resources, poor farming methods, and inadequate knowledge. In addition, climatic factors such as erratic rainfall patterns and recurrent droughts have exacerbated the challenges that small farmers face in rural Zimbabwe. To boost agricultural production, small farmers need support in the form of training, financial capital, access to markets, and a shift to sustainable farming methods.

Zimbabwe's Agricultural Policy

Considering the numerous challenges confronting the agricultural sector, the quest to improve agricultural production has shaped Zimbabwe's policy directives over the past two decades. In 1994 the government unveiled the Zimbabwe Agricultural Policy Framework (ZAPF) 1995–2020 which envisioned a "prosperous, diverse and competitive agriculture sector, ensuring food and nutrition security significantly contributing to national development" (Government of Zimbabwe [GoZ], 2012, p. 2). The ZAPF was concerned with increasing productivity, promoting proactiveness, and adopting participatory and responsive strategies in the agriculture sector. The ZAPF focused on enhancing small farmer incomes and promoting food security (Mutisi, 2009). In 2018, the government enacted the National Agricultural Policy Framework, which sought to strengthen and transform agricultural production in the country (GoZ, 2018). This policy is premised on adopting context specific strategies for a wide range of farmers in the country. Alongside these agricultural policies, the government has rolled out a range of input subsidization programs (ISPs) which premised on providing farmers with inputs to increase their productivity, which reaped immediate benefits for the nation (Kuhudzayi & Mattos, 2018).

While small gains were made through these policies, they have failed to capacitate and empower small farmers who are significant players in Zimbabwe's economy. As an example, though ISPs have managed to feed the nation, their modus operandi has proven unsustainable (Pindiriri et al., 2021). Notably, the 2030 Agenda for Sustainable Development prioritizes the need to increase the production levels of small farmers and the promotion of sustainable food systems (Jimbira & Hathie, 2020). Undeniably, low agricultural productivity by the small farmers negatively affects the livelihoods of a substantial population in the country.

There has been little research that examines the community engagement approaches during the implementation of agricultural intervention programs, which is the focus of this chapter. Drawing on a qualitative case study undertaken in 2016 in the Mazowe District, this chapter focuses on community engagement strategies in agricultural production. It demonstrates that agricultural production has improved through Development Aid from People to People's (DAPP's) participatory development praxis. The small farmers who were involved in the DAPP project were empowered and capacitated to farm in a more sustainable and productive manner. Broadly, household income was boosted, and livelihoods were improved. Some farmers built houses and others managed to send their children to school. Within this context, this chapter attempts to answer the following question: what kind of engagement approaches existed in the DAPP Farmers Club project? The remainder of this chapter is organized as follows; the first section contextualizes community development. Thereafter, the philosophical approach that underpins community development practice is presented. This is followed by an overview of community engagement in Zimbabwe's agricultural development. Further, a brief overview of the methodology is presented. The last sections dwell on the community engagement practices in the DAPP Farmers Club project and how they improved small farmers' livelihoods.

Contextualizing Community Development

Community development is defined as a collaborative process in which people with shared interests become conscious of their needs and assets, and work together to better their lives (Swanepoel, 1996). Frank and Smith (1999) define community development as a "process whereby community members come together to take collective action and generate solutions to common problems" (p. 3). Adding to this discussion, Phillips and Pitman (2009) explain that numerous specialists regard community development "as an outcome—physical, social, and economic improvement in a community—while most academicians think of community development as a process—the ability of communities to act collectively and enhancing the ability to do so" (p. 3). In the same vein, Robinson and Green (2011) view it as a collective process whereby people work together with the intention of improving their lives. Implicit in this thread is the fact that community development is a process whereby people unleash the potential and capacity within them and work in collaboration with each other to address development issues of common interest.

Philosophical Approach to Community Development

According to Robinson and Green (2011), the current body of knowledge on community development theory became popular between the 1950s and 1960s. It emerged as a critique of top-down development planning consonant with modernization theory, which shaped agricultural development. Under modernization, governments and development institutions defined community agricultural needs, prescribed solutions, and allocated resources. In other words, communities were passive recipients of programed agricultural initiatives and resources. Broadly, community development projects did not bring meaningful transformation due to their failure to take into consideration local knowledge, contexts, and community input (Chiome & Gambahaya, 2000, as cited in Tagarirofa & David, 2013).

Overall, community development (CD) was centered on getting development accomplished in a cost-effective way, persuading communities to rubber stamp decisions that had little benefit in their lives and adopting Western farming practices and technologies (De Beer & Swanepoel, 2006). Furthermore, development projects were implemented under the ambit of local leadership and there was no desire to touch base with the real beneficiaries of community development projects (Shepherd, 1998). There was a widespread belief that "working through the established traditional leaders in the villages, generally the better-off, would automatically benefit the community" (Burkey, 1993, p. 43). However, this mechanism excluded vulnerable members of society and was often used by local elites as a campaign strategy to gain political mileage. De Beer and Swanepoel (2006) noted that under the leadership of powerful elites "community development became a tool of marginalisation and disempowerment" (p. xiii). Dissatisfaction with this kind of mechanism ushered in a reformed community development strategy whereby development consultants work in partnership with community members, thereby acknowledging their rights and simultaneously "recognising community leaders for what they are" (Shepherd, 1998, p. 185). Thus, CD theory has evolved, with greater emphasis now centered on inclusivity, empowering weaker and vulnerable members of communities to actively participate in shaping the socioeconomic and political aspects that have a bearing on their lives (Deng, 2012).

While several theories underpin development practice, community development (CD) theory proved to be important in examining community engagement practices employed in the DAPP Farmers Club project. The theory focuses on addressing a community's basic needs as ascertained by residents themselves. CD is underpinned by the need to empower the weak and marginalized (Chambers, 1995). From a community development perspective, governments or development agencies are expected to facilitate the CD process through participatory engagement approaches (Swanepoel, 1996). The Food and Agriculture Organization (2007) notes that several countries and aid agencies have switched from conventional approaches to agricultural development, where farmers were relegated to passive recipients of knowledge. Dube (2017) notes that the participation of farmers is viewed as a strategic way to improve agricultural extension services. In other words, current thinking in agricultural development encourages governments and aid agencies to facilitate the active involvement of farmers in recognizing and resolving their agricultural challenges.

Principles of Community Development Practice

Participation, empowerment, and capacity building provide the building blocks that underpin community development practice. Community engagement strategies in a project should facilitate the meaningful participation of beneficiaries of development projects and empower and build their capacity to achieve their developmental objectives. This is vital for the sustainability of development projects.

At the heart of community development practice lies the notion of participation. Participation gained momentum during the 1979 World Conference on Agrarian Reform and Rural Development, which took place in Rome. The delegates at this conference agreed that it "is a basic human right" for rural people to participate in matters that affect their lives (United Nations, 2009, p. 5). Gran (1983) views participation as a "self-sustaining process to engage free men and women in activities that meet their basic needs and, beyond that, realise individually defined human potential within socially defined limits" (p. 327). Various scholars contend that recipients of development projects should be engaged as partners when envisioning, planning, executing, and assessing development initiatives (Chambers, 1997; Chazovachii & Tagarirofa, 2013). As such, organizations or governments should adopt community engagement strategies that give power to farmers, enable bottom-up planning, and create spaces where farmers are part of the decision-making processes.

Furthermore, community development should build the capacity of the local populace (De Beer & Swanepoel, 2006). What is important to understand here is that, through the community development process, the farmers' capacity should be enhanced in such a way that they are able to steer their own development. The capacity of a community is measured by the extent to which members can cooperate and work together in establishing and nurturing mutual relations, addressing problems, making group decisions, and collaborating efficiently in planning and formulating community objectives (Phillips & Pitman, 2009). The networks and relations that exist among farmers should be tapped to accelerate collaboration and the establishment of partnerships (Mattessich & Monsey, 2004).

In addition, CD is viewed as an empowering process whereby the voices of the farmers are amplified (McMillan & Chavis, 1986). Through participation, farmers become empowered to apply indigenous knowledge in sustaining agricultural initiatives and, at the same time, respond to challenges that might confront them (De Beer & Swanepoel, 2011). However, it is important to note that the very act of participating is not empowering in and of itself; rather, it is the extent of an individual's participation as well as "how much decision-making power he or she possesses ... [that] often determine empowering results" (Rocha, 1997, as cited in Karriem & Benjamin, 2016). Indeed, as Tacconi and Tisdell (1993) state, empowerment is linked with the authority to make decisions. In this regard, Narayan-Parker (2002) associates empowerment with expanding the "assets and capabilities of poor people to participate in, negotiate with, influence, control and hold accountable institutions that affect their lives" (p. 4). De Beer and Swanepoel (2006) advocate for a bottom-up empowerment process whereby power is given to the people, thus capacitating them to make decisions. CD therefore becomes an enabling force in empowering farmers. Ideally, governments or development agencies assume supportive roles and facilitate the establishment of spaces where empowerment can take place.

Community Engagement in Zimbabwe's Agricultural Development

The South Coast Natural Resource Management (2014) describes community engagement as an organized process whereby people of the same locality, or with the same interests, work together to address matters that affect their lives. Arnold et al. (2019) state that community engagement promotes cooperation between people, which, in turn, builds their capacity to actively shape their future. Put simply, community engagement is a strategic mechanism that is used to establish contact, bring stakeholders together, create partnerships and networks that facilitate the conceptualization and implementation of community development projects.

Historically, rural development has been associated with agricultural development. In Zimbabwe, both top-down and participatory approaches have been used to promote agricultural development (Mukute, 2013). In the 1960s, the colonial government promoted agricultural development using a top-down approach that involved passively transferring knowledge and practices to farmers. Broadly, there was a widespread belief that agricultural challenges could be solved through the intervention of technocrats with new practices and technologies. Nhongonhema (2010) notes that during this period, farmers received forced extension services whereby they had to prepare storm water drains, dip their cattle, and design some ridges in their fields. While failure to follow the regulation attracted a fine from the authorities, some farmers were still reluctant to participate in the forced extension program. Radio Listening Groups were used in Zimbabwe, whereby farmers acquired extension services through listening to the radio in groups (Hanyani-Mlambo, 2002). While farmers were given the opportunity to ask questions through calling the broadcaster, the programs were sometimes not contextually suitable for the resource constrained small rural farmers. The colonial (then Rhodesian) regime enforced top-down, modernist policies which small farmers had to passively accept.

Following the independence of Zimbabwe, engagement approaches shifted toward participatory mechanisms whereby the relationship between the extension worker and farmer was not one of benefactor and beneficiary (Pedzisa et al., 2010). In 2005, the government unveiled the Agriculture Sector Productivity Enhancement Facility (ASPEF) through the Reserve Bank of Zimbabwe to support agriculture through the provision of equipment to farmers (Mutami, 2015). During the same year, it rolled out Operation Maguta aimed at boosting food security in Zimbabwe through the provision of inputs, such as fertilizers and seeds, to farmers (Mupindu, 2015). In 2016, Command Agriculture was launched aimed at improving agricultural output. Input subsidy programs are not a new phenomenon in the region, as they were adopted by Africa's newly independent states some decades ago. These strategies are centrally planned at a national level and very prescriptive in nature and form. In other words, they fall short of a genuine participatory approach to community development and engagement, as they are still aligned with top-down development intervention mechanisms.

In championing agricultural productivity, state players are caught up embracing the conventional top-down approaches that have rendered farmers passive recipients of programed projects and resources. Furthermore, it is important to consider the long-term sustainability of ISPs in the wake of financial challenges that have hampered the timely procurement and delivery of inputs to farmers. From a community development perspective, improving agricultural production should not simply be anchored on providing advice and inputs to the small farmers; rather, it should be an empowering practice which entails capacitating farmers, making use of existing assets and tapping on the available capitals within the community. More importantly, the intervention mechanisms should be conceptualized with farmers in participatory spaces where values such as reflective thinking, mutual understanding, and shared responsibility guide the conceptualization and implementation of community development projects.

Methodological Considerations

A qualitative case study methodological approach was adopted in the study. The adoption of this methodology was informed by the need to draw from the respondents' lived experiences during the project life cycle. The qualitative methodology enabled us to "purposefully select" the study area and research participants (Creswell, 2009, p. 179). As such, this study was conducted in Ward 3 of the Mazowe District, where the project took place. The purposive sampling technique was further employed in selecting 10 participants who participated in the DAPP Farmers Club project that were best placed to provide answers to our research question. Ten face-to-face semi-structured interviews were conducted with key informants using semi-structured questions framed around the main research question indicated in the introductory section. The interviews were undertaken by one of the authors (SM) of this chapter in the case study area. The sample also consisted of four local leaders, two agricultural extension officers, three farmers who were club leaders and one official from DAPP—all of whom were selected because they had deep insights on the research topic. Semi-structured interviews are an effective method of data collection that facilitates a dialogue between researchers and participants and, more importantly, enables researchers to collect open-ended data and gain deeper insights into participant's experiences, feelings, and perceptions on a topic such as the role of community engagement in improving agricultural productivity (DeJonckheere & Vaughn, 2019).

Findings and Discussion

The Farmers Club Concept. Development Aid from People to People (DAPP) is a non-governmental organization which uses a participatory development praxis to empower and capacitate small farmers to farm in a more productive manner. The Farmers Club is a vehicle through which agricultural interventions are rolled out. More specifically, the Farmers Club is used "to empower the small farmers to become food secure by building their capacity with knowledge and skills on modern methods of farming which includes conservation agriculture and agro forestry" (DAPP, 2018, n.p.). It offers training and capacity-building programs in the use of sustainable farming methods so that yields can be boosted, and livelihoods improved. To this end, DAPP engaged small farmers in Ward 3 of the Mazowe District who were interested in increasing their agricultural output and improving their livelihoods using sustainable farming methods. The development agency facilitated the organization of these farmers into groups of 10 farmers in each group. An operational committee consisting of five farmers per club was set up to run the projects.

DAPP followed a multi-stakeholder approach whereby government departments (Agriculture and Veterinary Technical and Extension Services) provided technical expertise to farmers throughout the project. These government departments worked in collaboration with two extension workers from DAPP. In some instances, all the participating farmers worked in groups to improve output, diversify crop varieties, and design basic and sustainable farming techniques. Whilst farmers were working in groups, they still tilled their individual plots. DAPP follows a transformative approach whereby it promotes knowledge sharing, resource pooling, collective action, and engagement with a goal to unleash every small farmer's potential. Small farmers played an active role in improving their overall agricultural production through the Farmers Club facilitated activities such as project meetings, topic days, exposure visits, demonstration plots, self-help group gardens, small income-generating projects, and the Pass on Loan Program.

Farmers Club Engagement Activities

Several activities existed to facilitate engagement between DAPP and small farmers. This chapter focuses on six of these activities: (1)

demonstration plots; (2) self-help group gardens; (3) Women's Forum; (4) topic days; (5) the Pass on Loan Program; and (6) exposure visits.

Demonstration plots. Demonstration plots were set up with the intention of promoting knowledge transfer through equipping farmers with practical knowledge of growing food crops such as maize, soya beans, cowpea, and sorghum. In addition, farmers acquired technical knowledge on how to grow drought resistant grains since erratic rainfall patterns have become a challenge in the area. Farmers then applied the knowledge acquired during their participation in the demonstration plots in their own individual plots. This participatory activity promoted interaction and knowledge sharing among farmers and extension workers. Patrick, a village head, reflected on how these engagement practices empowered the farmers:

> What I can say is DAPP opened our eyes. I have lived in this village ever since I was born. It's more than 40 years now. But many people did not have the skill of sharing, people were just doing their own things. When harvesting time comes then you hear so and so got 15 tonnes or 20 tonnes. You also hear so and so did not even get a tonne. But through participating in the DAPP Farmers Club people learnt to share skills and knowledge for the benefit of everyone and that is good.

Adding to this discussion, Gabriel, one of the DAPP Extension workers, stated that "farmers participated in various activities as no one wanted to be left behind. It is during these activities that farmers learn many things. And during these activities information flows from all angles." When farmers engage with each other, information is exchanged and resilient networks can be established, thus illustrating the importance of small farmer community engagement practices. Bandewar et al.'s (2017) study in Kenya discovered that engagement between farmers and social networks promoted the embracing of new technologies by farmers. Engagement between farmers in the demonstration plots provided a fertile ground through which learning by doing flourished. During that process, social capital was built which facilitated higher levels of information sharing and cooperation among farmers.

Self-help group gardens. Self-Help Group Gardens enabled the farmers to work collaboratively to plant a variety of vegetables during different seasons. This consequently opened their access to vegetables for household consumption throughout the year. In addition, proceeds from the gardens supplemented their household income as they could sell their produce to local people. Reflecting on how the self-help group gardens had improved their lives, Lorriet, a Farmers Club leader, stated:

> Many people have started to compete with us DAPP Farmers. They have seen we are making money. So, they are now starting their own gardens and

planting vegetables like us. In fact, I can say things like vegetables and tomatoes are now readily available, which also improves the nutrition of people.

Another Farmers Club leader, Tracy, added her voice stating that:

People have woken up to the fact that one can plant vegetables and tomatoes and raise money more than a person who planted tobacco because there was an opportunity to learn that growing these crops requires [a] short time, thus one sells a variety of vegetables during the year.

The establishment of the self-help group gardens led to the efficient utilization of the available capitals in the area. At the same time, the living conditions of the farmers improved through this initiative. Summing up the activities undertaken in the garden project, Tracy further stated, "in our gardens we grew rape, cabbages, tomatoes, onions, beans, carrots and peas." This means that the project went beyond improving farmers' production of staple crops but also served as a catalyst to the establishment of self-help group gardens, which improved food security as well as nutrition and dietary diversity in the area.

Women's forum. A Women's Forum emerged from the Farmers Club where women participated in a range of workshops. This provided an opportunity for women members of the club to network and strategize on how they could confront the challenges that were crippling their operations. For example, group purchasing of inputs was organized in this forum, which enabled the farmers to pool their financial resources and purchase inputs in bulk. Purchasing the inputs in bulk enabled them to bargain for better prices from the suppliers, which consequently lowered the individual farmers' cost of production. The Women's Forum also enabled the farmers to secure markets and transport their products in groups, which eased negotiations with potential buyers and reduced transport costs. The farmers previously faced challenges getting their agricultural goods to market, which resulted in a loss of revenue to the resource constrained farmers. Lack of access to markets (Mensah & Karriem, 2021) is a major challenge that farmers face in rural Zimbabwe and the ability of the farmers to "order their world" is revered by proponents of participatory approaches (Bhattacharyya, 2004, p. 12). Put simply, the Women's Forum provided a space where resilient networks could be created, maintained, and capabilities synchronized.

Topic days. Topic days gave farmers an opportunity to set the agenda on issues of essence and common interest. Farmers would convene on these days to discuss project activities. This was meant to promote information sharing among farmers. A range of issues were discussed such as bookkeeping, crop rotation, weed control, and compost making. Reflecting on the benefits of these topic days, Benjamin, one of the village heads, stated that "we have realized that we can use compost on some of the crops, and now we are practicing zero tillage which has helped us to cut costs." In some instances, small farmers received training on aspects such as field preparation, compost formulation, crop processing, bookkeeping, and so forth.

Pass on loan program. Furthermore, apart from working in the fields, the Pass on Loan Program enabled farmers to get involved in poultry and pig production. Narrating how the project worked, Tracy stated that:

> We got involved in a poultry project. I was given 4 chickens at first. When the chickens started rearing, I passed on some chicks to 3 other farmers. And the cycle continued until everyone had chickens. After that we got involved in the goat project. When the goat had an offspring I passed the offspring to another farmer. We also ventured into the pig project as a group. As Batanai group we shared 6 pigs per person.

All the club members benefited from the Pass on Loan Program. This initiative promoted multiple streams of income for farmers, as they could sell their small livestock. The income was used to send their children to school and to improve livelihoods at the household level.

Exposure visits. Exposure visits enabled the farmers in Mazowe to visit other DAPP sponsored projects within the province. The purpose of these visits was for farmers to learn from each other and to build their agency. The project facilitated what is deemed as "farmer to farmer learning or horizontal learning" (Mukute, 2013, p.77). Mukute's study in the Masvingo District in Zimbabwe indicates that farmers were easily motivated by the actions of other farmers. Their confidence was built upon realizing that other farmers had adopted sustainable farming methods. The Mazowe DAPP Farmers met experienced piggery and poultry farmers from the Shamva District who offered lessons on piggery and poultry farming practices and skills to their counterparts.

Discussion

The values and principles of community development find a strong resonance in the findings of this chapter. First, it is clear from the participants' remarks that farmers meaningfully participated in the DAPP Farmers Club project and their participation was an empowering process. Without doubt, the engagement strategies used in the project satisfied the objective of participation, which is to empower beneficiaries of development projects (Chambers, 1995). The farmers did not only participate in the provision of labor but were active players who played key roles in the project and acquired knowledge on how to farm in a more productive and sustainable manner. Indeed, the community engagement strategies introduced by the Farmers Club project have empowered farmers who have learned new ways of producing through the demonstration plots, shared knowledge with each, diversified the crops they produced, and improved their livelihoods.

Second, the Farmers Club project created an environment where social capital developed among farmers. The links and association between farmers in the project enabled them to collaborate for the greater benefit of all the farmers involved (Mattessich & Monsey, 2004). Here, social capital was influential in enabling the farmers to think as a collective and act in a collaborative way. The community engagement practices that the farmers actively participated in helped to build a solidaristic ethos. Tracy's passing on of chicks, goats and pigs to other farmers exemplifies the development of social ties or an ethos of solidarity. Indeed, this ethos of solidarity among the farmers in Mazowe District provides a strong contrast to rational choice theory, where rational actors act in their self-interest and "free ride" and profit" from the collective participation of other farmers (Karriem, 2009; Levin & Milgrom, 2004). The Farmers Club project yielded solidarity and resilience, which enhanced cooperation between farmers and improved agricultural production. Without doubt, Tracy's remarks point to high levels of solidarity among farmers. As Bhattacharyya (2004) notes, solidarity entails "a concern for every person" (p. 14). The farmers community engagement practices highlight the dialectical relationship between the theory and practice of community development. Indeed, community development is a collaborative process through which farmers with shared interests become conscious of their needs and work together to improve their lives (Swanepoel, 1996). Moreover, Dogbe et al. (2013) note that the role of a development agent (the DAPP Farmers Club) is to guide farmers in recognizing and dealing with agricultural issues at the local level. Undoubtedly, the engagement methods used in this project increased the capacity of the farmers to work together, which is in consonance with the theory and practice of community development.

Third, respondents were clear that the project changed the lives of the participating farmers, but the benefits of sharing information on farming and community engagement practices spiralled to farmers who were not member of the Farmers Club. It is quite evident in Lorriet's remarks that the DAPP Farmers Club project set an example in the case study area. Ordinarily, farmers in the rural areas lack access to information which has contributed to poor yields and low agricultural production. Although organizations such as DAPP are urged to reach a wider population so that the benefits of these interventions are widely felt, the Farmers' Club is a vehicle through which government policy of strengthening and transforming agricultural production in the country could be rolled out (GoZ, 2018).

Overall, while food insecurity is quite high among small farmers, the Farmers Club project empowered farmers to participate meaningfully in a project that addressed their food and nutrition needs. The transformation of farmers' lives is a clear indication that livelihoods and well-being can be improved, and poverty reduced if development projects capacitate and empower beneficiaries to become active agents of their own development. A key component of community development is involving people to participate in an active manner which manifested itself in the project. Farmers were able to deliberate, reflect and make decisions which are crucial in achieving development that is sustainable.

Limitations of the Study

The major limitation of this study is that it is based on just one ward of the Mazowe District. Moreover, the study is based on a small sample size, which means that the results of this study cannot be generalized to the larger population. Be that as it may, the research provides key practical insights on the lived experiences of small farmers community engagement practices in improving agricultural productivity and hence the livelihoods of their families. Finally, this study could form the basis on which future studies with a larger sample size and different methodological approaches may be carried out.

Conclusion

The continued deterioration of Zimbabwe's agricultural production levels has drawn attention to the need for the development of intervention mechanisms that empower and capacitate farmers to farm more productively and sustainably. This chapter reviewed community engagement strategies employed in agricultural development in the Mazowe District of Zimbabwe. The central argument of this chapter is that government, development agencies, and NGOs should assist small farmers with training, knowledge transfer, and ensure that they adopt more sustainable farming methods. More specifically, stakeholders interested in rolling out agricultural intervention programs should follow participatory community engagement mechanisms that provide farmers the opportunity to participate in the conceptualization and the implementation of development programs. The chapter further demonstrates that small farmers' livelihoods will only be improved if farmers are capacitated to farm in a more sustainable manner and are empowered to diversify their farming activities. Overall, this chapter indicates the need for a multi-stakeholder approach that is participatory in nature and that establishes strong partnerships with small farmers and communities to ensure that they become active agents in their development.

REFERENCES

Arnold, L., Gallaher, M., Garcia, N., Head, M., Hutcheson, S., Khajehei, L., Oswald, J., Sheng, B., Siracuse, M., Wedekind, E., Wofford, Y., Wei, S., & Williams, S. (2019). *Community engagement techniques*. https://tinyurl.com/mpdtfefh

Bandewar, S. V., Wambugu, F., Richardson, E., & Lavery, J. V. (2017). The role of community engagement in the adoption of new agricultural biotechnologies by farmers: the case of the Africa harvest tissue-culture banana in Kenya. *BMC biotechnology*, *17*(1), 1–11.

Bhattacharyya, J. (2004). Theorizing community development. *Community Development*, *34*(2), 5-34. https://doi.org/10.1080/15575330409490110.

Burkey, S. (1993). *People first: A guide to self-reliant participatory rural development* (1st ed.). Zed Books.

Chambers, R. (1995). Poverty and livelihoods: whose reality counts? *Environment and urbanization*, *7*(1), 173–204. https://www.ucl.ac.uk/dpu-projects/drivers_urb_change/urb_society/pdf_liveli_vulnera/IIED_Chambers_poverty.pdf

Chambers, R. (1997). *Whose reality counts?: Putting the last first*. Intermediate Technology Publications.

Creswell, J. W. (2009). *Research design: Qualitative, quantitative, and mixed-method approaches* (3rd ed.). SAGE.

Chazovachii, B., & Tagarirofa, J. (2013). Exploring the politics of local participation in rural development projects. Small dam's rehabilitation project in Zimbabwe. *Russian Journal of Agriculture and Socio-Economic Sciences*, *2*(14), 74–88.

De Beer, F., & Swanepoel, H. (2006). *Community development: Breaking the cycle of poverty* (4th ed.). Juta & Co.

De Beer, F., & Swanepoel, H. (2011). *Community development: Breaking the cycle of poverty* (5th ed.). Juta & Co.

DeJonckheere, M., & Vaughn, L. M. (2019). Semi structured interviewing in primary care research: A balance of relationship and rigour. *Family Medicine and Community Health*, *20*(7), 1–8. https://fmch.bmj.com/content/7/2/e000057

Deng, D. K. (2012). *Handbook on community engagement: A good practice guide to negotiating lease agreements with landowning communities in South Sudan*. South Sudan Law Society. https://www.cmi.no/file/1985-ssls-handbook-on-community-engagement.pdf

Development Aid from People to People. (2018). *Farmers Club*. https://dapp-zimbabwe.org/project/farmers-clubs/

Dogbe, W., Etwire, P. M., Wiredu, A. N., Martey, E., Etwire, E., Owusu, R. K., & Wahaga, E. (2013). Factors influencing farmers' participation in agricultural projects: The case of the agricultural value chain mentorship project in the northern region of Ghana. *Journal of Economics and Sustainable Development*, *4*(10), 36–43. https://www.iiste.org/Journals/index.php/JEDS/article/view/6509/6526

Dube, L. (2017). Farmer to farmer extension approach: Analysis of extent of adoption by smallholder farmers in Manicaland and Masvingo provinces of Zimbabwe. *Journal of Agricultural Economics and Rural Development*. 3(1), 149–160. https://www.researchgate.net/profile/Lighton-Dube/publication/318402573_

Food and Agricultural Organization. (2007). *Applying people centred development approaches within FAO*. http://ftp.fao.org/docrep/fao/007/j3137e/j3137e00.pdf

Food and Agriculture Organisation. (2022). *Zimbabwe at a glance*. https://www.fao.org/zimbabwe/fao-in-zimbabwe/zimbabwe-at-a-glance/en/

Frank, F., & Smith, A. (1999). *The community development handbook* (1st ed.). Human Resources Development Canada. http://www.hrdc-drhc.gc.ca/community

Government of Zimbabwe. (2012). *Comprehensive agricultural policy framework (2012–2032): Executive summary*. https://swm-programme.info/documents/20142/407481/ZWE_

Government of Zimbabwe. (2018). *National agriculture policy framework (2018–2030)*. http://www.livestockzimbabwe.com/Updates/Draft-

Gran, G. (1983). *Development by people: Citizen construction of a just world* (1st ed.). Praeger.

Hanyani-Mlambo, B. T. (2002). *Strengthening the pluralistic agricultural extension system: A Zimbabwean case study*. Food and Agriculture Organisation. https://www.fao.org/3/ac913e/ac913e00.htm

International Fund for Agricultural Development. (2021). *Zimbabwe and IFAD join forces to transform small-scale agriculture*. https://www.ifad.org/en/web/latest/-/zimbabwe-and-ifad-join-

Jimbira, S. S., & Hathie, I. (2020). *The future of agriculture in Sub-Saharan Africa*. (Policy brief No.2). Southern Voice. https://www.ifad.org/documents/38714170/42030191/future_agriculture_sahara_e.pdf

Karriem, A. (2009). The Brazilian Landless Movement: Mobilization for transformative politics. In Y. Atasoy (Eds.), *Hegemonic transitions: The state and crisis in neoliberal capitalism* (pp. 263–280). Routledge.

Karriem, A., & Benjamin, L. (2016). How civil society organizations foster insurgent citizenship: lessons from the Brazilian Landless Movement. *VOLUNTAS: International Journal of Voluntary and Non-profit Organizations*, 27(1), 19–36.

Kuhudzayi, B., & Mattos, D. (2018). A model for farmer support in Zimbabwe—Opportunity for change. *Cornhusker Economics*. https://agecon.unl.edu/cornhusker-economics/2018/farmer-support-model-zimbabwe.pdf

Levin, J., & Milgrom, P. (2004). *Introduction to choice theory*. https://web.stanford.edu/~jdlevin/Econ 202/Choice Theory.pdf

Mensah, C., & Karriem, A. (2021). harnessing public food procurement for sustainable rural livelihoods in South Africa through the National School Nutrition Programme: A qualitative assessment of contributions and challenges. *Sustainability*, 13(24), 13838. https://doi.org/10.3390/su132413838

Mattessich, P., & Monsey, M. (2004). *Community building: What makes it work*. Wider Foundation.

McMillan, D. W., & Chavis, D. M. (1986). Sense of community: A definition and theory. *Journal of Community Psychology*. 14(1), 6–23.

Mukute, M. (2013). Bridging and enriching top-down and participatory learning: The case of smallholder, organic conservation agriculture farmers in Zimbabwe. *Southern African Journal of Environmental Education. 29*(2012/2013), 75–93.

Mupindu, W. (2015). The challenges of food security policy and food quality in Zimbabwe: A case study of Operation Maguta in Buhera district. *African Journal of Public Affairs. 8*(2), 90–103.

Mutami, C. (2015). Smallholder agriculture production in Zimbabwe: A survey. *Consilience: Journal of Sustainable Development. 14*(2), 140–157.

Mutisi, C. (2009). *Situation analysis of agricultural research training and support strategies for the National Agricultural Research System in Zimbabwe*. University of Zimbabwe.

Narayan-Parker, D. (2002). *Empowerment and poverty reduction: A sourcebook*. Poverty reduction and economic management. World Bank Publications. https://doi.org/10.1596/0-8213-5166-4

Nhongonhema, R. (2010, July 26-28). An overview of extension approaches and methods in Zimbabwe [Workshop]. In W. H. Kimaro, L Mukandiwa, & E. Z. J. Mario (Eds.), *Towards improving agricultural extension service delivery in the SADC region*. Dar es Salaam, Tanzania.

Pedzisa, T., Minde, I., & Twomlow, S. (2010). An evaluation of the use of participatory processes in wide-scale dissemination of research in micro dosing and conservation agriculture in Zimbabwe. *Research Evaluation. 19*(2), 145–155. https://repository.up.ac.za/handle/2263/16364

Phillips, R., & Pittman, R. H. (2009). *An introduction to community development* (1st ed.). Routledge.

Pindiriri, C., Chirongwe, G., Nyajena, F. M., & Nkomo, G. N. (2021, January). *Agriculture free input support schemes, input usage, food insecurity and poverty in rural Zimbabwe. (Working Paper Series)*. https://zepari.co.zw/sites/default/files/2022-03/Agricultural%20free%20input%20support%20schemes.pdf

Robinson, J. W., & Green, P., G. (2011). *Introduction to community development: Theory, practice, and service-learning*. (1st ed.). SAGE.

Shepherd, A. (1998). *Sustainable rural development* (1st ed.). Palgrave.

South Coast Natural Resource Management. (2014). *The community engagement handbook*. Green Skills. https://southcoastnrm.com.au/wp-content/uploads/2018/09/SCNRM_-_Community_Engagement_Handbook.pdf

Swanepoel, H. (1996.) Evaluation of community development projects: A human development approach. *Africanus. 26*(1), 53–64.

Tagarirofa, J., & David, T. (2013). An intersectional analysis of community participation, empowerment, and sustainability: Towards elimination of the barriers. *European Journal of Social Sciences, Arts and Humanities. 1*(1), 8–16.

Tacconi, L., & Tisdell, C. (1993). Holistic sustainable development: Implications for planning processes, foreign aid, and support for research. *Third World Planning Review. 15*(4), 411–428.

United Nations Economic and Social Commission for Asia and the Pacific. (2009). *Participatory approaches to rural development and rural poverty alleviation* (Working Paper). http://sergiorosendo.pbworks.com/f/Guimaraes+2010+participatory_rural.pdf

World Bank. (2020). *The World Bank in Zimbabwe*. https://www.worldbank.org/en/country/zimbabwe/overview

CHAPTER 10

ENGAGING TRADITIONAL LEADERSHIP AS A KEY AND PRACTICAL APPROACH TO COMMUNITY DEVELOPMENT

The Jatropha Project in Puriya Community as a Case Study

Eunice Abbey and Vyda Mamley Hervie

ABSTRACT

Community development plays a significant role in building and improving the lives of community members. The importance of engaging traditional leaders in community development cannot be overemphasized. The enormous scholarship on community development has revealed how effective, successful, and sustainable developmental projects and programs have been as a result of engaging traditional leaders. This chapter highlights the relevance of engaging traditional leaders in community development. Using the participatory approach to community development, the chapter discusses how the Jatropha project was successfully implemented in Puriya community in Northern Ghana through the engagement of traditional leaders and the community at large. Apart from highlighting the benefits of using the participatory approach in the project implementation, the chapter also presents some of the challenges that contributed to failure of the project some years after its implementation. The chapter concludes by calling for the continuous and effective engagement of traditional leaders and participation of community members at all levels of development initiatives to achieve effective

Community Development Practice in Africa: Putting Theory Into Practice, pp. 149–162
Copyright © 2024 by Information Age Publishing
www.infoagepub.com
All rights of reproduction in any form reserved.

developmental outcomes and sustainability of community projects whilst advancing the argument that the participatory approach must be used in conjunction with the principles of community development.

Keywords: traditional leaders, community development, engagement, Jatropha, Puriya, Ghana

> "Community leadership is the courage, creativity and capacity to inspire participation, development and sustainability for strong communities."
>
> —Gustav Nossal (n.d.)

The above quote was by Gustav Nossal, one of Australia's great community leaders and scientists. It emphasizes the crucial role of community leadership, which includes traditional leaders in the development of the community. It implies that without the participation of community leadership, development stagnates. This drives the very essence of the chapter on engaging traditional leaders as one of the practical approaches to community development.

Traditional leadership is the style of leadership where leaders are given power based on the traditions of the past and are crucial actors in development (Keulder, 2010; Mawere et al., 2021). They are also seen as representing their communities and playing key roles, such as harmonizing the customs and traditions of the land in line with the tenets of a country's constitution (Ndima, 2017).

In Africa and some parts of the world, traditional leaders play a critical role in the social, political, and economic lives of the people. They are characterized as local elites who gain their authority from tradition, culture, and religion (Honig, 2019). The local leadership or government is seen as the bridge or first point of contact between the local communities, government, and other institutions (Honig, 2019; Thornhill, 2008) also making them the most capable and appropriate for negotiating development (Paradza et al., 2010).

Traditional leadership is revered by many including those living in the rural areas. It is even seen as more effective in the delivery of services and transformation of lives than the local government (Koenane, 2018). To this effect, Baldwin (2016) argues that traditional leadership cannot be replaced given the unique roles played in for instance, the administration of justice, land management, maintaining the cultural values and beliefs of the land and the overall well-being of the community members (Kariuki, 2021; Mawere, 2014; Mawere et al., 2021).

Community development connotes a concept of self-help, where community members also come together to make decisions and pool their resources to address their needs and opportunities. Traditional leaders are major actors in community development as they are known to be very effective in engaging their communities in making decisions on development matters (Tshitangoni & Francis, 2014). Routing community development initiatives or projects through them is helpful in not only engaging the entire community members but they also become invested in the process of making changes that benefit their community and its future (Scancar, 2004).

From the preceding discussion, this chapter addresses the relevance of engaging traditional leaders and community members as one of the key approaches to community development. The authors use the Jatropha project in Puriya community in Northern Ghana as a case study to support the scholarship on participatory approaches in community development. Furthermore, the authors discuss why the Jatropha project in the community encountered challenges that eventually led to its failure and bringing to light some of the core principles needed to successfully implement and sustain community projects.

Traditional Leaders

In this section, emphasis is laid on how the participation of traditional leaders in the Jatropha project led to its initial success. Traditional leaders in this context refer to the chief, elders, and women's leader in Puriya community. According to one of the oldest elders in the community, traditions do not permit them to have a queen mother. Instead, there is a female leader who oversees the affairs of women and children in the community. She is accountable to the Queen Mother in Sambu, a community within the Yendi Municipal District (A. Baaba, personal communication, April 2, 2023). The chieftaincy position was also opened to all men in Puriya community if the candidate was healthy and of a sound mind. The candidates were required to communicate their interest to the Paramount Chief of Sambu, who was responsible for selecting the most qualified candidate for enstoolment (A. Baaba, personal communication, April 2, 2023).

The roles performed by the Queen Mother of Sambu are similar to those performed by other Queen Mothers in different communities of Ghana. Among others, the roles of Queen Mothers are to serve as the advisor to the chief and ensure the welfare of women and children in the community. The chiefs, on the other hand, are responsible for the physical, spiritual, and emotional wellbeing of the community members as well as maintaining law and order (Kreitzer, 2004).

The Concept of Community Development

An earlier definition of community was advanced by Tönnies (1955) as a preindustrial social formation where there was a face-to-face encounter with people in the tribal and rural societies: "Gesellschaft." However, given the changes in today's industrialized society (Goel, 2014), the concept of community has been diffused to apply variously to terms such as villages and ethnic groups. It is also seen as physically constrained areas of specific groups of individuals with similar needs, aspirations and the sharing of interpersonal and relational standards which include reciprocity, trust, and social engagement, which form the basis of community strengths (Anyidoho, 2010; Goel, 2014). Goel (2014) further asserts that a broader definition of community is required in the context of community development to transcend beyond interest and place-based definitions to include virtual communities such as the web, Facebook, online and social media where people relate with unknown others from different locations. For communities to function, thrive and do well, there is the need for continuing social, economic, and environmental improvement; structural aspects and circumstances for growth must be created (Cavaye, 2001; Chaskin, 2009; Goel, 2014).

Development, in its broad view, encompasses the enhancement or improvement of the social, economic, political, spiritual, and cultural lives of people (Coetzee et al., 2001). Thus, development connotes the transition from a poor to better situation, progressing and having the accessibility to resources for a decent standard of living (Coetzee et al., 2001) and a collective action of people in resolving their needs or problems (Weyman, 1996). According to Dinbabo (2003), development also includes, among others, values such as empowerment, sustainability, and capacity building.

Community development has been defined in different ways, with differing ideas in concept and emphasis. Hence, many societies should embrace and develop mixed pluralistic and modern societies (Goel, 2014; Rose, 1962). Community development is also defined as a deliberate attempt to strengthen citizens' ability to enhance their quality of life through the creation of resources such as physical, human, social, financial, and environmental assets (Phillips & Pittman, 2009; Sampson et al., 1999). Community development is also defined by Kenny (2011) as a way of empowering communities to take collective responsibility and control for their own development. By promoting collective rather than individualistic action, community development enables community members to be autonomous in making decisions toward addressing issues that affect them and in meeting their needs (Goel, 2014).

In the community development process, a cycle occurs where participation is encouraged at every level of the development initiative to promote effective interventions. It begins with organizing the community (community organization) to identify problems and mobilizing the community members to identify sustainable development interventions (Green, 2007). This is followed by the planning and vision phases where the community plans toward their desired end state for their community and their vision for the future (Green, 2007). The implementation phase follows where practical and required steps and actions are taken to actualize the goals and objectives set by the community. The monitoring and evaluation phase follows during and after the project implementation to assess whether corrections are necessary in the implementation phase and whether the project achieved its purpose or not (Green, 2007). The following section highlights the importance of participatory theory and its relevance to community development.

The Participatory Theory

Participatory theories became popular after the criticism of the modernization theories that promoted a top-down approach to development tied to the western view of progress (Waisbord, 2001). The emergence of the participatory theories has undergone several theoretical shifts, "spanning feminism, environmentalism, critical pedagogy and a critique of development itself" (Keough, 1998, p. 3).

The participatory theory emphasizes a bottom-up approach to development. Also known as "People-Centered Development," the theory lays emphasis on the fact that regular people could utilize resources already at their disposal to manage their own development, calling for the involvement or participation of all stakeholders in the development process (Dinbabo, 2003; Rahman, 1993). Some of the principles of participatory theory include having a sense of humility and respect, understanding local knowledge, adhering to democratic practice, and acknowledging diverse ways of knowing (Keough, 1998).

Participatory theory promotes cultural diversity and the incorporation of interpersonal channels of communication in local decision-making processes (Siddiqui, 2003) to promote and sustain community development. The active participation of community members in decisions regarding the execution of processes, programs, and initiatives has a positive impact on them and reflects their ability and power to think, act, and control their behavior within a cooperative framework (Barnett & Brennan, 2006; Dinbabo, 2003).

In addition to the above, participation allows community members to fully share in the benefits of the development services and opportunities, increasing their levels of output and becoming more receptive to new technologies and services (Cornwall, 2002; Dinbabo, 2003). More so, making use of labor and resources within the communities could reduce the costs and allow for growing cash surpluses (Anyidoho, 2010). Ensuring the development and progress of communities as well as in sustaining community projects are dependent on some principles of participatory development.

Some significant advantages of using participatory theory in community development include capacity building, self-reliance, empowerment, and sustainability. Capacity building occurs when all community members are enabled to develop competencies and skills geared toward inclusively contributing to community development and having greater control of their lives (Noya & Clarence, 2009). Self-reliance, on the other hand, involves the usage of local resources and initiatives to improve the condition of community members (Fonchingong & Fonjong, 2002). Empowerment in community development goes beyond participation or involvement. It captures community action and ownership that clearly aims at realizing social and political changes within the community (Labonte & Laverick, 2008).

Participatory theory is used in the Puriya case to explain and understand how "participation" from the traditional leaders influenced the entire community through the Jatropha project. It shows how the use of local knowledge and resources contributed to the success of the project. The benefits of the project to the community members and some post-project challenges that arose are also discussed.

Profile of Puriya Community

Puriya is a small community in the Mion District in the central part of the Northern Region of Ghana. The district shares boundaries with the Yendi Municipal District to the east, Tamale Metropolis to the west, Savelugu Municipal and Nanton District to the south. Puriya shares boundaries with other communities, such as Sang and Decekura (A. Baaba, personal communication, September 20, 2022).

Puriya was established by two men who first settled in the area as farmers. Puriya means "the good farm." Presently, the main economic activity in the community is farming. Puriya is a very small community with a population of about 200 people. The main language spoken is Dagbani (A. Baaba, personal communication, September 20, 2022).

The community is highly patriarchal in nature where men wield a lot of power and authority, a common practice in most African countries. They are mostly owners of lands and family heads (Offiong et al., 2021). They exhibit a communalistic way of living where community members are each other's keepers. The community lacks basic amenities such as clean drinking water and a health facility. However, they rely on traditional and herbal interventions for their health needs (A. Baaba, personal communication, September 20, 2022). The community has a basic school but limited learning materials and resources. For instance, the lack of textbooks and other learning materials made learning difficult for the pupils.

In terms of governance, the community is mainly governed under the traditional leadership, headed by the chief who is assisted by his sub elders. The chief and his elders assist in maintaining the cultural values and solving individual, family, and community problems (A. Baaba, personal communication, September 20, 2022).

The Jatropha Project

The Jatropha project in Puriya was the initiative of Ohayo Ghana Foundation, a Japanese organization based in Accra, Ghana. Jatropha is a biofuel plant used in the production of soap, lamp fuel and paint. It is also called a biodiesel plant, as the seed oil has similar characteristics to diesel (Dias et al., 2012; Moniruzzaman et al., 2017; Tikkoo et al., 2013).

The organization is mainly exploring new ways of revitalizing the traditional handicrafts, agriculture, and industries of Ghana. The organization also supports other humanitarian services in Ghana. For instance, the organization was part of the baseball project in Ghana, where it supported the project for the construction of the baseball and softball field at Labone Senior Secondary School (Japan's Official Development White Paper, 2014).

The Jatropha project in Puriya community was meant to end with the establishment of a factory in the community to generate biofuel and to improve the quality of lives of the people through the creation of job opportunities according to Abu (pseudonym) (personal communication, June 15, 2008). The traditional leaders and the entire community were very instrumental in the implementation of the Jatropha project. The following section throws more light on how the engagement of the traditional leaders led to its success.

Engagement of the Traditional Leaders: Relevance of the Participatory Theory

The beginning of the Jatropha project saw active participation and engagement of the traditional leaders and the community members in Puriya. Ohayo Ghana Foundation, then led by the late Mr. Tamura, first paid a courtesy call on the traditional leadership in Puriya. In the Ghanaian

Figure 10.1

Picture of a Jatropha Seed

Source: Dogbevi (2009).

context, it is believed that one cannot engage community members without first going through the traditional leaders who are believed to be the custodians of the people and the land. This affirms the assertion that local or traditional leadership is the first point of contact between local communities and institutions (governmental & non-governmental), making them most capable and appropriate for negotiating development (Honig, 2019; Paradza et al., 2010; Thornhill, 2008). The Foundation made their intentions known to the chief and his elders about the Jatropha plantation and how it will help develop the community. Prior to that, donations in the forms of exercise books and other learning materials had been made to the basic school in the community.

Pledging their commitment to the project, the chief offered the foundation about 200 acres of land. Some portions of the land were used for the plantation of the Jatropha seeds. The men and women in the community were actively involved in the plantation of the seeds. The participatory approach adopted by the Foundation encouraged the use of the community's resources: land and human resources. Thus, engaging them from the onset of the project created an overall positive attitude toward the project and becoming subjects of their own development as discoursed by Rahim (1994). Between 2008 and 2009, the authors visited Puriya and witnessed on countless occasions how community members, designated as caretakers of the Jatropha farms, were always on the farms, weeding and ensuring the seeds grew well. The sense of ownership was paramount with the understanding that the project would bring positive changes and development to their community. The project empowered them in this regard as advanced by Labonte and Laverick (2008) that empowerment captures community action and ownership geared toward realizing social and political changes within the community.

The project's second phase had to do with building the factory that was meant to process the Jatropha seeds into oil. The land used in building the factory was also given to the foundation by the traditional leadership in the community. One of the authors who was then doing her fieldwork in the community witnessed some of the construction activities and was responsible for taking the names of all those who worked on site for payment purposes. The foundation ensured they utilized the local skills and expertise. Carpenters and masons were picked from the community and neighboring ones when they needed more hands-on board. Building materials like sand were fetched from the community lands. The women fetched water from the well to the building site. Relying on the local resources encouraged self-reliance in that they mostly depended on their local resources. As noted by Fonchingong and Fonjong (2002), self-reliance involves using local resources and initiatives to improve the living conditions of community members. It also contributed to reducing cost, as opined by Anyidoho (2010) that making use of labor and resources within the communities could reduce the costs and allow for growing cash.

Success of the Project

The joy and speed with which they worked promoted a sense of togetherness. Some machines had to be used at a point in the construction. Although unfamiliar with such machines, the community members were receptive to the new technology, as working on the site provided job opportunities and improved their financial status. This also resonates with Dinbabo (2003) and Cornwall's (2002) assertion that participation allows community members to fully share in the benefits of the development services and opportunities, increasing their levels of output and becoming more receptive to new technologies and services.

The whole project was supervised by a Japanese who worked with the Foundation, assisted by some Ghanaians. Staying in the community for several months and interacting with them promoted cultural diversity as they learned about the cultural values and practices in the community and vice versa. Indeed, the participatory approach promotes cultural diversity, as noted by Siddiqui (2003).

Interactions with the community members about their thoughts on the project fetched positive responses and feedback. While attesting to the fact that the benefits to be gleaned would go a long way to alleviate their sufferings and difficulties in the community, others were also optimistic that Puriya will take on a new identity and rub shoulders with Sang regarding development. The following section provides information on the project's outcome as of February 2022, when the authors visited Puriya.

Post-Project Challenges: Why the Jatropha Project Ended

The authors had high expectations in terms of going to meet a new Puriya with significant improvement in the living conditions of the people. It was quite the opposite when the authors arrived in the community. The factory was in a deplorable state and now served as the residence for the new chief of Puriya. The community members were actively engaged in their farming activities. The Jatropha plantation was gone. These observations left the authors wondering what might have happened to the project that started effectively with a fully built factory and had a very promising future for the community.

The authors engaged Alhassan (pseudonym) one of the Foundation's right-hand men and the community on the project's current state. Alhassan was born and raised in Puriya and had stayed there all his life. His response to why the project did not succeed is captured below:

> The Foundation decided not to continue with the Jatropha oil processing because Ghana was beginning to explore more in the oil industry with several companies springing up in the oil business. Looking at the competition and financial prospects it was better to redirect the focus of the project. We went into milling of rice, the factory served that purpose and for some months, we were transporting milled local rice to Accra for sale. At first, the rice business was doing well. However, we started experiencing some challenges due to the low patronage of local rice among Ghanaians. It even got worst when the leader of the Foundation passed away ... milling of the rice became very low. The new person sent by the Foundation to the community knew nothing about us and would not even listen to us. He was just doing what he wanted. It was difficult interacting with him, so he left. Visits from the foundation to the community gradually reduced. Not many of us had the expertise to run the factory ... no money was coming. The factory collapsed and as you can see now, it is now the residence of our traditional leader, Chief Mohammed. (Alhassan)

Judging from Alhassan's response, the authors deduced four significant reasons why the project ended prematurely: (1) Lack of training of locals to manage the project; (2) lack of understanding and acknowledging local knowledge; (3) unrealistic expectations and (4) lack of funds. These are explained below.

Lack of training of locals to manage the project. Project management is known to produce better results for projects when it involves planning and delegating tasks to others (Martin & Tate, 2001). In the case of Puriya and the Jatropha project, the locals did not get any specialized skills and training to manage the project from their Japanese supervisors. This meant that in the absence of the supervisors, the locals could not run the project. In the aspect of management, they were utterly dependent on their supervisors.

Lack of understanding and acknowledging local knowledge. Success of projects adhere to principles, including having a sense of humility and respect, understanding local knowledge, using democratic practice, and acknowledging diverse ways of knowing Keough (1998). The "new" supervisor sent to the community disregarded the local knowledge and was not open to diverse opinions, as stated by Alhassan. The community members withdrew. This led to communication challenges and understanding. Eventually, he had to leave the community. This also implies that community members will resist any opposition to their knowledge, culture, and values.

Unrealistic expectations. Unrealistic expectations also contributed to the failure of the project. The expectations for the project were not aligned with the reality of the market demands for Jatropha oil in Ghana. Coupled with a lack of planning and making adjustment to the purpose of establishing the factory negatively affected the entire project. According to Wrona (2017), setting unrealistic goals leads to misunderstanding of the intricacies of projects and could lead to negative decisions and other risks that may negatively affect the project.

Lack of funds. Funding for the project was halted by the Foundation when the new supervisor left Puriya community. The death of Mr. Tamura (the project manager), coupled with the other challenges stated above, the project could no longer continue. A few of the community members who attempted to revive the project lacked the requisite skills in soliciting funds and getting the right resources to manage the project.

The failure of the Jatropha project provides insightful lessons for the future. Regardless of adopting the participatory approach that saw the effective and successful initial processes for the project, it still failed to achieve its purpose in the end. Beyond the approach used, principles that could have sustained the project were missing. According to Scancar (2004), core principles for the success and sustenance of community projects include, among others, building the right team and relationship (people are a key element of development), partnership, accountability, and constant monitoring. Most of these core principles were not applied in the Jatropha project leading to its collapse.

Conclusion

This chapter looked at engaging traditional leaders and, by extension, community members as a key approach to community development. The authors used the participatory approach to reiterate the importance of engaging traditional leaders in the effective implementation of community projects. The conventional leadership was instrumental in getting the community members on board and providing the local resources for the project. While this approach worked well in successfully implementing the project, it failed to meet its overall purpose after some years because of not applying some core principles in community development and project implementation.

Given its considerable benefits to communities, the authors call for the continual and active engagement (participatory approach) of traditional leaders and community members in community development. However, using the participatory process to engage traditional leaders and community members is insufficient. It must be used in tandem with the principles of community development and project implementation to ensure the sustainability of projects.

REFERENCES

Anyidoho, N. A. (2010). Communities of practice: prospects for theory and action in participatory development. *Development in Practice, 20*(3), 318–328.

Baldwin, K. (2016). *The paradox of traditional chiefs in democratic Africa*. University Press. https://doi.org/10.1017/CBO9781316422335

Barnett, R. V., & Brennan, M. A. (2006). Integrating youth into community development: Implications for policy planning and program evaluation. *Journal of Youth Development, 1*(2), 5–19.

Cavaye, J. (2001). Rural community development: New challenges and enduring dilemmas. *Journal of Regional Analysis & Policy, 31*(1), 109–124.

Chaskin, R. J. (2009). Building community capacity for children, youth, and families. *Children Australia, 34*(1), 31–39.

Coetzee, J. K., Graaf, J., Hendricks, F., & Wood, G. (Eds.). (2001). *Development: theory, policy and practice*. Oxford University Press.

Cornwall, A. (2002). *Making spaces, changing places: Situating participation in development* (IDS Working paper no. 170). Institute of Development Studies.

Dias, L., Missio, R., & Dias, D. (2012). Antiquity, botany, origin and domestication of Jatropha curcas (Euphorbiaceae), a plant species with potential for biodiesel production. *Genetics and Molecular Research, 11*(3), 2719–2728.

Dinbabo, M. F. (2003). *Development theories, participatory approaches, and community development*. [Unpublished paper, Institute for Social Development, University of the Western Cape].

Dogbevi, E. K. (2009). *Any lessons for Ghana in India's Jatropha Failure?* Ghana Business News. https://www.ghanabusinessnews.com/2009/05/23/update-any-lessons-for-ghana-in-indias-jatropha-failure/

Fonchingong, C. C., & Fonjong, L. N. (2002). The concept of self-reliance in community development initiatives in the Cameroon grassfields. *GeoJournal, 57*, 83–94.

Goel, K. (2014). Understanding community and community development. In K. Goel., P. Venkat, & P. Abraham (Eds.), *Community work: theories, experiences, and challenges* (pp. 1–14). Niruta Publications.

Green, G. P., Haines, A., Dunn, A., & Sullivan, D. M. (2002). The role of local development organizations in rural America. *Rural Sociology, 67*(3), 394–415.

Honig, L. (2019). Traditional leaders and development in Africa. In *Oxford Research Encyclopedia of Politics*. Oxford University Press.

Japan's Official Development White Paper. (2014). https://www.mofa.go.jp/policy/oda/white/2014/html/honbun/b2/s2_1_2_05.html

Kariuki, F. (2021). Harnessing traditional knowledge holders' institutions in realising sustainable development goals in Kenya. *Journal of Conflict Management and Sustainable Development, 6*(1), 1–54.

Kenny, S. (2011). *Developing communities for the future* (4th ed.). Cengage Learning.

Keough, N. (1998). Participatory development principles and practice: Reflections of a Western development worker. *Community Development Journal, 33*(3), 187–196.

Keulder, C. (2010). *State, society, and democracy: A reader in Namibian politics*. Macmillan Education Namibia.

Koenane, M. (2018). The role and significance of traditional leadership in the governance of modern democratic South Africa. *African Review, 10*(1), 58–71.

Kreitzer, L. (2004). *Indigenization of social work education and practice: A participatory action research project in Ghana* [Doctoral dissertation, University of Calgary]. Calgary, AB.

Labonte R., & Laverack, F. B. (2008). *Health promotion in action: From local to global empowerment*. Palgrave Macmillan.

Martin, P., & Tate, K. (2001). Getting started in project management. John Wiley & Sons.

Mawere, J., Matshidze, P. E., Kugara, S. L., & Madzivhandila, T. (2022). The role and significance of traditional leadership in South African local governance. In *Handbook of research on protecting and managing global indigenous knowledge systems* (pp. 249–273). IGI Global.

Mawere, M. (2014). *Culture, indigenous knowledge and development in Africa: Reviving interconnections for sustainable development*. Langaa Rpcig.

Moniruzzaman, M., Yaakob, Z., Shahinuzzaman, M., Khatun, R., & Aminul Islam, A. K. M. (2017). Jatropha biofuel industry: The challenges. *Frontiers in Bioenergy and Biofuels, 1*(12), 23–256.

Ndima, D. D. (2017). The anatomy of African jurisprudence: a basis for understanding the African socio-legal and political cosmology. *Comparative and International Law Journal of Southern Africa, 50*(1), 84–108.

Nossal, G. (n.d.). AZQuotes.com. https://www.azquotes.com/quote/594669

Offiong, E. E., Eyo, E. I., & Offiong, A. E. (2021). Patriarchy, culture and the social development of women in Nigeria. *Pinisi Journal of Art, Humanity and Social Studies, 1*(4), 78–86.

Noya, A., & Clarence, E. (2009). *Community capacity building: Fostering economic and social resilience*. Organisation for Economic Cooperation and Development (pp. 26–27). CFE/LEED, OECD. www.oecd.org/dataoecd/54/10/44681969.pdf?contentId=44681970

Paradza G., Mokwena L., & Richard, R. (2010). *Assessing the role of councilors in service delivery at local government level in South Africa* (Research Report 125). Centre for Policy Studies.

Phillips, R., & Pittman. P. R. (2009). *An introduction to community development*. Routledge.

Rahim, S. A. (1994). Participatory development communication as a dialogical process. In S. White., K. S. Nair, & J. Ascroft (Eds.), *Participatory communication working for change and development* (pp. 117–137). SAGE.

Rahman, M. D. A. (1993). *People's self-development: Perspectives on participatory action research*. University Press.

Rose, P. W. (1962). *What is community development?* Agency for International Development, Washington, D. C. https://pdf.usaid.gov/pdf_docs/PNABX081.pdf

Sampson, R. J., Ferguson, R., & Dickens, W. (1999). *Urban problems and community development*. Brookings Institution Press.

Scancar, R. (2004). Community development. In E. S. Friedrich (Ed.), *How to improve development on local level. Handbook with best practice examples from South-East Europe*. Friedrich Ebert Stiftung.

Siddiqui, M. (2003). *Paulo Freire's model of educational change*. http://www.imt.edu.pk/articles/paulofreire.htm

Thornhill, C. (2008). The transformed local government system: Some lessons. *Journal of Public Administration, 43*(si-2), 492–511.

Tikkoo, A., Yadav, S. S., & Kaushik, N. (2013). Effect of irrigation, nitrogen and potassium on seed yield and oil content of Jatropha curcas in coarse textured soils of northwest India. *Soil and Tillage Research, 134*, 142–146.

Tönnies, F. (1955). *Community and association*. Routledge & Kegan Paul.

Tshitangoni, M., & Francis, J. (2014). Effectiveness of traditional leaders in engaging communities on development matters in Vhembe District of South Africa. *Journal of Human Ecology, 19*(1–2), 49–61.

Waisbord, S. (2001). *Family tree of theories, methodologies, and strategies in development communication: Convergence and differences*. http://www.comminit.com/stsilviocomm/sld-2891.html

Weyman, F. (1996). The value of local knowledge and the importance of shifting beliefs in the process of social change. *Community Development Journal, 31*(1), 44–53.

Wrona, V. (2017). *Unrealistic goals*. https://www.projectmanagement.comcontentPages/article.cfm?ID=366692&thisPageURL=/articles/366692/PM-Obstacles--Unrealistic-Goals#_=_

CHAPTER 11

COMMUNITY DEVELOPMENT ASSOCIATIONS AND FUNDRAISING FOR SELF-HELP PROJECTS IN AFRICAN SUBURBIA FOR RURAL DEVELOPMENT

Babatunde Ayoola Fajimi

ABSTRACT

The African suburbia is an evolving smart frontier of new development areas connecting cities with rural communities in modern Nigeria. Precolonial societies developed their communities through collaborative self-help initiatives. The convergence of inclusive and sustainable communities with an emphasis on home-grown capacities is pivotal to Sustainable Development Goals 2030 in Nigeria. However, the government has not been able to meet the growing needs of urban communities. As a result, rural communities continue to suffer neglect. The emerging suburbia is driven by Community Development Associations (CDAs) through self-help projects to provide social amenities which are capital intensive. Rural development involves mobilization of the inherent capacity of the people to engender changes through deployment of resources in the community. The chapter explores CDAs' local fundraising initiatives in community development self-help projects for rapid rural development in Nigeria. Different theoretical approaches to citizens' participation in rural development were expounded to rationalize CDAs' involvement. The law governing CDAs recognized the concept of self-help in fundraising for rural development in communities. The traditional model for fundraising involves members' contributions, levies, and donations. The chapter discusses innovative fundraising initiatives within and outside rural communities that are consistent with the objectives of the CDAs. There are challenges that hamper CDAs' fundraising efforts for self-help projects in rural communities. The problem of capacity development exacerbates these challenges. It is suggested that CDAs should evolve creative nonformal education to upscale their members' capacity and collaborate with external stakeholders to unlock different external sources for funding community projects.

Keywords: African suburbia, community development associations, fundraising, rural development, self-help concept, adult education.

Introduction

Rural development is the focal point of community development. Precolonial societies in present-day Nigeria prioritized communal welfare and engaged in collaborative efforts through self-help initiatives to develop their locale and provided social amenities for their collective existence (Ugwukah, 2021). The convergence of inclusive and sustainable communities is entrenched in the Sustainable Development Goals (SDGs) 2030 agenda, with an emphasis on home-grown capacities. Nigeria needs inclusive and sustainable rural development to meet its SDGs (Nnaemeka-Okeke et al., 2020; Terzungwe, 2022; Udeajah, 2019) because the country fell behind in the Millennium Development Goal 2000–2015 (Fajimi, 2020).

The African suburbia is an evolving smart frontier of new development in areas connecting cities with rural communities in modern Nigeria (Bloch et al., 2015; Razak & Galadima, 2014; Tofowomo, 2008). This development is driven by the private actors' felt needs through homeowners who form associations to cater to their welfare and the development of their communities. The government is unable to meet the growing needs of urban communities. Consequently, less attention is given to the rural communities, particularly the new suburbia that is sandwiched between cities and rural areas, which are the two traditional communities in Nigeria.

Community Development Associations (CDAs) pool resources together with mainstream suburbia development with the provision of social amenities through self-help projects. Basic social amenities are capital intensive and CDAs will need to find creative ways to raise funds for their projects. This chapter will discuss the concept of CDAs in rural community development, CDAs, self-help projects, theoretical approaches to CDAs participation in rural development, and explore CDAs' local fundraising initiatives for rural development self-help projects for rapid rural development in Nigeria.

Concept of CDAs in Rural Development

Busari-Akinbode and Moses (2020) described CDAs as the coming together of voluntary members within a geographical area for their mutual interest to improve their environment and living conditions. Ogu and Fadeyi (2014) stated that CDAs execute rural development in their locality and contribute to development in society. Some scholars suggest that CDAs are like development unions or development associations. However, they are self-help but not always interest groups, unions, or associations unless they are heterogenous and residing together within a specific geographical territory (Olamidoye, 2021).

CDAs are a type of community organization with a focus on the process of community building (Olaleye, 2011). Residents in the community organize themselves into development associations. The membership is landowners who have bought lands, built houses, and are residents in the community. Some CDAs incorporate tenants into their groups. Attendance of members comprises males and females where their spouses are unavailable or nonexistent. CDAs do not discriminate based on gender, hence their participation is mixed. Where membership is predominantly male, the womenfolk have often organized themselves into gender-based groups to pursue independent agendas that reflect their interests toward community development.

Although the CDAs are essential for self-help projects that yield community development in their neighborhood, their roles are prescribed by legislations of the government in Nigeria to regulate their activities and ensure that they operate within a legal framework. The CDAs are not local government authorities and cannot act as one even when the local councils fall short of their statutory obligations. The 1999 Constitution of the Federal Republic of Nigeria (as amended) stipulates the rights and obligations of every citizen to freedom of association, movement, and speech within the society (Federal Government of Nigeria, 2023). There are also federal and state laws that guide the formation of CDAs in communities, their objectives, functions, and operationalities. The operations of CDAs are managed by the Ministry of Agriculture, Rural and Social Development and the government expects the formation of CDAs in communities across the country (Oyalowo, 2021). Busari-Akinbode and Moses (2020) surmise that they are regarded as the informal fourth tier of the government.

The law governing the existence of CDAs requires that community organizations should have an inclusive structure (Ogu & Fadeyi, 2014). The

CDAs are subsumed under the local government authority through the Community Development Committees (CDCs) to which all the executives of each CDA belong (Oyalowo, 2021). The applicable law governing the CDA states that it will have an executive council which will comprise a chairperson, two vice-chairpersons, a secretary, an assistant secretary, a treasurer, a financial secretary, an auditor, a social secretary, a welfare officer, a public relations officer, and three ex-office members.

The composition of a typical CDA executive leadership has an average of 14 members. Ogu and Fadeyi (2014) showed a case study of 11 members' CDA organizational structure. It is important that all offices on the organizational structure should be occupied to reflect compliance with requisite law establishing CDAs in Nigeria. Although the leadership is hierarchical in nature, the election process is democratic. Eligible members are allowed to contest for any position based on extant rules and regulations. The lack of corporate governance makes leadership selection and management less viable because of weak ties and social disintegration (Fajimi & Olajide, 2021).

CDAs and Self-Help Projects

Akinsorotan and Olujide (2006) state that CDAs play important roles in rural development in Nigeria because of the failure of the government to provide basic social infrastructure for people living in rural communities. The government does not have unlimited resources to provide for the growing needs of its population and concentration on urban renewal and development programs has always meant that less attention is paid to the rural area. The pace of expansion in new rural is faster than the capacity of the government to cope.

CDAs

Therefore, CDAs take up the challenge of organizing themselves into community groups and organizations for social actions to cater to their sociocultural and economic felt-needs to build a community where they live harmoniously together. They develop common facilities such as recreation centers, health centers, provision of potable water, schools, shopping centers, community halls, and the traditional ruler's palace. Sometimes, they make provision for the construction of public facilities such as hospitals and police stations. Where they do not have resources to fund these projects, they partner with private individuals who build these facilities for public use.

Oni (2013) argued that it is practically impossible for the government to single-handedly execute development projects in all communities in the country. Consequently, communities have always taken up the challenge to initiate and implement development projects that serve their felt needs. These projects involve the construction of public utility facilities which are usually capital intensive, such as schools, roads, bridges, boreholes, health centers, and worship centers to mention but a few. This puts the CDAs at the center of self-help projects in the community. Through prosocial action, they organize themselves as a group to identify their felt needs, conceptualize appropriate projects to meet these needs, and pool resources together to solve their problems.

Self-Help

This is self-help, which involves the full participation of all members of the community and minimal participation of external parties unless where such support is included in the process of problem solving as a capacity development initiative from the onset. The participation of community members in rural development entails the involvement of a people's decision-making process, implementation of programs, and efforts at program evaluation. It is expected that all members will be actively involved in the decision-making process to identify their felt needs and rank the projects in order of priority based on resources available at their disposal. They will be involved in mobilizing resources, finding financial and material capital to implement projects in line with their identified needs. Members of CDAs will also be actively involved in the execution of the projects as well as monitoring and evaluation of projects to be sure that their original felt needs have been met.

Akinsorotan and Olujide (2006) investigated projects executed and level of members participation in 50 CDAs from five communities in Lagos State, Nigeria and found that the CDAs carried out projects within their communities through self-efforts and without any external financial assistance from other sources. The study showed that age, gender, and level of education did not negatively impact the level of members' participation in their development efforts. The study of Ogu and Fadeyi (2014) corroborated the findings of Akinsorotan and Olujide (2006) that CDAs were involved in development projects in their communities through self-help initiatives. Ogu and Fadeyi investigated the Omologede CDA in Ogolonto community in Ikorodu, Lagos State and found that they were able to curb the challenges of flooding through active mobilization and cooperation of their members despite limited assistance from the government in flood management in the area.

Theoretical Approaches of CDAs Participation in Rural Development

The theory of community development stipulates that social action and rural community transformation are not unidirectional. The process of community development and the principle of community participation embrace the theorem of multidimensional stakeholders who collaborate with members of the community as prime movers of self-help initiatives to improve their communities. There are layers of community stakeholders who act as participants in rural development alongside CDAs. These groups are outside the community, but are also interested in development within the community. They are government agencies, development professionals, international development agencies, and philanthropic bodies (Olaleye, 2013). Four theoretical approaches that guide the involvement of multidimensional stakeholders in the fundraising efforts of CDAs for social action and improvement in rural areas are: (1) social approach, (2) service approach, (3) neighborhood maintenance service, and (4) self-help development approach.

Social Approach

The social approach conceives the community as a social organism where felt needs should be identified, coordinated, and met if the neighborhood would thrive and remain prosperous. The CDAs use this approach to build a sense of community belongingness. They can either improve on existing social services in the community or lobby to attract resources for the implementation of services in their areas. It begins with the identification of felt needs where CDAs collectively identify a problem as social disorganization and mobilize members and resources to solve the problem or work through internal and external networks to attract resources. The CDAs in rural communities use this approach to appeal to the social orientation of members to participate in community improvement because they have no other community to live in and unless they do it, it will not be possible for outsiders to join in to help them.

Service Approach

The service approach to community development is known as "self-help" in Nigeria (Akpomuvie, 2010). The CDAs orientate their members to active participation in the provision of social amenities in their community. They make this process a prerogative of their members to create living conditions that serve their purposes. This is because the service approach involves the initiative and participation of all members of the community through the CDA. The approach is concerned with the provision of social amenities in the community. These amenities are typically the installation of electric poles for electricity in the new rural areas. Others include the post-office (postal agency), health center, borehole for potable water, and police post for provision of postal services, medicare services, water, sanitation, and hygiene (WASH) services, and security services. The service approach is best suited for the initiation and implementation of self-help projects in the new rural areas.

Neighborhood Maintenance Approach

Olaleye (2013) stated that the neighborhood maintenance approach perceives the community as a geographical territory with intrinsic commercial value. The emphasis of CDAs is to maintain the value of properties and improve facilities in the neighborhood to make it more attractive to the public in general and government in particular. The government's perception of the commercial value of the neighborhood can redirect increased facilities like road expansion/dualization and private-sector-led amenities to the community. This approach is predominant in Lagos State, Nigeria and Abuja, the Federal Capital Territory, where slums closest to highbrow estates were converted to new rural and upper middle-class communities. The landowners transform the neighborhood into commercially viable estates that compete for government's infrastructural investments.

Self-Help Development Approach

This approach supposes that community development is concerned with total community life and needs, hence members of the community pull their resources together to participate in decision-making about improving their environment, planning their resources, and implementing their decision to achieve infrastructural, sociocultural, and economic projects they have identified and prioritized. The self-help development approach aims to use social action to initiate social change in the community. It is about what they must do, and how they intend to achieve it. The CDAs use this approach to mobilize internal and external resources for members of the community to improve facilities and living conditions through the social capital of their members and other forms of capital from other stakeholders.

CDAs Local Fundraising Initiatives for Rural Development Self-Help Projects

Community development requires different forms of capital to implement self-help projects. Lack of financial capital can hamper the conceptualization, mobilization, and implementation of self-help projects in community organizations. Financing in community development is critical for the implementation of plans and programs. Its importance is underscored by Cavaye (2004) who posited that rural community development involves the mobilization of the inherent capacity of the people to become fundamentally better at engendering changes in their environment through the deployment of available resources in the community.

Cavaye (2004) described these resources for community development mobilization as capital and identified five of them, namely physical, human, social, environmental, and financial capital. Effective community development involves the integrative building of the five capitals of a community through community participation. They build social capital when they rethink problems and expand contacts and networks. They build human capital when they learn new skills. They build physical and financial capital when they develop new economic alternatives. They build environmental capital when they transform their environment.

Sources of Funding for Self-Help Projects for Rural Development

There are different legitimate means available to CDAs to source funds for their self-help projects in the community. The law expects members to pay dues, subscriptions, and levies as well as make voluntary contributions for special projects in the community. The CDAs can receive gifts and contributions from philanthropists, corporate organizations, or international agencies as well as access grants from the three tiers of government. The CDAs can also generate revenue from community economic projects or assets. Funding in rural communities for self-help projects should not violate the Community Development Associations Law, that CDAs should not accept a gift from any source if the conditions are not consistent with the objectives of the CDA or the Law (Akande, 2016; Federal Reserve Bank of St. Louis, 2022; Smith, 2005).

Traditionally, CDAs can source funding for self-help projects through regular contributions of a pre-agreed sum of money at monthly meetings, payment of levies for infrastructure maintenance, payment of special projects' levies, and donations received within and outside the community. Smith (2005) and Akande (2016) opined that grants from the three levels of government at local, state, and federal, and donations from local and international donor agencies increase the sources of funding available to CDAs for self-help projects. Organizations are involved in corporate social responsibilities (CSRs), and they support CDAs if the community projects reflect the ethos of their organizations. Ola et al. (2018) studied self-reliance and community initiative among CDAs in Ido Local Government Area, Oyo State and found that traditional means of fundraising predominantly contributed to the execution of self-help projects such as water projects and road rehabilitation in the communities. The study of Busari-Akinbode and Moses (2020) found that poor funding and low community participation hampered the effectiveness of CDAs in implementing self-help projects and recommended that CDAs should engage their members and become innovative in fundraising within and outside the community for their projects.

Akande (2016) said that communities have devised innovative fundraising which include conferment of chieftaincy titles on deserving members of the society, sale of community resources or royalties on resources in the community, loans from financial institutions, payment of fees by property developers, and returns on community investments. The CDAs have also been creative in soliciting for funds during social events or traditional festivals to promote their cultural heritage as a community. The traditional means of fundraising are commonplace but have become unproductive. These funds obtained through the traditional means are seldom adequate to enable CDAs to embark on self-help projects in the community. The contemporary methods are innovative if the CDAs can demonstrate ingenuity and attract the right kind of support within and outside the community for verifiable and mutually benefiting projects in the community.

It should, however, be stated that CDAs are primarily voluntary community groups that are not-for-profit organizations. Illegitimate means of raising funds within the community will run afoul of the Laws, and CDA executives should therefore resist the temptations to obstruct free movement and voluntary participation of their members. The Federal High Court, Ikoyi, Lagos restrained the Registered Trustees of Gbagada Phase II Residents' Association from compelling Megawatts Nigeria Limited, an engineering firm resident in the community to join the CDA or pay dues/levies in its judgement in September 2020 because membership and payment of dues or levies in community-based associations is voluntary (Aelex, 2020; Edokwe, 2020; Ramon, 2020). The CDAs in Ido Local Government Area, Oyo State, had sourced funds through compulsory levies paid by their members to execute their self-help projects in 2018 because there was no financial assistance from the government (Ola et al., 2018). The authors, however, pointed out that the Ido LGA faced challenges because of non-payment of compulsory levies by some of their members.

Challenges of Funding Self-Help Projects for Rural Development

Fundraising for self-help projects for rural development has always faced challenges that hamper the speedy and successful completion of projects in the community. Despite the creative means available to raise funds for rural community development, CDAs have difficulties obtaining requisite funds as and when due to carry out their self-help projects. The researcher interviewed twenty CDAs in Sagamu Local Government, Ogun State, Nigeria. The feedback obtained present challenges that CDAs face when raising funds for self-help projects:

Timeliness of Funds Availability for Self-Help Projects

The funds projected for a felt need and specific idea in the community do not always come in as required. Often, there is a time lag, and members are discouraged because of the inability of their CDA executives to get the needed funds at the right time. The time variation in sourcing funds is a major cause of frustration for community development projects in most rural areas. As a result, most self-help projects become moribund and outlive successive executives as uncompleted projects in the community.

Lack of Full Community Participation

Most CDAs struggle to record full community participation. Without bringing all stakeholders on board, it may be difficult to meet financial projections for projects in the community. This partial participation is caused by apathy or division among members of the community. Unless there is effective communication and stakeholders buy-in of all members of the community, CDAs' executives always find it difficult to source funds because of a lack of full community participation.

Bureaucracy in External Support

The government is constrained by bureaucracy, and this affects its ability to offer financial assistance to most communities for rural development. The process of approaching government officials and presenting proposals for funding projects is tedious and time-consuming. The CDAs' executives spend money on logistics to seek financial assistance. At the end of the day, they do not get to meet the representatives of the government who will take a decision, or the process will drag on because of the government's bureaucracy.

Lack of Requisite Skills in Proposal Writing

When CDAs' executives lack competencies to write proposals for fundraising and grants, and there is no member of the community to volunteer, this would hamper the ability of the community to raise funds from the government or other non-governmental organizations who are available and willing to support. Rural communities without members with proposal writing skills may have to engage consultants and this will increase their pre-operational expenses for the projects they are not sure will get funding.

Lack of Governance Among CDAs' Executives

The institutionalization of governance increases the viability of CDA's access to funding and if there is no corporate governance in the way executives run their administration, they will not be able to raise funds for their self-help projects. Governance in the administration of CDAs' executives can build trust among members of the community and convince the government or non-governmental organizations that their funds will be well managed when they give financial assistance to the community. Often, communities are unable to get funds for their projects because their executives lack governance in the way they run their administration.

Unethical Means of Fundraising

Some communities resort to unorthodox means of compelling members of the community to contribute money or pay their levies. In remote rural areas, people succumb to such practices where they are subjected to illicit extortions by landgrabbers locally called *omo onile* (children of the traditional landowners) who, forcefully extort money from potential new entrants into the community, thrive in most Southwestern states of Nigeria. Lagos and Ogun States have instituted laws against such land-grabbing practices (unlawful, forceful possession of land from rightful owners) and severe penalties for defaulters. Unorthodox and illegal means of fundraising create apathy and result in non-participation in community building among community members. Unethical means of fundraising not only affect the ability of the community to generate funds for projects, but also hinder the development of the community.

Inept Leadership

Incompetence on the part of the CDA executives can result in the ineffectiveness of the community to raise funds for projects. The CDAs that elect competent leaders who are hardworking stand a better chance of generating funds for their projects. The financial landscape is competitive, and resources are lean. It requires the ingenuity of the CDA executives to think outside the box to know when and who to approach for funding when they have projects to execute.

Corruption

Like most of the white elephant projects in the communities, corrupt practices can hinder the ability of the CDA executives to raise funds. If embezzlement, misappropriation of funds, or loss of funds as a result of negligence or outright collusion among the executives or those entrusted with the community's funds is pervasive, the community will be distracted by fighting corruption rather than developing their environment. Unless the community elects credible leaders, who will manage their affairs with integrity and fiscal prudence, dishonest conduct of those in positions of power will halt any meaningful rural development in the community.

Mistrust and Lack of Cooperation

There are certain micro competencies among members of the community and their leadership that create an atmosphere of mistrust and lack of cooperation that affect the ability of the community to raise funds for its projects. Human relationships require a delicate balance of trust and confidence where divergent interests are involved. Given the heterogenous nature of a typical community, CDA needs to build an environment where there is trust and cooperation through governance, competence, and equity. Lack of these micro competencies negatively affects the community's ability to raise funds.

Conclusion

This chapter has been able to establish that rural community development is critical to national development, and the government has not been able to meet up with the pace of emerging smart new rural African suburbia alongside developmental needs of existing traditional rural and urban communities. The CDAs have demonstrated readiness to collaborate, participate, and pool resources together through legitimate means of raising financial capital to improve their living conditions and improve their geographical area. These CDAs are also amenable to accessing requisite support from external sources through the government and private sector actors to raise funds for their projects.

What stands between the CDAs and their aspirations to community participation and rapid rural transformation of their community, as it has been identified by this chapter, is capacity development. The options are open and varied for fundraising for CDAs, but the summation of the challenges of funding self-help projects for rural development is the problem of capacity development. The CDAs should evolve creative means to unlock informal and nonformal education to build the capacity of their members and collaborate with relevant agencies of government and private sector organizations to upscale their readiness to explore the different sources of funding for community projects. When members of the community are informed through innovative learning, they will realize that they have a common responsibility toward the development of their community. This realization will make them act within the ambit of the law of the land to participate in the election of leaders into their executives. Consequently, they can build strong linkages and networks, and fully mobilize stakeholders to raise funds for self-help projects in their community. A consistent collective social action and community participation will achieve two things: (1) The community will build its dream environment without waiting for external supports which are often delayed because of the limited resources of bureaucracy of government and conflicting priorities of donor organizations; and (2) the efforts of the community in infrastructure development and improvement of its environment will come to the attention of the government and private sector organizations, and their achievements may become a prototype for other communities to adopt as a model for rural transformation in the country.

REFERENCES

Aelex. (2020). *Megawatts Nigeria Limited V: Registered Trustees of Gbagada Phase II Residents' Association and its potential impact upon the payment of residential association dues and levies by members*. https://www.aelex.com/wp-content/uploads/2020/10/Megawatts-Nigeria-Limited-v.-Registered-Trustees-of-Gbagada-Phase-II-Residents-Association_-Its-Potential-Impact-Upon-the-Payment-of-Residential-Ass.pdf

Akande, J. O. (2016). *Understanding community development: A handbook for educators and practitioners*. Obafemi Awolowo University Press.

Akinsorotan, A. O., & Olujide, M. G. (2006). Community development associations' contributions in self-help projects in Lagos State of Nigeria. *Central European Agriculture Journal, 7*(4), 609–618.

Akpomuvie, O. B. (2010). Self-help as a strategy for rural development in Nigeria: A bottom-up approach. *Journal of Alternative Perspectives in the Social Sciences, 2*(1), 88–111.

Bloch, R., Fox, S., Monroy, J., & Ojo, A. (2015). *Urbanisation and urban expansion in Nigeria. Urbanisation Research Nigeria* (Research Report). ICF International. Creative Commons Attribution-Non-Commercial-ShareAlike CC BY-NC-SA.

Busari-Akinbode, S. A., & Moses, T. O. (2020). Effectiveness of community development associations (CDAs) in implementing development projects in Surulere, Lagos State. *African Journal of Social Sciences and Humanities Research, 3*(6), 157–166.

Cavaye, J. (2004). *Understanding community development.* http://increate.med-ina.org/static/assets/uploads/share/Step6-tools/Understanding-Community-Development-2004.pdf

Edokwe, B. (2020). *Estate residents can't be compelled to pay dues—Court rules.* https://barristerng.com/estate-residents-cant-be-compelled-to-pay-dues-court-rules/

Fajimi, B. A. (2020). Imperatives of Environmental Education in Effective Implementation of Water, Sanitation and Hygiene (WASH) among School Children in Rural Communities. *African Journal of Adult Education and Development Studies, 2,* 156–165.

Fajimi, B. A., & Olajide, O. E. (2021). Social network and community development in Nigeria: A case study of Onafowokan Estate Community, Ita Oluwo, Ogijo, Ogun State, Nigeria. *Nigerian Journal of Social Work Education, 20*(1), 1–17. https://doi.org/10.13140/RE.2.2.14730.34248

Federal Government of Nigeria. (2023). *1999 Constitution of the Federal Republic of Nigeria (as Amended).* https://www.constituteproject.org/constitution/Nigeria_2011.pdf

Federal Reserve Bank of St. Louis. (2022). *Sourcing financial resources for community development initiatives.* https://www.stlouisfed.org/community-development/how-to-launch-community-development-project/process-sourcing-financial-resources-for-comm-unity-development-initiatives.

Nnaemeka-Okeke, R. C., Okeke, F. O., & Sam-Amobi, C. (2020). The 2030 agenda for sustainable development in Nigeria: The role of the architect. *Science, Technology and Public Policy, 4*(1), 15–21.

Ogu, M. I., & Fadeyi, O. (2014). Omologede Community Development Association and Flood Management in Ogolonto Community, Nigeria. *Journal of Humanities and Social Science, 19*(9), 109–121.

Ola, A. B., Adewale, Y. Y., Bako, A. I., & Issa, B. S. (2018). Self-reliance & community initiative: Focus on Community Development Associations in Ido Local Government Area, Oyo State. *Journal of Environmental Spectrum, 2*(1), 155–169.

Olaleye, Y. L. (2011). *Introduction to community development (SOW204).* University of Ibadan Distance Learning Centre.

Olaleye, Y. L. (2013). *Community organisation (SOW311).* University of Ibadan Distance Learning Centre.

Olamidoye, L. (2021). *Securing an effective CDA System (1).* https://independent.ng/securing-an-effective-cda-system-i/

Oni, A. (2013). *Practical approaches to community development.* Stirling-Horden.

Oyalowo, B. (2021). *Community Development Associations in low-income and informal communities in Nigeria.* Heinrich Boll Stiftung. https://ng.boell.org/sites

Ramon, O. (2020). *Court stops CDA from forcing firm to pay dues.* https://punchng.com/court-stops-cda-from-forcing-firm-to-pay-dues/

Razak, S. Y., & Galadima, M. U. (2014). *Urbanist neighbourhoods in rapidly urbanizing global south cities: A mirage? An exemplar case illustration of new urbanism in residential neighbourhoods in Abuja, Nigeria*. Conference Paper on Management of Cities in Developing Economy: Issues, Challenges and Opportunities: NITP 45th Annual Conference Proceedings.

Smith, B. C. (2005). The sources and uses of funds for community development financial institutions: The role of the nonprofit intermediary. *Nonprofit and Voluntary Sector Quarterly, 37*(1), 19–38. https://doi.org/10.2139/SSRN.1564864

Terzungwe, S. (2022). *Nigeria not close to achieving SDGs in 2030–UN*. https://dailytrust.com/nigeria-not-close-to-achieving-sdgs-in-2030-un/

Tofowomo, A. O. (2008). *The planning implications of urban sprawl in Akure*. 44th ISOCARP Congress.

Udeajah, G. (2019). *Report doubts Nigeria's ability to meet SDG 2030 targets*. https://guardian.ng/appointments/report-doubts-nigerias-ability-to-meet-sdg-2030-targets/

Ugwukah, A. C. (2021). A historical appraisal of development in the Nigerian society from pre-colonial to post-colonial periods. *Journal of Sustainable Development, 14*(4), 26–41.

SECTION IV

SUSTAINABLE AND ETHICAL COMMUNITY DEVELOPMENT IN AFRICA

CHAPTER 12

EXPLORING THE PROBLEM OF "JUSTICE" IN A CONTEXT OF COMMUNITY DEVELOPMENT IN AFRICA

A Dialogue Between Philosophy and Politics

Irene Ayallo

ABSTRACT

This chapter explores a pragmatic theory of justice in an African community development context using examples from a Kenyan context. It is provoked by an evidence-based argument that most well-intended community development projects remain unsustainable because they are founded on theories of justice based on Anglo European and North American (excluding Indigenous and First Nations) epistemologies transplanted into the African context without critical analysis. This chapter identifies the gaps in some of these "classical" theories and explains why they remain irrelevant in these contexts. The discussion sheds light on the realities of African community development that challenge transplanted theories with examples from Kenya. Using data collected from a qualitative participatory action research project, practice observations, and critical literature review, some of the factors highlighted include the challenge of balancing local and international needs, deeply rooted politicized ethnicity and patrimonial politics that favors a top-down elitist approach to community development, and the individualized view and implementation of "justice" issues. The chapter concludes that considering these issues, a pragmatic theory of justice in an African community development context is characterized by the complex notions of human dignity and not merit and entitlement, centering the margins, and the notion of difference and not sameness. The significance of this chapter lies in its contribution to normalizing discussions about justice as integral parts of the African community work discourses in the academy and practice.

Keywords: community development, justice, politics, top-down approach, participation

Introduction

This chapter explores a theory of justice most relevant to an African community development context based on examples from a Kenyan context. The journey towards developing such a theory of justice began in 2012, with doctoral research completed by the author (Ayallo, 2012). Community development is defined in this chapter as the process of assisting people in improving their own communities by undertaking autonomous collective action (Twelvetrees, 2008). It is often a process provoked by calls for "justice." Advocates for addressing societal problems, such as meeting the needs of the people, equality and equity, access and participation, capability building, and social change, often invoke "justice" or its related concepts, human rights, fairness, and democracy. Yet justice, its theory, remains the proverbial elephant examined by blindfolded explorers (Lebacqz, 1986; Novak, 2000; Sewpaul et al., 2021). Even when people have a strong sense of justice (and injustice), this sense is based on many perceptions (Sen, 2011). Accordingly, the author argues that a clear concept of justice, and one that is specific to the contexts within which the struggles in and for justice occur, is required for effective community development practice.

The problem in African community development is a lack of a clear articulation of a theory of justice most relevant to this context and, therefore, a lack of a solid foundation for practice. According to the author, one of the main reasons for this is that community development practice in Africa is often primarily founded on theories of justice based on Anglo European and North American (excluding Indigenous and First Nations) epistemologies transplanted into African contexts without critical analysis (Ayallo, 2012). This chapter contributes to this crucial conversation by engaging with some supposed "classical" concepts of justice, exploring their weaknesses and reasons for failing in an African community development context. The aim is to normalize these discussions about justice as integral parts of the African community work discourses in the academy and practice. Ultimately, an idea of justice relevant to African community development is proposed. Practice examples are primarily drawn from a Kenyan context. In 2012, the author was fortunate to conduct doctoral research when the call for "justice" was demonstrated in the significant review of the Kenyan National Constitution (Ghai, 2009). A relevant theory of justice will also be discussed here, considering the most recent somewhat controversial Kenyan Presidential Elections in 2022 (Olewe, 2022).

An African Context of Community Development

The concept and practice of community development in Africa have undergone significant changes, a pattern also observed in other places (Hardcastle et al., 2004). One of the most notable of these in a Kenyan context is the struggle to balance local and international needs, critical aspects of it documented in the arguably controversial book by Dambisa Moyo (Moyo, 2009). Some of the aspects of these challenges directly impact a relevant theory of justice. The first is the colonial past, which presented some opportunities and challenges. For instance, an evidence-based recounting of Kenya's colonial past reveals a history of social exclusion demonstrated in the preference for the perspectives of the "experts or elites" over "ordinary" Kenyans, deeply rooted in politicized ethnicity and patrimonial politics (Gĩthĩnji & Holmquist, 2009; Ogude, 2002). This past has favored a top-down and elitist approach regarding community development where the voices of those most affected by issues are often ignored or untold. The cited doctoral research, for example, involved participants who were all positively living with HIV and, therefore, most affected by HIV-AIDS policies. Yet, their participation in making these policies was lacking (Ayallo, 2012).

Issues of the international-AID Approach to Community Work

In a country without a welfare state system, colonial and postcolonialism have directly and indirectly reinforced an aid model of community development. This model is often characterized by overreliance on international funding and gifts and, in some cases, technical assistance. While this may not be inherently problematic and can be an additional option, these usually come with stipulations and target areas such that it is easy to ignore the real needs of the people, particularly in cases where community programs and projects become tailored to meet the funder's demands (Olsgard, 1997). The author agrees with Moyo (2009) in these cases that this leads to a band-aid and short-term solution to social and community issues. Accordingly, several international policies and programs have been marked by failure or mixed outcomes, including the UN Millennium Development Goals 2000 (African Union, 2010). According to the author, this is not because they are flawed. Instead, their failure is because of their unrelatable theoretical frameworks that do not consider the complex interplay between local context, content, actors, and processes (Wouters et al., 2010). Most importantly, the voices of the people most affected by these programs and policies are often left out in their design. At best, their participation is limited to non-statutory bodies or community-based organizations that the government does not necessarily fund (Ayallo, 2012; Young, 2000). In the author's doctoral thesis, it was argued, with evidence, that the groups that these politics of privilege have most excluded are youth, those between the ages of 15 and 35 (defined according to the African Youth Charter) and women (Abbink, 2021; Ayallo, 2012).

Concept of Justice

The problem is the theoretical concepts of justice upon which these community programs and policies are founded. According to the author, a relevant theory of justice should enable three critical approaches to community development (Hardcastle et al., 2004). These include a process committed to practicing ways of empowering people to take individual and collective control over their lives. An approach that views the community as more than a place or in simple geographical terms. Community includes the ties and bonds that bring people together, social bonds, social capital, and social bridges (Ager & Strang, 2008). Finally, an approach to community development that considers the changing dynamics within a community allows the space to establish and re-establish structures within which new ways of relating and organizing social life become possible (Ife & Tesoriero, 2006). Considering the colonial past and postcolonial reality, community development in these contexts should be marked by at least five unique characteristics: (1) a critical form of practice; (2) transformative; (3) collective action; (4) a preventative approach; and (5) an educational process (Forde & Lynch, 2015).

The Problem of Justice in an African Context

Theories of justice. The current body of literature discussing the complexities of justice as a theory and concept is vivifying, especially its social embeddedness. Logically, most of these originate from population groups traditionally marginalized and socially excluded from these discussions, including women, indigenous communities and First Nations, the Global South and the LGBTQIA+ people (Balibar et al., 2012). The main question being investigated by these groups is: "whose justice," or more accurately, "whose theoretical framework of justice?" Notably, the question is still under-explored in the African context. However, there are some comprehensive works worth noting that align with the author's argument, including Philip Ogo Ujomu exploring the problem of Africa's political justice (Ujomu, 2007, 2008, 2018, 2019; Ujomu & Bature, 2018; Ujomu & Olatunji, 2014a), theories of democracy and their deficiencies in the African context (Ujomu & Olatunji, 2014a), and the problem of citizenship and social order (Ujomu, 2004; Otieno, 2008; and Eze, 2021) on the limitations of the human rights approach in an African context. The primary argument in these works is that European and North American (excluding Indigenous and First Nations) theories of justice are limited when transplanted into African contexts. Two of these views are particularly problematic. The first is that justice is an ideal state of affairs or associated with the perfect arrangement of institutions, which stems from an understanding of justice as fairness and proportionality. The second is the concept of entitlement based on "universal unalienable rights" (Rawls, 1971). Debatably, the human rights approach commonly invoked in African community development contexts derives from both these justice perspectives.

"Justice" as Fairness and Proportionality

As mentioned earlier, the author's doctoral research completed in 2012 provoked the discussions in this chapter (Ayallo, 2012). During this time, while conducting field research in Kenya, a significant event was also happening, the review of the Kenyan National Constitution, which is regarded as the framework for social, economic, and cultural "justice" in the country (Government of Kenya, 2013). The politics and process failures that marked the review of this Constitution are now well documented (Cottrell & Ghai, 2007; Ghai, 2008, 2009). A critical note is that for many Kenyans, reviewing the national constitution equated to solving most of the country's major social problems, including loosening ethnic tensions, power sharing, increasing local participation, and better access and distribution of resources. Again, these expectations were mainly based on the idea of equal rights. The final Constitution consists of an entire chapter (Chapter 4) on the Bill of Rights, yet significant problems remain (Branch & Cheeseman, 2009; Government of Kenya, 2013). The contested National Presidential Elections in 2017 and 2022 are some evidences of disillusionment (Olewe, 2022). An ideal state of affairs is a good starting point for the question of justice. However, events in African community development contexts, examples from Kenya, show that realizing justice requires more than thinking about ideals, philosophical speculation, and recourse to abstract philosophy, which tend to be the focus of most European and North American theories of justice (Choules, 2007; Solomon & Murphy, 2000).

At the core of the view of "an ideal state of affairs" is a theory of justice that justice is *fairness*. John Rawls, arguably the most influential proponent of this notion, demonstrates it in the idea of the "original position" or the "veil of ignorance." This is a condition in which people are assumed to revert to the natural or circumstantial location by stripping themselves of attributes such as social and cultural status in society, thereby creating situations where everyone is similarly situated (sameness), and no particular person is favored because of their specific attributes (difference) (Rawls, 1971). As Eze (2021) explains, it is a "condition in which people are free, equal, and are able to make without bias choices about the principles that would guide their lives" (p. 4). The author argues that this is the condition that "human rights" is often assumed to create. What is problematic in an African context is that there are sociocultural elements, which, in addition to mannerisms and personality traits, the "veil of ignorance" cannot suspend (Ayallo, 2012; MacIntyre, 2013). Politicized ethnicity, social and economic status (linked to poverty), gender, and age are some examples of realities that challenge such a positioning. Each issue is multifaceted and complex, and the author is not attempting to provide a comprehensive picture. The following discussions only highlight the elements which challenge this supposed classical theory of justice.

Examples of Justice Issues in Africa

In a Kenyan context, for instance, political trends such as the 1992 "ethnic clashes," Constitutional review debates in 2005 and 2010, and the General Presidential Elections in 2002, 2007/8, 2017, and 2022 have highlighted the role of ethnic identity in any effective decision-making processes in the country (Holmquist & Githinji, 2009; Holmquist & Oendo, 2001; Olewe, 2022). While ethnic identity and solidarity are not inherently negative phenomena and have positively contributed to "African" identity, the cause of most conflicts is attributed to the deliberate politicization and mobilization of ethnic consciousness to achieve specific political, social, and economic objectives (Ajulu, 2001; Eriksen, 2002; Govers & Vermeulen, 1997). Politicized ethnicity is the "deep politics of tribe and clan, pitting insiders against outsiders, clansmen [sic] against foreigners, and the original landowners against sojourners" (Ogude, 2002, p. 225). It is widely observed that this form of ethnic competition is strongest during periods of acute contestation over resources or power. It becomes a dominant instrument of dispensing resources and patronage by those in power to reward support and loyalty. Without other accessible platforms upon which to base political appeal, ethnicity seems to be the most natural basis of political organization (Kimenyi, 2001). In the context of community development, ethnicity directly impacts access to national resources, allocation of society's benefits and burdens, public participation in decision-making, and representation in decision-making bodies (Ayallo, 2012). Several attempts have been made to address this problem legislatively, with most of these initiatives focusing on ideal institutional arrangements. Examples include the National Cohesion and Integration Act 2008 and the Kenya National Commission on Human Rights Act 2011. As Kimenyi (2001) rightly observes, these initiatives are limited because of their underlying assumptions that the otherwise heterogenous groups should be homogenized to coexist peacefully. Accordingly, the focus is often on provisions that minimize, even deny, group identity or limit expressions of group differences—the idea of justice as fairness and sameness.

A second challenge to justice as fairness is continuing sociocultural and economic disparities (Ayallo, 2012). Specifically, this reality calls into question some of the principles of justice as fairness, namely *entitlement, merit, and contract* (Nozick, 1974). The primary proposition in both ideas of justice is just acquisition, that people only hold what they have worked hard for or fairly acquired through merit—one of the measures of merit being inalienable individual rights (MacIntyre, 2013). How these supposed universal rights are arrived at is widely contested (Eze, 2021; MacIntyre, 2013; Otieno, 2008; Sewpaul et al., 2021; Ujomu & Olatunji, 2014b). A critical note is that every member of society is assumed to have equal or the same access to goods and services on the basis that they have or should work hard, failure of which blame is attached to the individual for not working hard to get what is *rightfully* theirs. For fair distribution, a perfect institutional arrangement is needed—with people who can position themselves in the "original position." As Choules (2007) explains, within this understanding of justice, intervention addressing inequalities is regarded as an act of charity, kindness, welfare, and benevolence—an understanding from which the language of *deserving* and *undeserving* poor derives.

The idea of entitlement is unrelatable in an African context in many ways, mainly because its view of fairness focuses on ontology while maintaining a critical distance from the real-life situations where people live in the face of inequalities, threats, dangers, real and imagined (Sewpaul & Kreitzer, 2021). For example, in a Kenyan community development context, these realities include social inequalities born out of established arrangements of cultural, political, and religious institutions (Ayallo, 2012). In other words, the "spaces within which people breathe, live, learn, marry, work, play, and become mothers and fathers [caregivers]; daughters; sons;

brothers; sisters; friends and colleagues" (Sewpaul & Kreitzer, 2021, p. 1). High poverty prevalence in Kenya is most notable in regions either traditionally alienated from the sanctums of power or where national resources and infrastructure have been restricted because of their association with critics of current and previous governments (Holmquist & Githinji, 2009). The tension between some elements of African culture and the human rights approach for women is well documented by Sewpaul and Kreitzer (2021) and several African women postcolonial writers (reviewed in Ayallo, 2012). Gender inequalities continue to exist even with several initiatives, mainly in legislation to safeguard women's *rights*. The fact that youth (15 to 35 years old) form a numerical majority in Kenya and are overrepresented in criminal activities and rebellious movements mainly because of a history of social exclusion and lack of representation in socioeconomic and political processes is well known (Abbink, 2021; Ayallo, 2012; Kagwanja, 2003). Generational politics, partially arising from cultural kinship arrangements, significantly contributes to the existing social exclusion (Abbink, 2021; Kagwanja, 2006)—a reality that seems impossible to address legislatively.

Overall, justice as fairness, including principles of proportionality and entitlement, is an individualistic approach with an ontological focus. Predominant concerns are about individual interests and freedom and creating conditions within which these are not interrupted (Ayallo, 2012). While there is a place for this perspective, in most African contexts, individual interests cannot be viewed separately from the collective (Eze, 2021; Ujomu, 2007). The addition of *Ubuntu* as a theme in the Global Agenda for Social Work and Social Development (International Federation of Social Workers, 2021) acknowledges that from an African perspective, "an individual human being is part of larger and more significant relational, communal, societal, environmental, and spiritual world" (Mayaka & Truell, 2021, p. 2). Accordingly, an approach to justice focusing primarily on the individual and perfect institutional arrangement is ineffective, and their universal claim is questionable (Ayallo, 2012). Justice in this context is about addressing the practicalities of human life.

Justice as Partiality, Participatory and Dialogical: Centering the Margins

The author has argued so far, and elsewhere, that in complex societies characterized by heterogeneity, deeply rooted political, social, and cultural inequalities, and a colored history of colonialism and postcolonialism, the perspective of justice as fairness and proportionality is remote from everyday experiences. As a case study, the Kenyan context has tended to adopt a politics of privilege, with the state as the source and distributor of goods and services, which history shows are distributed to the benefit of the "elite" and supporters of the incumbent government. On the other hand, the structure and arrangement of the state are shaped by, for instance, politicized ethnicity and cultural beliefs that inherently generate inequalities. Therefore, the structures favor some and disadvantage others (Ayallo, 2012). In this chapter, an example of the most relevant concept of justice in these contexts relies on a combination of multi-faceted notions. These include the dignity of every individual—that access to advantages and disadvantages in society is essential, not because people are entitled to them based on merit or contract but because of their intrinsic dignity as humans (Eze, 2021); the idea of public deliberation and participation founded on deliberative democracy (Sen, 2011); and the notion of difference (Fraser, 1999; Young, 2011).

Human dignity. The idea of inherent human dignity is already embedded in most African worldviews and philosophies. However, in many ways, it has either been ignored, judged, or actively suppressed by the supposed "classical" theories through the colonization of African, Eastern, and Indigenous philosophies (Nwosimiri, 2017). This is changing with the renaissance of African philosophies such as Ubuntu, which is now included as a significant theme in global social and community work practice. For instance, human dignity is rooted in Ubuntu, expressed in generic life values of love, respect, care, trust, integrity, reciprocity, and relatedness (Mayaka & Truell, 2021). As a notion of justice, addressing a problem within African community development contexts, ubuntu does not begin by analyzing it into components or parts but instead focuses on the larger context within which the problem occurs. Similarly, a successful individual is also someone who contributes as part of the whole and is committed to supporting others with integrity—negating the idea of "individual merit." "Ubuntu predicts that life faces ongoing challenges, disaster and loss and that people need communal coping mechanisms to minimize damage" (Mayaka & Truell, 2021, p. 3).

Participation through deliberation/dialogue. Participation, through deliberation or dialogue, as a concept of justice, supports the idea of working together to address the social, political, cultural, and religious barriers to everyone's development (Ayallo, 2012). Sen (2011) explains that what animates people the most in contexts where inequalities are deeply rooted is not, first and foremost, the realization that society falls short of being perfect or fair. Instead, it is the knowledge that these inequalities can collectively be remedied through public reasoning. Therefore, this understanding should be central to any theory of justice. This is built in the author's idea of justice as public dialogue, first developed based on participants' responses in the 2012 doctoral research (Ayallo, 2012).

The widely debated concept of increasing public participation in issues that directly concern them, including what it means and its benefits, is commonly referred to in the literature as participatory democracy (Ayallo, 2012; Habermas, 1990; Kellner, 2000; Young, 2000). A recount of these debates is outside the scope of this chapter. A critical note is that it concerns recognizing and creating public spaces for the active and direct participation of communities within a society in decision-making processes through dialogue. The aim of deliberations in these spaces is not to settle all questions and scores or come to a consensus. Instead, they present an opportunity for diverse voices within society to be heard, argue their case, make their situations known, and listen to others' perspectives (Sen, 2009). These critical elements are missing in African community development contexts because of the over-emphasis on policies and procedures or the "ideal speech situation" at the expense of actual participation (Ayallo, 2012). As Schugurensky (2004) explains:

> By participation ... I do not mean token consultations without authentic decision-making power, clientelistic relationships that disempower and control people, or even basic associationalism in the sense of membership in community associations. Instead, I mean inclusive processes of deliberation that are bound to real and substantive decisions. (p. 607)

In the African context, such participation is lacking because decisions have often been made from higher up the hierarchy, making them inaccessible and removed from the lived realities of local populations. The author found in the 2012 doctoral research and has observed over the years that spaces where such participation and dialogue can occur already exist in local African communities (Ayallo, 2012). They are present in schools, families, churches, village gatherings, marketplaces, self-help groups, support networks, local media, and advocacy and interest groups. However, the "rules" of participation in these spaces are still a barrier. Active participation is still tied to high social, economic, and cultural status and formal academic qualifications (LiPuma & Koelble, 2009). In a Kenyan context, this excludes the majority who do not meet these criteria (Ayallo, 2012). The problem is a lack of recognition and validation of a range of local public spheres. A second related challenge is the lack of a mechanism for connecting these local public spheres and institutions to national public spheres. Accordingly, justice as public dialogue begins with a contextual definition of a *valid* public sphere that validates the local spheres where traditionally excluded groups are found and considers the flexibility necessary for their active participation (Schugurensky, 2004; Sen, 2011). Elsewhere, the author has suggested how such public spaces can be created, validated, and facilitated with local examples from a Kenyan community development context. Two unrelated examples from outside Kenya are also provided to show the power of public dialogue in justice matters. These include using the Zulu concept of *Indaba* by the Anglican Communion as a process of discussion about the issue of sexuality and the Bible (The Anglican Communion, 2011); and the *gacaga* courts in Rwanda (Corey & Joireman, 2004).

The key argument is that local public spheres are central to an idea of justice, primarily because they are the critical sites where socialization occurs and identities are constructed, deconstructed, and reconstructed (Ayallo, 2012). While it may not be possible to eliminate social, cultural, and political differences because they are deeply rooted in society, opening up spaces for active engagement enables groups to redefine their struggles and build capacity within and beyond their immediate spheres. This is a primary and practical concern (Coates, 2007; Westheimer & Kahne, 2004). Public dialogue is a notion of justice that begins from a critical deliberation of real-life experiences, as opposed to the classical concepts that start from general premises about the nature of society and human beings and, therefore, on balancing society's equilibrium or perfect arrangement.

Notion of difference. Forms of diversity characterize African community development contexts. So far, examples of a Kenyan context show cultural, political, social, and religious diversity. Therefore, a notion of *difference or impartiality* should be central to understanding justice in these contexts (Young, 2011). This is the idea that in circumstances where deeply rooted inequalities have resulted in adverse health and well-being outcomes, those most affected should be treated differently, implemented through the principles of need, redistribution, recognition, and capability development (Raphael, 2001). While some of these principles have been implemented in some African contexts, the author argues that they have primarily been marked by failure because they were transplanted without a critical evaluation of the local context—for instance, the *affirmative action* approach. Since 2003, women in Kenya have advocated for active inclusion in decision-making through affirmative action (Vision 2030 Delivery Secretariat, 2018). This strategy is like others worldwide, where recognition of difference has been implemented through schemes such as reserved seats, party lists, or voting rights (Young, 1997). The author contends that affirmative action has culminated in manipulation, tokenism, and decoration because of the dominant politics of privilege, like other legislative approaches in Kenya. Additionally, it lacks an accompanying locally based monitoring mechanism and evaluation to explore how it contributes to women's capability-building and sustainable initiatives that address the actual root causes of gender differences (Ayallo, 2012; Young, 2000).

Overall, this chapter reiterates that there are deeply rooted socially constructed differentiations and disparities in most African community development contexts that evidence shows to be challenging to eliminate.

As the author concluded elsewhere (Ayallo, 2012), this acknowledgment is not meant to naturalize, legitimize, and normalize these disparities. Instead, it is a provocation to develop a relevant concept of justice in this context that does not remain at the level of abstract philosophy or must transcend philosophical speculation of a perfect society and address the lived realities. Such a concept of justice should be multi-dimensional, as summarized in Figure 12.1. However, it is possible to create, validate, and nurture spaces where dialogue can occur about issues facing communities and public spheres to initiate intentional communication that includes the voices of all members of society, especially traditionally marginalized groups.

Conclusion

The author has argued that "justice" issues that characterize community development in most African contexts, especially in Kenya, cannot be effectively addressed from an understanding of justice focusing on formulating rules or principles to create equilibrium in society or perfect the arrangement of societal institutions. The most relevant concept of justice cannot

Figure 12.1

Critical Elements of a Multi-Dimensional Concept of Justice

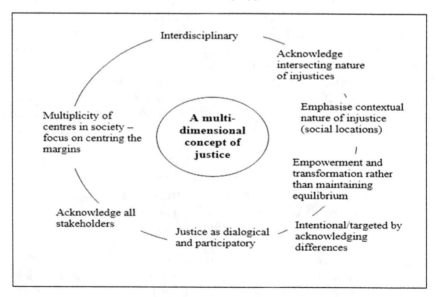

Source: Ayallo (2012).

ignore the deeply rooted differences based on culture, politics, ethnicity, kinship, religion, and social status; it cannot focus on homogeneity; and individual rights and freedom. A theory of justice proposed in this chapter is an understanding of justice as public dialogue, the ability of all individuals and groups to participate in deliberations and decision-making processes on issues that affect their livelihoods. This concept of justice requires proper recognition and validation of multiple and overlapping public spheres where ordinary people are mostly found, including intermediary institutions such as schools, families, churches, self-help or support groups, and markets.

In Ayallo (2012) the author found that even though traditionally marginalized groups such as women and youth have been denied access to national-level public spheres, they have found creative ways and spaces of getting together to talk about their issues and finding albeit temporary solutions to their problems. Several are part of local support, self-help, and "merry-go-round" groups. These spaces are accessible and flexible for their participation. What is lacking is the validation of these spaces as equally viable and "centered" and authentic mechanisms of connecting these local public spheres and institutions to the national-level public spheres. Therefore, an understanding of justice as public dialogue, centering the margins, is the most relevant in this context of community development. As Bohman (1996) explains, public dialogue as a concept is about social and collective action and recognizes status differentials and the multiplicity of centers. It is an understanding of justice as transforming rather than maintaining equilibrium.

REFERENCES

Abbink, J. (2021). *Vanguard or vandals: Youth, politics and conflict in Africa*. Brill.

African Union. (2010). *Economic Report on Africa 2010: Promoting high-level sustainable growth to reduce unemployment in Africa*. Retrived on October 12, 2022, from https://sustainabledevelopment.un.org/index.php?page=view&type=400&nr=452&menu=35

Ager, A., & Strang, A. (2008). Understanding integration: A conceptual framework. *Journal of refugee studies*, *21*(2), 166–191. https://doi.org/10.1093/jrs/fenO16

Ajulu, R. (2001). Kenya: one step forward, three steps back: The succession dilemma. *Review of African Political Economy*, *28*(88), 197–212. https://doi.org/10.1080/03056240108704525

Anglican Communion. (2011). *Continuing Indaba*. Retrieved October 17, from https://www.anglicancommunion.org/mission/reconciliation/continuing-indaba.aspx

Ayallo, I. A. (2012). *Public policy dialogue for socially-inclusive public policy making processes in Kenya: The role of the Anglican church of Kenya.* Auckland University of Technology.

Balibar, E., Mezzadra, S., & Samāddāra, R. (2012). *The borders of justice.* Temple University Press.

Bohman, J. (1996). *Public deliberation: Pluralism, complexity, and democracy.* The MIT Press.

Branch, D., & Cheeseman, N. (2009). Democratization, sequencing, and state failure in Africa: Lessons from Kenya. *African Affairs, 108*(430), 1–26. https://doi.org/10.1093/afraf/adn065

Choules, K. (2007). The shifting sands of social justice discourse: From situating the problem with "them," to situating it with "us". *The Review of Education, Pedagogy, and Cultural Studies, 29*(5), 461–481.

Coates, R. D. (2007). Social justice and pedagogy. *American Behavioral Scientist, 51*(4), 579–591.

Corey, A., & Joireman, S. F. (2004). Retributive justice: The Gacaca courts in Rwanda. *African Affairs, 103*(410), 73–89.

Cottrell, J., & Ghai, Y. (2007). Constitution making and democratization in Kenya (2000–2005). *Democratisation, 14*(1), 1–25.

Eriksen, T. H. (2002). *Ethnicity and nationalism: Anthropological perspectives.* Pluto.

Eze, C. (2021). *Justice and human rights in the African imagination: We, too, are humans.* Routledge.

Forde, C., & Lynch, D. (2015). *Social work and community development.* Palgrave Macmillan.

Fraser, N (1998), *Social justice in the age of identity politics: Redistribution, recognition, participation* (WZB Discussion Paper, No. FS I 98-108). https://hdl.handle.net/10419/44061

Ghai, Y. (2008). Devolution: restructuring the Kenyan state. *Journal of Eastern African Studies, 2*(2), 211–226.

Ghai, Y. (2009). *Decreeing and establishing a constitutional order: Challenges facing Kenya.* The Royal African Society: African Arguments.

Gĩthĩnji, M., & Holmquist, F. (2009). The default politics of ethnicity in Kenya. *Brown Journal of World Affairs, 16*(1), 101–117.

Government of Kenya. (2013). *Constitution of Kenya, 2010.* Retrieved October 12, 2022, from http://www.kenyalaw.org:8181/exist/kenyalex/actview.xql?actid=Const2010#part_I

Govers, C., & Vermeulen, H. (1997). From political mobilization to the politics of consciousness. In C. Govers & H. Vermeulen (Eds.), *The politics of ethnic consciousness* (pp. 1–30). Palgrave Macmillan.

Habermas, J. (1990). *Moral consciousness and communicative action.* MIT Press.

Hardcastle, D. A., Powers, P. R., & Wenocur, S. (2004). *Community practice: Theories and skills for social workers* (2nd ed.). Oxford University Press.

Holmquist, F., & Githinji, M. W. (2009). The default politics of ethnicity in Kenya. *Brown Journal of World Affairs, 16*, 101–117.

Holmquist, F., & Oendo, A. (2001). Kenya: Democracy, decline, and despair. *Current History, 100*(646), 201–206.

Ife, J., & Tesoriero, F. A. (2006). *Development: Community based alternatives in an age of globalisation*. Pearson Education.
International Federation of Social Workers (IFSW). (2021). *Global agenda for social work and social development*. Retrieved on June 27, 2023, from https://www.ifsw.org/2020-to-2030-global-agenda-for-social-work-and-social-development-framework-co-building-inclusive-social-transformation/
Kagwanja, P. M. (2003). Facing Mount Kenya or facing Mecca? The Mungiki, ethnic violence and the politics of the Moi succession in Kenya, 1987–2002. *African Affairs*, *102*(406), 25–49.
Kagwanja, P. M. (2006). 'Power to Uhuru': Youth identity and generational politics in Kenya's 2002 elections. *African Affairs*, *105*(418), 51–75.
Kellner, D. (2000). Habermas, the public sphere, and democracy: A critical intervention. *Perspectives on Habermas*, *1*(1), 259–288.
Kimenyi, M. S. (2001). Harmonizing ethnic claims in Africa: A proposal for ethnic-based federalism. In P. O. Agbese & J. M. Mbaku (Eds.), *Ethnicity and governance in the Third World* (pp. 125–148). Routledge.
Lebacqz, K. (1986). *Six theories of justice: Perspectives from philosophical and theological ethics*. Augsburg Books.
LiPuma, E., & Koelble, T. A. (2009). Deliberative democracy and the politics of traditional leadership in South Africa: A case of despotic domination or democratic deliberation? *Journal of Contemporary African Studies*, *27*(2), 201–223.
MacIntyre, A. (2013). Justice as a virtue: Changing conceptions. In *After virtue* (pp. 283–296). Bloomsbury Academic.
Mayaka, B., & Truell, R. (2021). Ubuntu and its potential impact on the international social work profession. *International Social Work*, *64*(5), 649–662.
Moyo, D. (2009). *Dead aid: Why aid is not working and how there is a better way for Africa*. Macmillan.
Novak, M. (2000). Defining social justice. *First things*, 11–12.
Nozick, R. (1974). *Anarchy, state and utopia*. Basic Books.
Nwosimiri, O. (2017). Do the works of the nationalist–ideological philosophers undermine Hume's and Kant's ideas about Race? *SAGE Open*, *7*(1), 1–11.
Ogude, J. (2002). Ethnicity, nationalism and the making of democracy in Kenya: An introduction. *African Studies*, *61*(2), 205–207. https://doi.org/10.1080/0002018022000032929
Olewe, D. (2022). *Kenya elections 2022: Win or lose, why Raila Odinga's election challenge matters*. Retrieved October 12, 2022, from https://www.bbc.com/news/world-africa-62599219
Olsgard, P. J. (1997). *Policy formation: HIV/AIDS in Kenya and Malawi*. University of Denver.
Otieno, N. (2008). *Human rights and social justice in Africa: Cultural, ethical and spiritual imperatives*. All Africa Conference of Churches.
Raphael, D. D. (2001). *Concepts of justice*. Clarendon Press.
Rawls, J. (1971). *A theory of justice*. The Belknap Press.
Schugurensky, D. (2004). The tango of citizenship learning and participatory democracy. *Lifelong Citizenship Learning, Participatory Democracy and Social Change*, *2*, 607–694.
Sen, A. (2011). *The idea of justice*. Harvard University Press.

Sewpaul, V., & Kreitzer, L. (2021). Culture, human rights, and social work: Colonialism, eurocentricism, and afrocentricity. In V. Sewpaul, L. Kreitzer, & T. Raniga (Eds.), *The tensions between culture and human rights: Emancipatory social work and Afrocentricity in a global world* (pp. 1–24). University of Calgary Press.

Sewpaul, V., Kreitzer, L., & Raniga, T. (2021). *The tensions between culture and human rights: emancipatory social work and Afrocentricity in a global world*. University of Calgary Press.

Solomon, R. C., & Murphy, M. C. (Eds.). (2000). *What is justice?: Classic and contemporary readings* (2nd ed.). Oxford Univesity Press.

Twelvetrees, A. (2008). *Community work* (4th ed.). Palgrave Macmillan.

Ujomu, P. O. (2004). Citizenship and social order: Reflections on Plato. *Democracy & Development: Journal of West African Affairs*, 4(1), 11–30.

Ujomu, P. O. (2007). The problem of justice in an African traditional and postcolonial experience: a theoretical exploration. *Orita: Ibadan Journal of Religious Studies*, 39(2), 41–75.

Ujomu, P. O. (2008). *Africa's political justice problem and the politics of justice in the development architecture*. Retrieved May 31, 2024, from http://biblioteca.clacso.edu.ar/clacso/sur-sur/20130919041848/03_Philip_Ogo_Ujomu.pdf

Ujomu, P. O. (2018). Nigeria"s problem of human nature and the quest for reciprocity and the common good as developmental values: A philosophical reflection. *Journal of Globalization Studies*, 9(1), 61–76.

Ujomu, P. O. (2019). Human dignity and social order as key values for an endogenous African development. *Agathos*, 10(2), 267–281.

Ujomu, P. O., & Bature, A. I. (2018). Conflicting values, Ubuntu philosophy and peace building: An African experience. *Culture and Dialogue*, 6(2), 174–190.

Ujomu, P. O., & Olatunji, F. O. (2014a). Democratic theories and the problem of political participation in Nigeria: Strengthening consensus and the rule of law. *Human Affairs*, 24(1), 120–135.

Ujomu, P. O., & Olatunji, F. O. (2014b). Justice in Hobbes' and Rawls' ideologies and the quest for social order in Africa: A philosophical reflection. *Khazar Journal of Humanities and Social Sciences*, 17(1), 55–69.

Vision 2030 Delivery Secretariat. (2018). *Kenya Vision 2023: Affirmative action*. Retrieved October 21, 2022, from http://vision2030.go.ke/project/affirmative-action/#

Westheimer, J., & Kahne, J. (2004). What kind of citizen? The politics of educating for democracy. *American Educational Research Journal*, 41(2), 237–269.

Wouters, E., Van Rensburg, H., & Meulemans, H. (2010). The National Strategic Plan of South Africa: what are the prospects of success after the repeated failure of previous AIDS policy? *Health Policy and Planning*, 25(3), 171–185.

Young, I. M. (1997). Deffering group representation. In I. Shapiro & W. Kymlicka (Eds.), *Ethnicity and Group Rights* (pp. 349–376). New York University Press.

Young, I. M. (2000). *Inclusion and democracy*. Oxford University Press.

Young, I. M. (2011). *Justice and the politics of difference*. Princeton University Press.

CHAPTER 13

INTERACTIONS OF COMMUNITY DEVELOPMENT AND LEGAL REFORMS IN REHABILITATING JUVENILE OFFENDERS IN ZAMBIA

Chilala K. Sheilas, Chikampa Victor, Moonga Fred, and Hamauswa Shakespeare

ABSTRACT

Children occupy a special place in every well-meaning society. It is the aim of all the governments in the world to protect the interest of the child. Despite the effort to protect children, many of them come in conflict with the law and are incarcerated in law enforcement agencies. However, juvenile justice systems have been developed in several countries to protect the special rights of children who come into conflict with the law. Zambia has ratified numerous international instruments relating to the welfare of prisoners, including juvenile offenders. Additionally, the Zambian government has enacted its own legislation, which deals with child offenders. It has been noted that confinement facilities may not provide the best option for rehabilitating juvenile offenders. Separating children from their close communities, families and other supportive networks can do more harm than good to young people, particularly because of their age. The main objective of this chapter is to propose a new broad-based approach for rehabilitating juvenile offenders in Zambia and Africa at large. The emphasis is on engaging juvenile offenders in productive activities in the communities and local spaces in which they reside, as opposed to institutional-based social treatment provided for by the law. The chapter reiterates the significance of the family and community involvement in juvenile reformation, which is perceived to be a principal mechanism of social control and overall community development. This can ease the process of re-integration and reduce chances of recidivism, while re-affirming social justice.

Keywords: rehabilitation, legal reforms, social justice, recidivism, juvenile justice

Introduction

Zambia, formerly Northern Rhodesia, is a landlocked southern African country with a population of about 18,383,955 (GRZ-Zambia Statistical Agency, 2021), approximately 0.24% of the total world population. Based on the United Nations International Children's Emergency Fund, [UNICEF] (2018) report, Zambia has predominantly young people with much of the population under the age of 18 (53.4%) which is one of the youngest in the region and globally. The estimated median age is 17.6 years. Of the total population, about 8,336,38, representing 45.3% live in urban areas (Worldometer, 2020), implying that there are more people in rural than urban areas.

Zambia covers an area of about 753,000 square kilometres (Ndangwa, 2000). It shares its borders with Mozambique, Malawi, Tanzania, Democratic Republic of Congo, Namibia, Zimbabwe, Angola, and Botswana. Zambia attained her political independence in 1964. At independence, Kenneth Kaunda of the United National Independence Party (UNIP) became the inaugural president, guided by humanism and a socialist ideology which guided policy and general social relations.

The Zambian economy has historically been based on the mining industry. The International Council on Metals and Mining (ICMM) in Sikamo et al. (2016) indicated that 86% of the foreign direct investment that came into Zambia was due to the mining industry, 89% of the country's export earnings came from the mining industry, as well as over 25% of all revenues collected by government. The remainder is covered by manufacturing, agriculture, and tourism among other sectors.

As one of the developing countries in Africa, about 54% of the nation's population lives on less than $1.90 a day and has an average life expectancy of 63.5 years. Despite the country having achieved slow but steady economic growth from 2017 to 2018, growth fell to 1.4% in 2019, and contracted further to around 4.5% in 2020 (Bertelsmann Stiftung [BTI], 2022). Based on UNICEF's report (2018), many of the children in Zambia are affected by both monetary and non-monetary poverty, with 36% of them multidimensionally deprived. The situation was compounded by many factors including the country's debt position which pushed a significant number of Zambians into vulnerability and poverty, resulting into increased crime rate. The same applies to adolescent or juvenile delinquency.

Juvenile Delinquency in Zambia

Like other countries, Zambia is not an exception regarding the global aspect of juvenile delinquency. The survey by the Adala (2009) noted that the prevalence of criminal activities is much higher in cities and towns, especially those located along railway lines, the transport routes and the copperbelt province where mining activities are concentrated. The contributing factors include high levels of unemployment, the influx of people to the urban centres and the resultant population growth. In line with international conventions and treaties, the Zambia Correctional Services, formerly known as Zambia Prison Services, recognized the importance of offender rehabilitation and reintegration. The Zambia Correctional Service also works to provide institutional correctional services to offenders and to increase industrial and agricultural production to contribute to the wellbeing and reformation of offenders. The services provided include education, literacy programs, basic and higher education, rehabilitation training through agricultural production, carpentry, tailoring, metal fabrication and behavior change, and reintegration. However, the focus of this chapter is the interactions of community development and legal reforms in rehabilitating juvenile offenders in Zambia.

Defining Juvenile Delinquency Worldwide

The term "juvenile" has been used differently in different settings. Section 82 of the Malaysian Penal Code describes the juvenile as a child who has reached the age of criminal liability or responsibility, namely 10 years of age. Section 83 of the Penal Code, however, describes conditional protection for a child who is above 10 but below 12 years of age from being prosecuted, if he has not attained sufficient understanding of the nature and consequences of his act during the commission of the crime (Baba et al., 2007, p. 1). As such, a delinquent, according to the law in Malaysia, refers to "a young person who has committed a criminal offence and given a court order. This means any behavior that violates the criminal law, committed by a young person below the age of eighteen (18)" (Baba et al., 2007, p. 2). In Australia, according to the Australian Institute of Criminology (2011), except in Queensland, a juvenile is defined as a person aged between 10 and 17 years of age, inclusive, while as in Queensland, a juvenile is defined as a person aged between 10 and 16 years, and the minimum age of criminal responsibility is 10 years inclusive of all jurisdictions.

In Zambia, the Juvenile Act, Cap. 53 s. 2(1) of the laws of Zambia (Government Republic of Zambia, 2018), defines a juvenile as any person who is under the age of 19 years. This implies that a juvenile can be a child (defined as any person under the age of 16 or a young person (defined as any person who is at least 16 but not yet 19 years old).

On the other hand, delinquency is defined as a group of behaviors that are inconsistent with the collective practices and ethics of the dominant social group. These behaviors, in essence, deviate from societal norms and, more specifically, violate established criminal codes and laws (Georges, 2009; Shailja et al., 2022). Bhanukeshi (2021) states that the juvenile justice Act 2015 of India defines juvenile delinquency as an act of participating in an offence or act which is unlawful according to the law (p. i).

According to the Government Republic of Zambia (2018), juvenile delinquency can mean unlawful behavior that violates the criminal law of the land by a child or a young person whose age is below 19 years old. It is worth noting that, the age of criminal responsibility in Zambia is 8 years, unless it can be proven that, at the time of doing the act, the child had the capacity to do the act or make the omission, in which case the minimum age of criminal responsibility is 12 years.

Factors Perpetuating Juvenile Delinquency

Perpetuation of delinquency is fostered by some factors that put pressure on young people and influence them to commit delinquent activities. Mwangangi (2019) and Nourollah et al. (2015) cited poverty as a main reason why juveniles commit crimes. Other factors associated with juvenile delinquency are overcrowding in unplanned settlements, peer pressure, substance abuse, and disintegration of family ties. Other crimes adolescents commit include arson, rape, drug offences, murder, and burglary, among others.

In most societies, the situation is compounded by HIV/AIDS and COVID-19 which resulted in deaths of parents/guardians and subsequent lack of family or community support. Such frustrations and negative influences within society can lead to criminal and delinquent activities. UNICEF (as cited in Muyobela & Strydom, 2017) reported that, worldwide, at any given time, over 1 million children are detained by law enforcement bodies. This is an indication that, despite efforts to the contrary, children in conflict with the law still end up incarcerated (p. 540). The goal of a child justice system is to ensure that children are better served and protected. To this effect, the Juvenile Justice System (JJS) in Zambia seeks to rehabilitate delinquents and hence is less punitive.

Despite the challenges experienced by the social welfare officers who are designated to work with juvenile offenders, it has been noted that some measures have been put in place by Zambian government to promote special care and treatment for juveniles who come in conflict with the law. To this effect, the Zambian government ratified the UNCRC (1989) in 1991 (GRZ-National Child Policy, 2012). Additionally, Zambia has enacted its own legislation that deals with child offenders in the criminal justice system. These include the National Child Policy and The Constitution of Zambia (Amendment) Act 2 of 2016 (Muyobela & Strydom, 2017, p. 543). The Juvenile Justice system in Zambia uses a multidisciplinary approach which involves social workers, psychologists, the police, the Magistrate, and teachers for skills training.

Juvenile Justice System (JJS) in Zambia

UNICEF (2018) reported that worldwide, over 1 million children are detained by law enforcement agencies. In Africa, the percentage of the prison population comprising child detainees generally ranges from 0.5% to 2.5% and in Namibia, juveniles represent 5.5% of prisoners. According to Todrys and Amon (2011), in 2010, Zambia's prisons held 414 juvenile inmates (aged between 8 and 18) representing 2.5 of all Zambian inmates. Zambia has a total of 86 prisons throughout the country, and though one of these facilities is designated for juvenile offenders, juveniles are incarcerated with the adults at other facilities countrywide (p. 20).

The JJS is a system of laws, policies, and procedures intended to regulate the processing and treatment of non-adult offenders for violations of law and to provide legal remedies that protect their interests in situations of conflict or neglect (Jensen & Shoemaker, 2022; Odiango, as cited in Muyobela & Strydom, 2017, p. 540).

The JJSs have been developed in several countries worldwide to protect the special rights of children who come into conflict with the law. This implies that juveniles who come in conflict with the law must be treated differently from adult offenders, and they should be kept separately and tried in designated juvenile courts and correctional institutions if found guilty. Although some juvenile offenders may be very dangerous and incarceration is considered appropriate for them, detention comes as a last option, and their rights are respected as provided for in the international and national instruments under the JJS.

Thus, the UN member countries, Zambia inclusive, have signed and ratified a number of international human rights instruments such as the

United Nations Convention on the Rights of the Child (UNCRC, 1989). The CRC provides the framework for promoting the wellbeing of children, including those who come in conflict with the law.

In addition to being a state-party to the UNCRC, Zambia has also enacted its own legislation which deals with child offenders in the criminal justice system. These include the Juveniles Act, Cap 53 of the Laws of Zambia, the Constitution, the Penal Code, National Diversion Framework, and the Criminal Procedure Code (Mumba, 2011). All these provisions are meant to protect the best interests of the child, particularly children in conflict with the law. Both international and national instruments provide guidance on the implementation of the JJS. For instance, the UNCRC, the Juveniles Act, the African Charter and the 2015 National Child Policy (NCP) designates that children who come into conflict with the law must be treated with dignity and compassion, while respecting their legal rights and implementing legal safeguards in all processes

In Zambia, because the JJS focuses on reformation, the younger offenders are sent to the approved reformatory centres, while the older offenders are sent to adult correctional facilities, formally known as prisons. The purpose of sending juvenile offenders to reformatory centers is to enable them to continue schooling while incarcerated for them to lead meaningful lives in future and prevent recidivism. Juvenile offenders are supposed to be separated from adult inmates to avoid the early labeling of juveniles as criminals.

Challenges to the JJS

Most of the juvenile reformatory measures have not yet been implemented in Zambia. Mumba (2011) and Todrys and Amon (2011) noted that in practice, the procedures, and the infrastructural facilities for administering the law are fundamentally the same for both adults and children despite the recognition that children deserve special care and treatment. Similarly, the Auditor General's performance report (2018) and the Ministry of Community Development and Social Services (MCDSS) report (2018) revealed several shortcomings in the implementation of national, international, and regional standards for treating children who are in conflict with the law in Zambia. Child offenders still experience extended periods of detention for petty offences and are sometimes held together with adult inmates. Todrys and Amon observed that the juveniles' process through the justice system is very slow and does not meet the requirements as specified under the international and national JJS. This implies that the JJS in Africa and Zambia is not effective in resolving juvenile delinquent problems. Yet, the need to rehabilitate juvenile offenders cannot be overemphasized.

This calls for the need to reform the JJS in the country to enhance its effectiveness in rehabilitating offenders, especially juveniles, and reduce child delinquency and recidivism. The Zambian Government under the Judiciary in conjunction with line Ministries, civil society organizations, co-operating partners and other stakeholders came up with the National Juvenile Justice Strategy and Action Plan 2022–2026 to improve the Juvenile Justice System in the nation (Government Republic of Zambia, 2022).

Rehabilitation of Juvenile Offenders in Zambia

The institutionalized model of rehabilitation. Since the aim is to rehabilitate juvenile offenders, the JJS stipulates that the court judge may impose a variety of sentences as mandatory schooling, treatment programs, counseling, and many more as a condition of release. During this period, a juvenile is introduced to the probation officer (a social worker) assigned to the case. The social worker works with the juvenile during the entire justice process and assists in successfully completing the court order, and the social worker is expected to report to the judge on the juvenile's progress. The system is meant to be less punitive. However, this old model of rehabilitating juveniles who come in conflict with the law was based on a centralized institutionalization approach with its emphasis on seclusion of offenders.

The centralized institutional approach is stigmatizing and discriminatory. It emphasized institutional and secluded reformation which isolates the juvenile offenders from their families and mainstream of society during the period of incarceration. It also tends to encourage over-reliance on institutional correction and care of young offenders at the stage when parental and or community monitoring and guidance is rather critical in shaping their character. Furthermore, the services provided under the institutional model do not take into consideration the specific interests and needs of the juvenile offenders. For instance, the court judge may impose a variety of sentences as mandatory schooling, treatment programs, counseling, and many more as a condition of release. Confinement reduces the supportive networks and opportunities, resulting in loneliness, helplessness, depression, and the eventual challenges in the rehabilitation process. The approach is therefore limited in its reach and impact in reforming juvenile offenders. Thus, mandatory treatment may not yield the desired results.

Additionally, the institutional model confines the detained juveniles to a particularly deplorable environment, exposing them to unfavorable conditions that might negatively impact on their health and general welfare. Interaction with dangerous juvenile offenders and adult inmates in some correctional facilities could also have a negative impact on the character of younger ones who might become worse than they were prior to incarceration. The institutional model is also costly, as it involves the provision of many services, including the basic requirements of life that are heavily subsidized by the government. It also requires large numbers of trained professionals needed for the reformation process. The institutional model is therefore unsustainable.

With the aforementioned, the institutional approach is inappropriate for juvenile rehabilitation. Considering the shortcomings of this approach, there is a need for a new and multidimensional model that incorporates all the key players that might impact on the transformation of the offenders. The new integrated correctional model breaks from the institutional correctional approach and posits a new strategy for juvenile offender rehabilitation. The proposed model advocates for a holistic approach which accentuates community-based rehabilitation for juvenile offenders. The community-based approach recognizes the significant role the family and the local community can play in the rehabilitation process.

Community-Based Correctional Model

The limitations of the earlier approach prompted the authors to search for a broad-based model that may be relevant and appropriate for reforming young offenders in Zambia. The new model requires a paradigm shift in correctional service provision, from a centralized institutional confinement model to a community-based training and rehabilitation approach (community-based sentencing). It advocates for the adoption of community-based correctional practices and policies, to help young offenders lead more integrated lives in local communities, rather than detaining them in isolated settings. This is in line with the nation's adoption of less punitive measures towards rehabilitation of not only juveniles, but adult offenders as well. Nevertheless, the details about this transformation from prison to correctional services are beyond the scope of this chapter.

Community-based corrections, also known as deinstitutionalization, are programs that manage criminal offenders outside of correctional facilities and in the community. According to Shewit (2017), community-based rehabilitation is a broad concept which includes different kinds of non-custodial or institutional programs for offenders. It is a court ordered period of correctional supervision in the community. The objective of community-based rehabilitation is to sanction and control offenders without confining them. This allows offenders to maintain existing contacts and establish new ones which may be helpful in the correctional process.

Community-based correction decreases expenditure on corrections, decreases the rates of recidivism and overcrowding in correctional facilities and promotes community protection and development. There are various types of community-based corrections. These include probation, parole, work release, study release, furloughs, and halfway houses. They all aim at helping individuals with correction and re-integration (Shewit, 2017).

Literature shows that a number of countries have adopted the CBCM in combination with the country's Criminal Justice System (CJS). For instance, the United States of America (U.S.), grants probation if the court feels the case is suited to probation (Shewit, 2017). Similarly, the Ethiopian Criminal Code recognizes the idea of probation whereby the court is given discretionary power to order probation having regard to all the circumstances of the case and if it believes that it will promote the reform and reinstatement of the criminal.

Martelli et al. (2012) explained how an integrated, holistic model for Community-Based Rehabilitation (CBR) is used to rehabilitate people after traumatic or acquired brain injury (TBI/ABI). According to this model, community rehabilitation and integration has been defined by four main areas: social relations, peer interventions, cognitive, and reintegration strategy. The model states that psychological, affection, or social relationships and meaningful economic engagements mark the most important needs of someone during rehabilitation. We therefore think this model can be applied in rehabilitating young offenders.

Social Relations Strategy. Most often, attention during rehabilitation focuses only on counselling and skills training, neglecting the critical role of social relations, which can be fulfilled by the family, friends, and the local community at large. Building social relations helps clients develop a sense of belonging and acceptance. It also enhances feelings of purposefulness and self-worth, which can significantly influence their involvement in productive activities (Martelli, 2012). Social relations encourage participation, which does not only enhance knowledge of the participants, but it also builds people's productive capacity, which makes rehabilitation and integration more attainable (Shailja et al., 2023). CBCM underscores the value of social networks, including the family and community, in the rehabilitation of juvenile offenders, particularly because of their age.

For instance, the probation system in Singapore has taken several measures to enhance the effectiveness of probation (Bee, 2003). One of them is the Community Probation Service (CPS) which involves Volunteer Probation Officers (VPOs) from the community. The VPOs complement the work of probation officers in re-shaping the lives of young probationers. They serve as positive role models to the probationers and encourage them to be meaningfully engaged in community work. CPS offers a wide scope of involvement to cater to the VPOs' interests, skills and training, availability, and the various stages of their volunteer life cycle. These include preparation of pre-sentence reports, gather feedback and progress of probationers, preparing programs for probationers and their parents (Bee, 2003).

Cognitive Strategy. This strategy emphasizes the importance of knowledge and meaningful productivity. Productivity is very important because it helps promote a sense of achievement and self-worth, which is an important component of rehabilitation. This stage requires rehabilitation professionals like psychologists, social workers, probation officers, and legal professionals, among others. The purpose of rehabilitation is to return the affected person to some form of productivity or to engage them in productive activities.

Reintegration Strategy. This strategy involves recreational activities. It includes hobbies, volunteer activities and other recreational activities. Recreation is viewed as an important component of human development and psychological health. It is also a source of productivity, and it strengthens social networks, increases self-esteem and stress relievers, which play a very important role in achieving social identity, hope, motivation, reformation, and reintegration. These are fundamental elements that can be helpful in deterring criminal behavior. Through this strategy, society can achieve social justice, harmony, empowerment, and development for the benefit of all.

Community-based interventions allow offenders to maintain existing contacts and establish new ones in the community. They protect society from further harm and control offenders while they remain in the community (Shewit, 2017). This model will build on Zambia's rich tradition of humanism, guided by the value of respect for humanity and hard work. It is also in line with Zambia's motto "One Zambia one Nation," signifying unity, peace, respect, and love among all the people of Zambia. We think that the community can be part of the network in providing social, economic, psychological, and other forms of support required during the rehabilitation process. Community-based intervention strategies are not only best suited to rehabilitate juvenile offenders but also to address vulnerability in communities.

The CBC model can be achieved through community building, which promotes sustainable livelihood (Patel, 2005). With robust economic and social networks and strong family bonds, it is reasonable to expect reduced vulnerability and subsequent peaceful and prosperous communities, where reformation of offenders can be attainable with much ease. This approach brings together the community members, professional workers, and the state for greater results. It is in this context that community-based strategies are being proposed.

Despite the advantages of the CBCM, it has some challenges that need to be addressed for it to be effective. For instance, some community members may not have the competences required for them to participate in implementing the proposed model. To this effect, there is a need to train the local community members to enable them to support CBCM. The training can also equip the community members with skills to engage in effective community practices. It is also necessary to ensure that the family and other community members close to the offender do not interfere with the juvenile justice system during the period of rehabilitation.

Conclusion

Juvenile delinquency is one of the complex problems experienced in many countries around the world. In the recent past, Zambia experienced high rates of juvenile delinquency due to vulnerability, high levels of unemployment, peer pressure, substance abuse, negative influence of social media, and disintegration of the family ties. This has become a source of great concern to the Zambian government and community at large. Being a member of the UN and the AU, Zambia has ratified numerous international instruments relating to the welfare of offenders, particularly juveniles, but has also enacted its own legislation, which deals with this type of offenders in the criminal justice system. This is to protect "the best interest of the child." Despite these measures, juveniles who come in conflict with the law are kept in institutionalized correctional facilities.

These secluded facilities are not the best option for rehabilitating juvenile offenders because of their age. It is for this reason that the authors propose a broad-based and multi-dimensional model for rehabilitating juvenile offenders. The community-based and collaborative model, which involves all the stakeholders such as the government, community, family, and other social networks for support is the best approach for Zambia. This model will not only yield positive results in alleviating juvenile delinquency but can also play a significant role in reducing poverty and vulnerability in the country. However, there is a need to ensure that the new model takes into consideration the possible challenges that might be encountered during its implementation. Some of these challenges may include interference of the close community and the family members. It might also be necessary to design mentorship programmes to provide continuous support for the rehabilitated juveniles, to avoid recidivism.

REFERENCES

Adala, O. (2009). The criminal justice systems in Zambia: Enhancing the delivery of security in Africa. *Institute for Security Studies Monographs, 2009*(159), 41.

Baba, M., Ahmad, S., & Rosmidah J. (2007). *Juvenile Delinquency: Definitions, trends and governmental efforts to curb the problem.* https://www.researchgate.net/publication/301543703

Bee, L. A. (2023). *Community-based rehabilitation of offenders in Singapore.* https://www.unafei.or.jp/publications/pdf/RS_No61/No61_15VE_Ang1.pdf

Bertelsmann Stiftung [BTI]. (2022). *Bertelsmann Stiftung Country Report, Zambia.* Retrieved August 14, 2022, from https://www.ecoi.net/en/file/local/2069795/country_report_2022_ZMB.pdf

Bhanukeshi, B. (2021). *Theories relating to juvenile delinquency in reference with Juvenile Justice Act, 2015.* Retrieved June 11, 2021, from https://lawtimesjournal.in/theories-relating-to-juvenile-delinquency-in-reference-with-juvenile-justice-act-2015/

Georges, S. (2009). Deviant behaviour and violence in Luxembourg School. *International Journal of Violence and School, 5*, 54–70.

Government Republic of Zambia. (2018). *Juvenile justice, National Diversion Framework.* Government Printers.

Government Republic of Zambia. (2021). *Zambia statistical agency report.* Retrieved July 16, 2022, from https://www.zamstats.gov.zm

Government Republic of Zambia. (2015). *National Child Policy.* Ministry of Community Development and Social services. Government Printers.

Government Republic of Zambia. (2022). *National Juvenile Justice Strategy and Action Plan 2022–2026.* The Judiciary. Government Printers.

Jensen, G., & Shoemaker, D. J. (2022). *Juvenile justice. Encyclopaedia Britannicap.* Retrieved August 20, 2022, from https://www.britannica.com/topic/juvenile-justice

Martelli, M. F., Zasler, N. D. & Tiernan, P. (2012). Community based rehabilitation: Special issues. *Neuro Rehabilitation, 31*, 3–18. https://doi.org/10.3233/NRE-2012-0770

Mumba, D. C. (2011). *The Juvenile Criminal Justice System in Zambia VIS-A-VS The International Protection of Children's Right* [Master's thesis. University of Zambia].

Muyobela, T., & Strydom, M. (2017). The rehabilitation of incarcerated of child offenders: Challenges faced by social welfare officers in Zambia. *Social Work Journal, 53*(4), 539–562.

Mwangangi, K. R. (2019). The role of family in dealing with juvenile delinquency. *Open Journal of Social Sciences, 7*(3), 52–63.

Ndangwa, N. (2000). *Social welfare in Zambia.* Multimedia Publications.

Nourollah, M. Fatemeh, M., & Farhad, A. (2015). A study of factors affecting juvenile delinquency. *Biomed Pharmacology Journal, (8)*(Spl Edition). http://biomedpharmajournal.org/?p=2257>

Patel, L. (2005). *Social welfare and social development.* Oxford University Press.

Shailja, D., Tiwari, G., Dubey, S. K. & Verma, A. K. (2022). Socio-economic and family factors attributing enhanced juvenile delinquency: A review. *Journal of Community Mobilization & Sustainable Development, 17*(4), 1065–1069.

Shewit, K. G. (2017). Community-based rehabilitation of offenders: An overview of probation and parole in Ethiopia. *Hawassa University Journal of Law, 1* (7), 23–41.

Sikamo, J., Mwanza, A., & Mweemba, C. (2016). Copper mining in Zambia—History and future. *The Journal of the Southern African Institute of Mining and Metallurgy*, *116*(6), 491–496. http://dx.doi.org/10.17159/2411-9717/2016/v116n6a1

Todrys, K. W., & Amon, J. J. (2011). Human rights and health among juvenile prisoners in Zambia. *International Journal of Prisoner Health*, *7*(1), 10–17.

UNICEF. (2018). *Children in Zambia Report*. Retrieved September 20, 2022, from https://www.unicef.org/zambia/children-Zambia

United Nations. (1989). *Convention on the Rights of the Child (1989)*. Treaty no. 27531. Retrieved September 12, 2022, from https://wwwohchr,org

Worldometer. (2022). *Zambian population*. Retrieved August 30, 2022, from https://www.worldometers.info/world-population/zambia-population/

CHAPTER 14

THE COLLECTIVE PATH TO SUSTAINABILITY

Leveraging Community Systems for Positive Change

Rosemary Anderson Akolaa

ABSTRACT

The study aims to understand the impact of community systems on sustainable development by conducting a comparative analysis between the Nabdam and Bosomtwe Districts of Ghana. The objectives included assessing existing systems and structures, examining the effectiveness of political-administrative and indigenous administrative structures, and uncovering hidden differences between communities, disparities in community systems, development inequalities, and the cultural impact on community development. A qualitative research design was adopted, utilizing an ethnographic approach to systematically observe, collect, and analyze cultural and community structure data. In-depth interviews were conducted with chiefs, queen mothers, opinion leaders, and knowledgeable elders. The study reveals noticeable discrepancies in community structures between northern and southern Ghana and underscores the importance of economic stability, social involvement, community support, socialization, and social regulation in community prosperity and development. It recommends minimizing governmental and political intrusions and involving traditional leaders and elders in the decision-making process to ensure consistent and sustainable development. The findings of the study are linked to the *theory of change* model, which serves as a comprehensive framework designed to facilitate positive transformation and growth within a community. Understanding the unique characteristics and challenges of each community is critical for the application of the theory of change model in a manner that is culturally sensitive and tailored to address the specific needs of the community. Ultimately, the study provides valuable insights and recommendations for fostering positive change and sustainability by leveraging community systems and addressing the unique challenges faced by different regions.

Keywords: community systems, sustainable development, theory of change, cultural impact, administrative structures, Ghana

Introduction

Communities are complex systems comprising various structures and dynamics that influence their growth and development. The key structures within communities encapsulate the entire tangible and intangible environment and their interaction, whereas dynamism refers to the changes in these structures (Bocken & Geradts, 2020). Communities are driven and unified by certain norms, principles, and beliefs, but are a supersystem with different pillars and factions within them (Bartle, 2011). Community systems are community-led structures and mechanisms used by communities through which community members and community-based organizations and groups interact, coordinate, and deliver their responses to the challenges and needs affecting their communities. These systems are composed of ingrained human beliefs, knowledge, behaviors, and expectations (Bartle, 2011; The Global Fund, 2022; Shaw, 2008). The chapter outlines the community systems among the Mole-Dagdon ethnic group in Northern Ghana, emphasizing the Nabdam district, and the Akans, focusing on the Bosomtwe district, and gathers insights into how community structures, dynamics (functionalities), and processes contribute to sustainable development. The study examines community structures, dynamics (functionalities), and processes along the lines of the social, cultural, economic, and political environment and how these interact to bring about sustainable development.

Community Systems

Community systems are composed of structures, mechanisms, and processes that underpin community responses (Gunderson, 2010). These systems are categorized into three key areas: social, infrastructure, and organizational systems. Social systems encompass various aspects of community life, including housing, communication, education, and culture. Infrastructure systems cover areas such as transportation, energy, and buildings. Organization systems include local government, public health, and businesses. These three areas intersect to bring about progress in a community (The University of the South Pacific, 2014). The structures of a community can be further categorized into social, cultural, political, and economic structures (Robinson & Green, 2011). Community structures refer to areas within towns, cities, or neighborhoods that include population, housing, facilities, jobs, and services, production and consumption, leisure areas, and roads (Ministry of Environment, 2013).

Community Functionality and Dynamics

The chapter discusses the essential components for a community to thrive, including economics, social participation, communal support, socialization, and social control (Duranton & Puga, 2020). These components are necessary for providing members with a means to make a living, companionship, cooperation to accomplish urgent tasks, instilling norms and values, and enforcing adherence to community values (Chavis & Lee, 2015). The degree of development of a community is influenced by the type and nature of its structures, with deeper and higher participation leading to stronger and more developed communities (OECD/Noya& Clarence, 2009).

Sustainable Development in the Context of Community Processes

According to the Cambridge Dictionary, development is a process of growth and change, and community development is a social activity where people within a community organize and implement common needs with reliance on community resources and possible external supplements (Hanachor & Olumati, 2012; Sakalasooriya, 2020). Community development involves interactions between different components of a community (Bonye et al., 2013). It is a process where community members collectively generate solutions to common problems (Parada et al. 2012) and the theory of change is one way to bring about positive change.

Theory of Change Model

The theory of change (ToC) model serves as a comprehensive framework designed to facilitate positive transformation and growth within a community. It necessitates effective leadership that adheres to a methodical process and maintains robust, collaborative partnerships among all stakeholders. This model consists of six essential phases: recognizing the circumstances, strategizing the action, implementing the action, altering the system, modifying behaviors, and enhancing community infrastructures. It is recommended to distinctly separate the phases of problem recognition and strategizing, as both phases demand significant resources. The framework is designed to be recurrent and ongoing, with the results being influenced by the characteristics of the occurrences within the structure, which differ from one community to another. The framework is displayed in Figure 14.1.

Figure 14.1

The Theory of Change Model

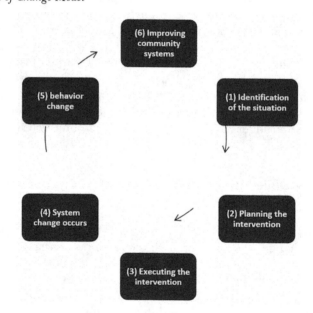

Source: Adopted from the Center for Community Health and Development (2022).

There are notable variations in the community systems between Northern and Southern Ghana, encompassing norms, beliefs, kinship, and land ownership, and their influence on development responses (Bonye et al., 2013). Research conducted by Gottlieb and Robinson (2016) indicates that communities adhering to the matrilineal system tend to exhibit smaller gender inequality gaps and demonstrate higher levels of collaboration (Kongela, 2020). The objective of the chapter is to reveal the underlying disparities between communities, scrutinize the inequalities in community systems and development, identify methods for positive intervention, and assess the impact of culture on community development. Ultimately, understanding these nuances is critical for the application of the ToC model in a manner that is culturally sensitive and tailored to the unique characteristics and challenges of each community.

METHODOLOGY

Objectives of the Study

To understand how community systems impact sustainable development, a comparative analysis between the two communities was conducted. The researcher selected two completely distinct communities, assessed their existing systems and structures, and examined the effectiveness of the district political-administrative structures and the indigenous administrative structures of the Nabdam and Bosomtwe Districts of Ghana, representing the North and South of Ghana, respectively.

Research Design

A qualitative research design was adopted for the study. The research adopted an ethnographic research design, which involved the collection and analysis of data about the culture of the people in the region and explored other related empirical data. The ethnographic research design enabled the researcher to systematically observe, collect, and analyze data about the community structures and how they impacted development in the study area. Ethnography is a process of analyzing patterns or lifeways of a familiar community (Leininger, 1985). Chiefs, queen mothers, opinion leaders, and knowledgeable elders participated in the in-depth interview. There were also informal conversations with elders, women group leaders, and youth groups within the communities. In all, the number of interviews was 17, and by gender, the participants were 10 males and 7 females. See the Appendix.

Study Areas

The study was conducted among the two major ethnic groups in Ghana, which are segregated by the North and South of the country. The largest ethnic group in Ghana is the Akans, who mostly reside in the central and southern parts of the country, followed by the Mole-Dagbon ethnic group, located in the northern part of Ghana.

Brief History of the Akans

The Akans are a wealthy ethnic group in Ghana and were the first to settle in the country. They migrated from the Sahara Desert and the Sahel regions of Africa. The Akan culture is rich and diverse, with several subgroups classified under eight main clans. The Akan culture has a chief who is the custodian of the land, and they practice a matrilineal form of inheritance (Asante et al., 2019). The Akans make up about 47.5% of the Ghanaian population with rich cultural practices in arts and artifacts (Asante et al., 2019).

Brief History of the Mole Dagbons

The Mole Dagbani ethnic groups in Ghana migrated from northeast of Lake Chad to the south of Niger Bend, Zamfara, and Nigeria. The Mole Dagbon state can trace its origin to one ancestor, Tohazie, who led their migration (Abukari, 2021). They belong to the Western Oti-Volta Gur ethnolinguistic group and comprise the Dagomba, Mamprusi, Gonja, Nanumba, and Mossi. The Mole Dagbani ethnic group is the second largest ethnic group in Ghana, constituting about 16% of the current population (Owusu & Agyei-Mensah, 2011); they have distinctive traditional and cultural practices and are predominantly Muslims. They operate the patrilineal system of inheritance.

These ethnic groups consist of thousands of communities that assimilate their ethnicity's values, cultures, norms, and protocols. Communities from the Akan and Mole-Dagbon ethnic groups were randomly selected and examined to understand the community systems, structures, and their influence on development.

Selection of Study Area

The Ashanti Region and the Upper East Region were purposefully chosen based on the fact that the Ashanti region represents the largest Akan community in Ghana, and its culture is relatively representative of southern Ghana. The Upper East region also represents the poorest region among the Mole-Dagbon ethnic groups, having poor and contrasting vegetation, with only one rainy season. The culture in the Upper East Region is relatively representative of Northern Ghana. Districts within these regions were randomly selected for the study. Displayed below are the Bosomtwe and Nabdam districts:

Figure 14.2

Nabdam District Map and Bosomtwe District Map

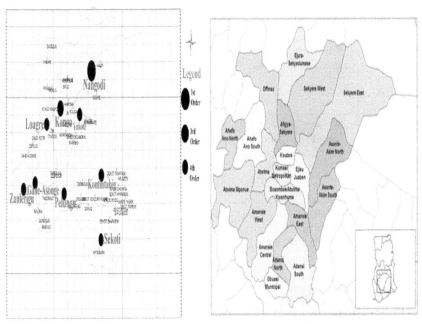

Source: District Planning Coordinating Unit (DPCU) (2017).

RESULTS

Systems and Structures in the Study Areas

The social structures of any community encapsulate the organized patterns of the social relationships and the social institutions that come together to form the society (the social community). These include chieftaincy, festivals, politics, lineage, customs, religion, and more (see Figures 14.1 and 14.2).

Effectiveness of the District Political-Administrative and the Traditional Administrative Structures

With proper leadership and interactions between the community structures, and with systematic implementation of the ToC, growth and development within communities might constantly occur. Observations

Table 14.1

Physical Structures—Tangibles

Thematic Area	Nabdam District	Bosomtwe District	Comment
Land Size and Location	The district occupies a land area of 353 km2.	Located in the Central part of Ashanti Region with a land size of 422.5km2.	The land size of the Bosomtwe district is about 16% larger than that of the Nabdam district.
Population	Nabdam District's projected population is 63,014, consisting of 31,254 males (49.6%) and 31,760 females (50.4%).	Bosomtwe District has a projected population of 119,730, representing a male population of 47.7% and a female population of 52.3%.	The gender distribution in both districts is about the same.
Vegetation	There exist forest reserves in the district, primarily Nangodi and Sakoti reserves.	A large amount of the region lies in the equatorial forest zone.	The forest in the Nabdam district is within the savannah woodland, with short and drought-resistant trees.
Rainy Seasons	It has a tropical climate and has one rainy season with an average annual rainfall of 800mm.	Has two rainy seasons with an average annual rainfall of 1,270 mm.	Bosomtwe district has an advantage over the Nabdam district with an additional rainy season in a year.
Water Bodies	The district has dams and dug outs which serve as sources of water for community members, livestock, irrigation, and for construction works.	Has many geographies of lakes, waterfalls, rivers, springs, and ponds.	Bosomtwe is advantaged with more water bodies.
Agriculture	Predominantly, the people in the district engage in agriculture (about 80% of the working force).	About 63% of the working force engages in agricultural activities.	Both districts are predominantly engaged in agriculture activities for a living.
Health Facilities	The district has 10 health facilities, consisting of 2 health centers and 8 CHPS Compounds serving the population.	The district has 23 health facilities.	Both districts have health facilities. Bosomtwe district has the advantage of training human resources for their health facilities.

(Table continued on next page)

Table 14.1 (Continued)

Physical Structures—Tangibles

Thematic Area	Nabdam District	Bosomtwe District	Comment
Educational Facilities	The district has a total of 70 educational institutions.	Bosomtwe District has 366 schools.	There are facilities within both districts to develop the human resource of the communities in the districts.
Economic Facilities	The major economic activities of the district include agriculture, hunting, forestry, and small-scale fishing.	The district is endowed with economic facilities to aid trade, tourism, and industrial development.	Both districts have great economic facilities that can be enhanced for job creation and revenue mobilization in their respective districts.
Energy	Electricity remains the main source of energy for lighting of households (65.0%).	The district is endowed with three main sources of lighting in households; these are the electricity grid (69.4%), flashlight/torch (16.5%), and kerosene lamp (11.5%).	Communities in both districts rely on almost the same source of energy. Energy is important for community vibrancy, and hence, the most sustainable and cheap source of energy should be encouraged.
Political Facilities	The District Assembly machinery is present in the communities as a partner in the development with the traditional authorities.	The District Assembly machinery is present in the communities as a partner in development with the traditional authorities.	The presence of the district assemblies calls for strong partnerships and effective leadership for growth and development.

Source: Researcher's Construct and Adoptions from the Nabdam District Assembly Composite Budget (2022), and the Bosomtwe District Assembly Composite Budget (2020).

Table 14.2

Social Structures (Intangible)

Thematic Area	Nabdam District	Bosomtwe District	Comment
Chieftaincy	Two paramountcy's: Sakoti-Naba and Nangodi Naba.	Each community has a chief, from Odikro to Omanhene.	Traditional leadership exists in both communities, influencing community leadership.
Festivals	Goug festival in March and Tinlebgere Festival in November.	Akwasidae held regularly at six-week intervals, celebrated as Adeakese if on a Sunday.	Festivals help strengthen collaborative relationships and community bonds.
Lineage	The Nabdams observe the patrilineal system.	The matrilineal system of customary inheritance is observed.	Differences in lineage and inheritance directly influence development processes.
Social Control	Chiefs, Council of Elders, Tendanas, Sub-Chiefs, and Village Herdsmen ensure adherence to law and order.	Social control is implemented through a traditional system of chieftaincy and elders.	Strong social control contributes to a peaceful community by ensuring adherence to rules and values.
Religion	Religious groups: Traditional, Islamic, and Christianity.	Religious groups: Traditional, Islamic, and Christianity.	Religious groupings enhance social participation, companionship, and satisfying relationships.
Politics	Two main political parties: NPP and NDC.	Two main political parties: NDC and NPP.	Democracy is expected to generate effective leadership for growth and development.

show that indigenous and traditional leadership in Ghana today has been overpowered by political structures (The District Assemblies), where community development has been changed to political party development (political interest) which is bringing about serious setbacks in most Ghanaian communities. The functions of the District Assemblies are derived from statute, as mandated by Local Government Act 462 (Faolex, 1993) now Act 936 (LGS, 2016). These functions are broadly aimed at attaining its objectives and fulfilling its mission of improving the quality of life of its people. So, the political-administrative structures are expected to be a key partner to the traditional authorities and are expected to take local content into consideration to ensure sustainable development. Taking local content into consideration will mean a strong collaborative relationship with the traditional authorities.

The results reveal that the relationship between the traditional authorities and the district assemblies is growing weaker and weaker. In terms of collaborative partnerships between the two parties, below are some responses from interviews and interactions undertaken with community members, elders, and politicians.

The local authorities do not have any say or control whatsoever over the natural resources in this district. A good example is mining. People just come with permission documents from the government to mine a place without the traditional leader's and landowners' knowledge. A lot of farmlands are destroyed and there is serious poverty in the communities because of that. **(In-Depth Interview with a Traditional Leader in Bosomtwe Community)**

The District Assembly in my community is always politically biased in the selection of human resources, especially for revenue collection ... they don't involve the traditional leaders who have good knowledge of the people and can help select the right people for the jobs. **(An Elder in the Nabdam community—In-depth Interview)**

The involvement of local authorities in projects in their communities is dependent on the type of project. If it needs local participation, then we involve them. However, if it does not need their involvement, they are only informed. **(In-Depth Interview—Assembly Member, Bosomtwe)**

Issues on arbitration, which was a means of maintaining law and order and ensuring adherence to norms, culture, and values, came up strongly during the interviews. Participants' response are as follows:

In the Ashanti Kingdom, where Bosomtwe District is part, arbitration is key to social control and development in our communities. The government is not helping us in that line; their interference is too much. However, some community members still prefer the traditional arbitration processes because they say it is genuine and has the hand of the ancestral spirits. It is also faster and does not waste time and money. There is nothing like "go come, go come" and there is no paying of so much money which is common with the government procedure. **(In-Depth Interview—A Community Elder, Bosomtwe)**

Community's Partnership With NGOs

Participants from both communities indicated that NGOs had some project interventions in their various communities. Examples of such projects are the provision of potable water by World Vision in the Bosomtwe District and the maternal health project by Oxfam in the Nabdam District. All these projects involved local authorities and community members from the onset through to the end. They were very successful projects and they contributed to enhancing the lives of the community members.

> *Between 2010-2011, an NGO called OXFAM brought a project to our community, the project was on the health of women and children, especially pregnant women. The chiefs, the health workers in the community, community elders, the traditional birth attendants (TBAs), and community volunteers were fully part of this project, and it was very successful.* **(In-depth Interview—A Community Elder, Nabdam)**

Gender Equality and Development

On the question of how the lineage system impacts gender equality and development, the responses below were solicited from the participants:

> *The matrilineal inheritance has its own strengths and weaknesses. In the larger community, women play a powerful role in decision making and their views are highly respected. In most cases, they are the final decision makers, even in the enskinment of chiefs. At the nuclear family level, the system is not favorable to wives and children as they tend to suffer the consequences of the system. In cases where a man passes on, all the property he and his wife acquired will be inherited by his sister and her children living his wife and his own biological children with nothing. In this system, the children belong to the woman.* **(In-depth Interview—Community Elder, Bosomtwe)**

The respondents reiterated the fact that development begins at home, where a fair relationship between spouses is expected. However, the drawbacks of matrilineal inheritance have contributed to poor relationships between spouses, which frustrate the development process, since there is no peace, no honesty, no trust, and unity. They added that things are changing. The story in the Nabdam District is different where the patrilineal system of inheritance has men as the head of the home, the breadwinner, the main decision-maker, and the holder of the property.

> *Taking away initiatives and suggestions from women who are home builders is a big-time loss to the development agenda. That is why the government has asked that every chief should have a Queen Mother, thereby involving women in the decision-making process.* **(In-depth Interview—Queen Mother, Nabdam)**

Discussion

The discussion explores the connection between the physical and social structures of Nabdam and Bosomtwe districts and sustainable development. Physical structures, such as land size, location, natural resources, health and educational facilities, and energy sources, play a crucial role in the economic activities, well-being, and environmental sustainability of the districts. On the other hand, social structures, including traditional leadership, social cohesion, access to resources, social control, religious involvement, and governance, are vital for achieving sustainable development goals. Understanding the unique challenges and opportunities in each district helps in developing appropriate strategies for sustainable development.

The ToC, as emphasized by the Center for Community Health and Development (2022), is pivotal in fostering positive change, growth, and development in a community when good leadership is enforced with strong collaborative partnerships among stakeholders. However, the study revealed that political interference in traditional administrative structures and procedures, resulting in unauthorized mining activities and unsuitable projects for political gain, has led to environmental degradation, poverty, weak collaborative partnerships, and development setbacks. To ensure consistent and sustainable development, it is recommended to minimize governmental and political intrusions and engage traditional leaders and elders in the decision-making process.

In summary, the ToC, intertwined with sustainable development, requires a holistic approach that considers both tangible and intangible structures and emphasizes good leadership, collaborative partnerships, and community engagement to address unique challenges and opportunities in each district.

Conclusion

To achieve sustainable development, it is important to promote sustainable economic, social, and environmental practices in both districts. For example, promoting ecotourism in the Bosomtwe district can help to create jobs and economic opportunities while preserving the environment. Similarly, promoting sustainable agriculture in the Nabdam district can help to increase food security while reducing the environmental impact of farming practices.

Overall, by leveraging the unique characteristics of each district and promoting sustainable practices, both the Nabdam and Bosomtwe districts can achieve sustainable development. This requires a comprehensive approach that considers the various thematic areas of sustainable development, including economic, social, and environmental sustainability.

The importance of community development and meaningful exchanges between community structures and established conventions for interactions is highlighted in the study. ToC is emphasized to yield positive change and growth in a community but requires good leadership and strong collaborative partnerships. Political and partisan interferences in administrative structures and procedures in communities can hinder development, emphasizing the need to minimize governmental and political intrusions and interferences and to consult and engage with traditional leaders and elders for meaningful and sustainable development. By working together, stakeholders in both districts can create a brighter future for their communities and promote sustainable development for generations to come.

REFERENCES

Abukari, A. M. (2021). *The history of Mole Dagbon State*. Retrieved April 10, 2023, from https://dagbonkingdom.com/history-of-mole-dagbon-state/

Asante, E. A., Ebeheakey, A. K., Opoku-Bonsu., K., & Cornah, J. (2019). The unwritten historical perspectives of Akan spokespersons staffs. *African Journal of History and Culture, 11*(1), 1–10. https://doi.org/10.5897/ajhc2018.0408

Bartle, P. (2011). *Community empowerment collective*. Retrieved November 11, 2022, from Vancuver Community Network. https://doi.org/http://www.cec.vcn.bc.ca/cmp /whatcom.html

Bocken, N. M. P., & Geradts, T. H. J. (2020). Barriers and drivers to sustainable business model innovation: Organization design and dynamic capabilities. *Long Range Planning, 53*(4), 3–16. https://doi.org/10.1016/j.lrp.2019.101950

Bonye, S. Z., Aasoglenang, A. T., & Owusu-Sekyere, E. (2013). Community development in Ghana: Theory and practice. *European Scientific Journal, 9*(17), 79–98.

Bosomtwe District Assembly. (2020). *Composite Budget for 2020–2023*. Programme Based Budget Estimates for 2020. Government of Ghana.

Center for Community Health and Development. (2022). *Our model of practice: Building capacity for community system change*. University of Kansas. https://doi.org/https://ctb.ku.edu/en/table-of-contents/overview/

Chavis, D. M., & Lee, K. (2015). *What is community anyway?* Stanford Social Innovation Review. Retrieved April 4, 2023, from https://ssir.org/articles/entry/what_is_community anyway.

Duranton, G., & Puga, D. (2020). The economics of urban density. *The Journal of Economic Perspectives, 34*(3), 3–26. https://doi.org/https://www.jstor.org/stable/26923539

Food and Agricultural Organization (Faolex). (1993). *Act 462*. Retrieved September 18, 2023, from https://faolex.fao.org/docs/pdf/gha91927.pdf

Global Fund. (2022). *Technical brief community systems strengthening allocation period from 2023–2025*. Retrieved April 4, 2023, from https://www.theglobalfund.org /media/4790/core_communitysystems_technicalbrief_en.pdf

Gottlieb, J., & Robinson, A. L. (2016). *The effects of matrilineality on gender differences in political behavior across Africa*. University of California.

Gunderson, L. (2010). Ecological and human community resilience in response to natural disasters. *Ecology and Society, 15*(2), 18. https://doi.org/10.5751/es-03381-150218

Hanachor, M. E., & Olumati E. S. (2012). Enhancing community development through community education. *Journal of Education and Practice, 3*(14), 59–62.

Kongela, S. M. (2020). Gender equality in ownership of agricultural land in rural Tanzania: Does matrilineal tenure system matter? *African Journal on Land Policy and Geospatial Sciences, 3*(4), 13–27.

Leininger, M. M. (1985). Ethnography and ethnonursing: Models and modes of qualitative data analysis. In M. M. Leininger (Ed.), *Qualitative research methods in nursing* (pp. 33–72). Grune & Stratton.

Local Governance Service (LGS). (2016). *Act 936*. Retrieved September 18, 2023, from https://lgs.gov.gh/local-governance-act-of-2016-act-936/

Ministry of Environment. (2013). *Finland: Community structures*. https://doi.org/ https://www.ymparisto.fi/en-us/living_environment_and_planning/Community_structure

Nabdam District Assembly. (2022). *Composite Budget for 2022–2025*. Programme Based Budget Estimates for 2022. Government of Ghana.

OECD/Noya A., & Clarence E. (2009). *Community capacity building: Fostering economic and social resilience. Project outline and proposed methodology, working document*, CFE/LEED, OECD. www.oecd.org/dataoecd/54/10/44681969.pdf?contentId=44681 970

Owusu, G., & Agyei-Mensah, S. (2011). A comparative study of ethnic residential segregation in Ghana's two largest cities, Accra and Kumasi. *Population and Environment, 32*, 332–352. https://doi.org/10.1007/s11111-010-0131-z

Parada, H., Barnoff, L, Moffatt, K., & Homan, M. S. (2012). *Promoting community change: Making it happen in the real world* (2nd Canadian ed.). Nelson Education.

Robinson, J. W., & Green, G. P. (2011). Developing communities. In J. W. Robinson & G. P. Green (Eds.), *Introduction to community development* (pp. 1–18). SAGE.

Sakalasooriya, N. (2020). *The concept of development: Definitions, theories and contemporary perspectives*. https://doi.org 10.13140/RG.2.2.17378.48323

Shaw, M. (2008). Community development and the politics of community. *Community Development Journal, 43*(1), 24–36.

The University of the South Pacific. (2014). *CEC31: Basic concept of community development*.

APPENDIX

List of Interviewees (Participants)

Bosomtwe District

No.	Role or Position in the Community	Gender of Person
1	Chief	Male
2	Assembly member	Male
3	Queen mother	Female
4	Elder	Male
5	Women group leader	Female
6	Sunday special football association	Male
7	Opinion leader	Male
8	Assembly member	Male

The table above is a simple construct by the researcher indicating the number, position held in the Bosomtwe community, and the gender of those who participated in the research.

Nabdam District

No	Role or Position in the Community	Gender of Person
1	Paramount chief	Male
2	Queen mother	Female
3	Women group leader (CMA)	Female
4	Assembly member	Male
5	Community elder	Male
6	Elderly woman	Female
7	Youth group leader (Association of Dressmakers)	Female
8	District assembly member	Male
9	Market queen	Female

The table above is a simple construct by the researcher indicating the number, position held in the Bosomtwe community, and the gender of those who participated in the research.

CHAPTER 15

SUSTAINABLE COMMUNITY DEVELOPMENT PRACTICE IN AFRICA

Cultural Competemility and Professionalism Informed Approach

Paula Ugochukwu Ude

ABSTRACT

Attaining effective outcomes in implementing sustainable community development projects remains a global concern and social workers' responsibility to address. One factor that limits community development projects maintaining sustainability is the need to integrate culture into practice. In other words, the necessity of recognizing the worth of community people and stakeholders' viability in building and sustaining their projects and being able to actively engage them in every plan or step involving the projects. This chapter suggests the implementation of the cultural competemility and professionalism model—a practical approach that guides community development social workers on how to actively engage community people and stakeholders in building sustainable community projects in Africa. This approach is rooted in resilience and constructive social perspectives. It embraces cultural diversity and inclusion, thus adopting an ubuntu ideology—engaging in human connectedness and togetherness while serving and mobilizing community people to attain effective project outcomes. This chapter unpacks the meaning of cultural competemility and professionalism and expounds its history, key concepts (interpersonal relationships, service interpretation, strength, and intervention identification) and application process. The innovation of

Community Development Practice in Africa: Putting Theory Into Practice, pp. 227–241
Copyright © 2024 by Information Age Publishing
www.infoagepub.com
All rights of reproduction in any form reserved.

the cultural competemility and professionalism model is its applicability. The model offers three simple mathematical steps (contextual knowledge, experiential knowledge, and convergence) and systematic guidelines on integrating culture into practice for effective outcomes when building sustainable ubuntu community development. Finally, this chapter highlights and discusses social work policy implications and some challenges or obstacles that can impede the successful application of the cultural competemility and professionalism model.

Keywords: diversity, intervention, inclusion, model, practice, social worker, Ubuntu

Introduction

Building a sustainable ubuntu community development (CD) in African communities remains a global concern and social workers' responsibility to address. Community development is defined as a process of working with communities to help them recognize the needed economic, political, social, and religious issues; and how to improve their community life and welfare both in the present and in the future (Banks et al., 2016). Social workers in the field of CD must practice cultural competemility and professionalism to help develop and build community projects that is sustainable (International Association of School of Social Workers [IASSW], 2018; International Federation of Social Workers [IFSW], 2020; Ude, 2021). In other words, they must be culturally competent, humble, and professional in executing community development activities" (IASSW, 2018; IFSW, 2020).

Experts in community development recommended utilizing the asset-based community development (ABCD) model, which centers on the adoption of a participatory community approach that allows assessing the strengths and capacities of a community and its stakeholders (Butterfield et al., 2009). However, to achieve the goal of what ABCD model is recommending requires one's understanding of how to integrate culture into practice—being culturally sensitive, inclusive, and diversified. Adopting a cultural competemility and professionalism approach that embraces cultural diversity, inclusion and sensitivity will help social workers build a sustainable community development as social workers are sanction to be culturally competent, humble, and professional in their practices to attain an effective community development that embraces the ubuntu ideology, "you are because we are" (IFSW, 2020).

Many literatures underscore some challenges that encourage setbacks in achieving success in building sustainable community development in Africa (Ling et al., 2009; Pawar, 2014). For example, lack of community inclusion and incorporation of Western concepts prove unsuccessful in attaining a community development that is inclusive, culturally sensitive, and sustainable in African communities (Kalibatseva & Leong, 2014; Van Schalkwyk, 2015). The cultural competemility and professionalism approach fosters cultural diversity and inclusion. Thus, allowing the social workers to apprehend the need to exhibit humility when helping individuals, families, groups, and communities encircled by poverty regain their potential (IFSW, 2020). It guides social workers to becoming co-builders of the community, while the community people are the builders. This chapter explicates the concept of cultural competemility and professionalism, application process, the model in relation to community development, social work policy implications and challenges to successful application outcomes of cultural.

Cultural Competemility and Professionalism Conceptualization

Definition and Brief History. The importance of incorporating cultural competence and humility in social work practice is essential, as revealed in a study conducted by Ude (2021) on the help-seeking behaviors of perinatal African diaspora women. The study identified the hindrance of cultural integration to the participants' help-seeking process during perinatal periods. The term competemility, which refers to competence and humility, was coined from Stubbe's (2020) research on the need for cultural humility in social work. Professionalism is also crucial in this field and requires social workers to prioritize the community's interests and maintain competence, humility, and integrity while providing expert advice on community development and sustainability (Vivanco & Delgado-Bolton, 2015).

The cultural competemility and professionalism model, drawn from resilience and social constructivism, emphasizes community resilience in the face of adversity and understanding the meanings people hold about interventions. This model offers practical guidelines for implementing cultural diversity and inclusion in practice and recognizes clients' self-determination. It also encourages social workers to learn from community members, including chiefs, elders, men, women, and youth groups, to address community needs effectively during the helping process (Trager, 1998; Ude, 2021). Ultimately, this cultural practice model teaches social workers to step outside themselves and learn from the community to help solve identified or presenting problems.

Key Concepts

The cultural competemility and professionalism model is built on the foundation of four key concepts: (1) interpersonal relationships; (2) service interpretation; (3) strength; and (4) intervention identification. *Interpersonal relationship* is an interaction or interconnectedness between social work professionals, the community, and people. Being culturally competent and humble helps build and improve the working relationship between the professional and client and encourages a better understanding of problems and collection of solutions (Poulin et al., 2016). *Service interpretation* is an ability for professionals to move beyond their own interpretations of problems and interventions to deepen understanding of how the community's people interpret the presenting problem and its solutions. During the decision-making process, the client's definition, perspectives and concern about the problem and intervention remain the focus of social workers (Marsh, 2002; IFSW, 2020). The service interpretation highlights the essentiality for community development social workers to explore, assess, and recognize the community people's interpretation of a community development project and how good a fit or culturally sensitive it is in addressing their community's needs. *Strength identification*, as a concept, centers on identifying community resilience—identification of community adaptive capacity such as economic development, social capital, and community competence (Butterfield et al., 2009; Norris & Stevens, 2007). In other words, identifying and assessing community strengths would help bring the community development project to success. The final concept of *competemility and professionalism* is *intervention, which is a* social worker's ability to formulate a culturally sensitive intervention and provide accessible resources to clients. Clients who interpret the services they receive as in line with their culture or have culturally accommodative professionals would be more likely to stay with the professional and benefit from the services or program (Kalibatseva & Leong, 2014).

Cultural Competemility in Relation to Community Development

Community development is an essential aspect of social work professional activities as social workers face challenges in extending cultural knowledge, values, and skills to build community (IFSW, 2020; Johnson-Butterfield & Chisanga, 2008). In contributing knowledge, skills, and values to build an ubuntu sustainable community development, the social work profession recognizes respect for culture, diversity, inclusion, community people-centeredness, and self-determination (IASSW, 2018). It recommends understanding the totality of people's culture and cultural influences when working with people to build their community projects (Johnson-Butterfield & Chisanga, 2008). People's culture is an "umbrella term that subsumes with [their] values, beliefs, customs, rituals, practices and behaviours [and] combination of the material and non-material components of human society that is as fluid as it is diverse" (Yancu & Farmer, 2017, p. e1). The IFSW (2020) code of ethics also enjoins social workers to be aware of cultural sensitivity and diversity and their relevancy during a client-worker relationship and uphold them throughout the helping process. This sanction on culturally sensitivity also implies that African community development social workers should be sensitive and embrace African culture, values, traditions, and beliefs while understanding African community people's interpretations of community, development, and help-seeking as in the African contextual framework, nothing exists outside traditions and customs and community people (Molefe, 2019; Van Breda, 2019).

Significantly, any projects developed or built without the involvement of custodians or conservators (community elders, chiefs, women) would struggle for survival (Trager, 1998; Ude, 2021). Globally, factors such as geographic misfortune, regional disparity, political instability, and policy inattention toward community development and social services impede the success of community development (Hameed et al., 2017). African rural communities are not exempt as they battle with economic and political failures and are confronted with daunting challenges. However, being culturally competent and humble helps social workers to learn from the community people and stakeholders on how they can collaboratively and effectively work to co-build and promote sustainable communities, especially the impoverished communities combatting economic, political, and social injustices (Trager, 1998).

Application of Cultural Competemility and Professionalism Model

This section talks about how competemility and professionalism model can be used in African localities and communities as part of the process of community development. It also provides recommendations and guidelines for incorporating culturally sensitive questions during the assessment and intervention change process to engage community members in sustainable community development effectively. The cultural competemility and professionalism model suggests applying three practical steps to help a social worker succeed when helping communities realize their potential while developing their community. This author developed and provided some case examples or scenarios to help community development social workers to have a clear understanding of how this model can be applied in community development settings. See the diagram below displaying the application model process and the case example that demonstrate each application step. See the Appendix for a diagram depicting cultural competemility and professionalism model application process developed by this author.

The first step is community development social work professionals' ability to be aware of contextual information (notional knowledge). This step is described as what is known (previous information about clients' issues/problem, diversity, cultural, race, etc. cultural diversity) about community development in general, culture, tradition, community people's way of life, the economic status of the community they want to develop, and history of the community Professionals gain this information, knowledge, and skills through education, training, professional development, community referrals, the media, talking with community members, organizational notes from organizations involved with the community, past and present, and other sources (IFSW, 2012). This is considered competence. Being culturally competent requires professionals' knowledge of the interplay of cultures in how different communities view and interpret problems and help-giving to build trusted relationships with them (Alpers, 2018). With this information, social workers develop knowledge about clients' social problems, cultural differences, traditions, dynamics, and diversity and become competent in providing services to communities (Stubbe, 2020). In the community development context, social workers develop knowledge of the community and its history, specific problems, or project to be implemented, community strengths or adaptative capacity, power blocks, and factors impeding community development success (IFSW, 2012; Ude, 2021). Also, having this knowledge and skills enables the social work professional to cultivate attitudes of respect and acceptance to work with the community (Cai, 2016; IFSW, 2012). This below case example provides more conceptualization about the first step of cultural competemility and professionalism.

Case Example for step one. A community development social worker was consulted to help a community tackle a water issue that plagued them. Before assisting the community in embarking on this project, the social worker, though with many years of experience working on different community development projects, was unfamiliar with the water project and never worked with this community. However, with limited knowledge about the water project, this community development social worker researched and gained more knowledge about the water project, how to consult and engage the experts, and the process involved in establishing clean water in any communities. Additionally, this social worker understands the community culture and economic status through education, training, and research and acquired professional experience and skills working with several African communities on successful projects. In this case, this community development social worker is culturally competent in community development, especially when he or she recognizes his or her own culture and cultivates respect to this community culture.

The second step of cultural *competence and professionalism is e*xperiential knowledge—new information professionals gain from clients to understand the client's perspectives regarding the identified problem and intervention (Ude, 2021). In the context of community development, experiential knowledge is considered as the information the social workers gather from the community people to understand the identified problem (history, previous intervention, etc.) a little better. To understand the problem from community peoples' perspectives and their interpretation of seeking and receiving help especially from someone outside their community, professionals must cultivate the attitude of humility—a willingness to learn the problem and intervention from the community members' perspective (Stubbe, 2020; Ude, 2021). According to Chan and Reece (2021):

> Cultural humility captures a person's ability to assume and maintain an interpersonal stance where they are open to the other with respect to aspects related to cultural identities the other holds as most important [and] with such a stance, a person is better able to understand the unique beliefs, values, and worldviews held by those whose cultures differ from their own. (p. 31)

Accordingly, learning requires humility and cultivating the "I don't know it all" attitude is a key to successful learning. In other words, acquiring humility as a virtue or skill helps to improve community social workers' ability to learn from the community people, to listen and collaborate with them to strategize solutions to their problems (Chan & Reece, 2021; Marsh, 2002; Stubbe, 2020; Ude, 2021; Yancu & Farmer, 2017). The case example below provides more understanding of this second step.

Case example for step two. Community development social worker received a grant to help a community start a community health center. Despite the social worker's limited knowledge about community development as regards to African communities, culture, traditions, and factors that lead to successful outcomes, the community people need to be involved and engaged in the project throughout the helping process (Ude, 2021). During the needs and strengths assessment and intervention process, social workers should be able to talk to and involve community people in the planning and implementation and ask for their advice and opinions on the intervention measures. For example, if a social worker failed to consult or engage the community stakeholders simply because the social worker perceived them as uneducated or unenlightened, there is a tendency that the community people may decline the social workers' help. In the African cultural context, it is common to engage chiefs, elders, youth, and women's groups in decision-making. The social worker is considered culturally humble if they, despite the expert knowledge, sought the opinions of this community people on the health center project and engaged them in the intervention progress.

Convergence (contextual information plus experiential knowledge) is the third step of *cultural competemility and professionalism*. This step includes professional interpretation of themes that emerged from their professional knowledge, practice, and the data/information collected from stakeholders about the problem and intervention, analysis, interpretation, evaluation, and integration of both information (Butterfield et al., 2009; Ude, 2021). This is considered professionalism—social worker's ability to interpret, analyze, evaluate, and integrate the previous knowledge about the community and community development, and information gathered from the community to develop an action-driven intervention or an intervention plan that is culturally sensitive and appropriate while putting first the interest of community people (Ude, 2021; Vivanco & Delgado-Bolton, 2015). Professionalism demands placing the interests of the community above those of the social worker, setting and maintaining the standards of competence, humility, and integrity, and providing expert advice to community people on the matter of community development and sustainability (Vivanco & Delgado-Bolton, 2015). This process will also allow social workers to design structured and constructive intervention plans that are based on hierarchical needs of the community and engage the community people in the decision-making process during the planning, implementation, and evaluation processes to build their capacity-based strengths (Butterfield et al., 2009; Norris & Stevens, 2007).

Case example of professionalism (Step 3 of the model). By gaining community people or stakeholders' perspectives about health center projects and interventions, the community development social worker could analyze, interpret, and evaluate the information and identify the emerging themes through his/her interpretations. Professionalism comes when community development social workers incorporate these three pieces of information (contextual, experiential, and professional interpretation) into the intervention plan and implement the intervention based on the plan. Throughout the intervention process, the community development social worker should continue cultivating respect for the community people and consult and involve them in any evaluation process.

To achieve effective and efficient results in helping a community achieve sustainable ubuntu community development, all steps of *cultural competemility and professionalism* must be taken. It is common for professionals to jump from Step 1 to Step 3 and this affects the professionals' ability to develop and maintain a culturally sensitive and sustainable community development. Also, developing an intervention plan that takes culture into account will help meet the needs of communities and make them more likely to seek help or come back for it.

Applying the model of competemility and professionalism allows social workers not only to be culturally sensitive when engaging in sustainable community development to help reduce social and economic disparities, but it also helps social workers to learn from and engage the conservators in community development as their storytelling and speaking back are valuable to the development of a community (Csesznek, 2021). The cultural competemility and professionalism model in ubuntu ideology embraces serving the community people, which urges social work professionals when engaging in community work to:

> Go to the people, live among them, learn from them, and love them. Start with what they know, build on what they have: But of the best leaders. When their task is accomplished, their work is done. The people all remark "We have done it ourselves. (as cited in Poulin et al., 2016, n.p.)

The cultural competemility and professionalism model is community-centered, and the above statement captures its totality. This is in line with the social work profession's mission, which sanctions social workers to respect diversity by taking account of community differences, recognizing, and treating its members as a whole person while focusing on capacity-building and empowering them through a human-centered developmental approach (IFSW, 2018).

Social Work Policy Implications of Cultural Competemility and Professionalism

Utilizing cultural competemility and professionalism when engaging in community development would effectively achieve social work mission goals—capacity building through a human-centered approach. However, it is essential to address the policy inadequacies that can undermine its success in the African community. Two of these policies, economic and education, are discussed below.

Economic Policy Implications

Economic challenges posed a threat to social workers' effort to utilize cultural competemility and professionalism in African community development context. The goal of the social work profession is to help lift individuals, families, groups, and communities from poverty and all sorts of oppression (IFSW, 2020). However, because the profession is relatively young, especially in most African localities, achieving this mission goal most often proves unsuccessful (Dhavaleshwar, 2022; Hameed et al., 2017). Since the social work profession is still striving to survive in Africa, economic and political system elites have yet to attend to how social workers' discussions and decision-making on community development intervention affect social work practice conditions and thus sidetracks the standard practice of social work in Africa (Hameed et al., 2017). Conversation on genuineness and transparency in economic, political, religious, and social systems is important to establish and to effectively apply cultural competemility and professionalism model during the community development process (Hameed et al., 2017; Ling et al., 2009; Pawar, 2014).

In any cultural localities where social work has passed its developmental stage and the economic, political, social, and religious systems accost genuineness and transparency, government sets policy guidelines that control, monitor, and evaluate community development projects' proposals (Pawar, 2014). Building an ubuntu sustainable community development that is culturally sensitive requires economic and political backing as transparent and genuine government fortifies, revives, and challenges institutional structures that perpetuate corruption or impede the achievement of community development activities' goals (Hameed et al. 2017; Ling et al., 2009; Pawar, 2014). A genuine government apportions personnel whose roles would be to evaluate and monitor all the community project activities, processes, and outcomes, and ensure they are culturally sensitive and meet the community's needs.

Education and Knowledge Implications

Social work professionals aim to empower individuals, families, groups, and communities to help them bounce back from adversity (Gutierrez et al., 1998). In creating consciousness-raising through education, social workers help the community to deeply understand the complex social, economic, and political realities that negatively impact their community. Education is essential in aiding the community to deeply understand their human rights and how they can voice their needs, gain support, and improve community needs (Dhavaleshwar, 2022; Gutierrez et al., 1998). This may be due to their lack of knowledge and understanding of community development, total funds allocated for the project, and fear of losing the project. So, a model of cultural competence and professionalism is in line with the empowerment perspective and is essential to helping the community regain the power to solve any of its problems (Hameed et al., 2017).

The model effectively helps social workers to be transparent in helping the stakeholders understand the intricacies of the project (Dhavaleshwar, 2022; Ude, 2021). These include, but are not limited to, educating, or orienting the community people on the project goals, objectives, and timeline; total funds allocated for the project; and explaining community people's rights as they relate to the project (Dhavaleshwar, 2022);Social workers' engagement in active listening and openness to stakeholders' suggestions and recommendations on how to make the project better ultimately improves the relationship and project (Ling et al., 2009; Marsh, 2002; Pawar, 2014; Ude, 2021).

Challenges to the Application of Cultural Competemility and Professionalism Model

Certain factors impede or challenge a successful application of cultural Competemility and professionalism during the community development process in different social work practice settings. In a community development practice setting, social workers need more knowledge about community development work and continuing education/training on integrating culture into practice. Achieving and maintaining a high standard of sustainable community development requires knowledge beyond a social worker's basic social work knowledge and skills and demands certain levels of education and practice experience (IASSW, 2018; IFSW, 2012). Social work education is still dragging itself to attain international standards survival in some African localities, and some schools need good structure and decolonized instructional materials to attain and maintain high-quality programmes that meet the standards that would prepare students to work as community development social workers (Alamu, 2022; Veta & McLaughlin, 2022).

For example, some schools or universities lack access to social work-related organizations or social agencies that would match their students to engage them in gaining practice experience that would help practice affecting the community development field settings. Consequently, not being adequately trained may affect community development social workers' ability to recognize and appreciate their own culture and may experience difficulties in learning how to be culturally competent and humble and integrate culture into practice when working with the community people (Cai, 2016; Stubbe, 2020; Yancu & Farmer, 2017). It is imperative to establish and strengthen unified African social work professionals or accreditation bodies in different African regions who would be responsible for evaluating, monitoring, and accrediting African social work education and field practice programmes to ensure they meet the global standards as sanctioned by International Association of School of Social Workers and International Federation Association of Social Workers and (IFSW, 2020). These professional bodies put regulations on social services and welfare agencies hiring not only non-social graduates but also have a clear definition of job descriptions for social workers graduate with undergraduate, master's level graduate and as well those field practice experience in community development settings (Veta & McLaughlin, 2022).

Additionally, there is a need for Africa as a continent or each country of the continent to set up a social work board that would monitor social work education and practice. Thus, one of these is ensuring that community social workers engage in professional development (continuing education/training), particularly on cultural competence and humility. Social work educators should also encourage students who intend to practice in community development to do fieldwork placement or require them to gain a certain required number of fieldwork hours in the community development area before graduating and practicing in any community development and welfare agencies (Alamu, 2022). This will help them learn from other professional social workers how to be culturally sensitive when working with the community or integrate culture into practice.

Conclusion

This chapter examines cultural competemility and professionalism and how it can be incorporated into community development when assisting communities in creating and maintaining innovative and sustainable community development projects. This model allows social workers to integrate cultural competence and humility into cultural knowledge and practice when working with any communities to address economic, social, political, and religious disparities, to attain innovative and sustainable community development projects. The chapter also discusses the key concepts of cultural competemility and professionalism, including interpersonal relationships, service interpretation, strength identification, and intervention, and the three steps of the application process. These steps are contextual knowledge, experiential knowledge, and convergence. The chapter underscores the importance of education and economic policies to enhance the social work profession that embraces cultural competemility in professionalism in Africa. The author also highlights the lack of standards and inadequate social work guidelines as factors that can hinder effective and efficient utilization of cultural competemility and professionalism model. Improving social work education programs, such as providing continuing education and training in the areas of cultural competency, humility, and professionalism in community development practice are recommended as measures to addressing these hinderances.

REFERENCES

Alamu O. I. (2022). Challenges of social work in Nigeria: A policy agenda. *African Journal of Social Work, 11*(3), 116–122.

Alpers, L.M. (2018). Distrust and patients in intercultural healthcare: A qualitative interview study. *Nursing Ethics, 25*(3), 313–323. https://doi.org/10.1177/0969733016652449.

Banks, G., Scheyvens, R., McLennan, S., & Bebbington, A. (2016). Conceptualising corporate community development. *Third World Quarterly, 37*(2), 245–263. http://10.0.4.56/01436597.2015.1111135

Butterfield, A., Kebede, W., & Gessesse, A. (2009). Research as a catalyst for asset-based community development: Assessing the skills of poor women in Ethiopia. *Social Development Issues, 31*, 1–14.

Cai, D. Y. (2016). A concept analysis of cultural competence. *International Journal of Nursing Sciences, 3*(3), 268–273. https://doi.org/10.1016/j.ijnss.2016.08.002

Chan, L. & Reece, A. (2021). Positive cultural humility in organizations. In C. Chen & S. I. Donaldson (Eds.), *Positive organizational psychology interventions* (pp. 125–140). Wiley Blackwell. https://doi.org/10.1002/9781118977415.ch6

Csesznek, C. (2021). Speaking back by storytelling—A method for increasing critical thinking and engagement in community development. *Revista Universitara de Sociologie, 17*(1), 51–58.

Dhavaleshwar, C. (2022). *Short review paper: The role of social worker in community development*, 61–64. https://doi.org/10.2139/ssrn.2854682

Gutierrez, L. M., Parsons, R. J., & Cox, E. O. (1998). *Empowerment in social work practice: A sourcebook*. Brooks/Cole.

Hameed, G., Saboor, A., Khan, A. U., Ali, I., & Wazir, M. K. (2017). Impact of community development in poverty reduction: Reflections of Azad Jammu and Kashmir community development program. *Social Indicators Research, 130*(3), 1073–1086. https://doi.org/10.1007/s11205-016-1235-3

International Association of Schools of Social Workers. (2018). *Global social work statement of ethical principal.* https://www.iassw-aiets.org/wp-content/downloads/global-social-work-statement-of-ethical-principles-2018/Global-Social-Work-Statement-of-Ethical-Principles-IASSW-27-April-2018-01-English.pdf

International Federation of Social Workers. (2020). *Global standard for social work education and training.* https://www.ifsw.org/global-standards-for-social-work-education-and-training/#practiceeducation

International Federation of Social Workers. (2020). Global Definition of Social Work. https://www.ifsw.org/what-is-social-work/global-definition-of-social-work/

Johnson-Butterfield, A. K., & Chisanga, B. (2008). Community development. In T. Mizrahi & L. Davis (Eds.), *Encyclopedia of social work*. Oxford University Press.

Kalibatseva, Z., & Leong, F. T. L. (2014). A critical review of culturally sensitive treatments for depression: Recommendations for intervention and research. *Psychological Services, 11*(4), 433–450. https://doi.org/10.1037/a0036047

Ling, C., Hanna, K., & Dale, A. (2009). A template for integrated community sustainability planning. *Environmental Management, 44*(2), 228–242. https://doi.org/10.1007/s00267-009-9315-7

Marsh, J. (2002). Learning from clients. *VeLex, 47*(4), 1–5. https://www.researchgate.net/publication/11019375

Molefe, M. (2019). Ubuntu and development: An African conception of development. *Africa Today, 66*(1), 97–115. https://doi.org/10.2979/africatoday.66.1.05

Nabudere, D. W. (2005). *Ubuntu philosophy: memory and reconciliation* [Document]. Kigali, Centre for Basic Research.

Norris, F. H., & Stevens, S. P. (2007). Community Resilience and principles of mass trauma intervention. *ProQuest Psychology Journals, 70*(4), 320–328.

Pawar, M. (2014). Social work practice with local communities in developing countries: Imperatives for political engagement. *SAGE Open, 4*(2). https://doi.org/10.1177/2158244014538640

Poulin, J., Matis, S., & Witt, H. (2018). Using supervision to guide professional development and behavior. *The Social Work Field Placement*, 51–68. https://doi.org/10.1891/9780826175533.0003

Stubbe, D. E. (2020). Practicing cultural competence and cultural humility in the care of diverse patients. *Focus, 18*(1), 49–51. https://doi.org/10.1176/appi.focus.20190041

Trager, L. (1998). Home-town linkages and local development in South-West Nigeria, whose agenda? What impact? *Africa, 68*(3), 360–382.

Ude, P. (2021). *Perinatal mood and anxiety disorders among women in the African Diaspora: Knowledge and help-seeking behaviors* [Unpublished Doctoral Dissertation]. Millersville University of Pennsylvania.

Van Breda, A. D. (2019). Developing the notion of ubuntu as African theory for social work practice. *Social Work (South Africa), 55*(4), 439–451. https://doi.org/10.15270/55-4-762

Veta, O. D., & McLaughlin, H. (2022). Social work education and practice in Africa: The problems and prospects. *Social Work Education*. https://doi.org/10.1080/02615479.2022.2029393

Vivanco, L., & Delgado-Bolton, R. (2015). Professionalism. *Encyclopedia of Global Bioethics*, 2312–2319. Springer. https://doi.org/10.1007/978-3-319-05544-2_353-1.

Yancu, C. N., & Farmer, D. F. (2017). Product or process: Cultural competence or cultural humility? *Palliative Medicine and Hospice Care—Open Journal, 3*(1), e1–e4. https://doi.org/10.17140/pmhcoj-3-e005

APPENDIX

Cultural Competemility and Professionalism Model Diagram

Diagram depicting cultural competemility and professionalism model application process

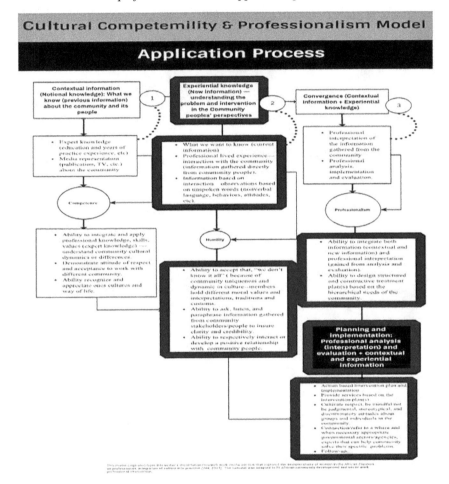

CONCLUSION

Somnoma Valerie Ouedraogo

In this book, we have explored various themes and concepts that collectively underscore the significance of stakeholders, the expansion of perspectives in community development theories and models, and the essential role of empowering communities in Africa. We have emphasized the voices of traditional leaders to strengthen communities in terms of engagement, networking, and knowledge mobilization for and with the community itself. Therefore, the community itself as the driver of development is the core message that connects all the contributions of this book. All themes highlighted in this book have consistently underlined the interconnectedness of social, cultural, economic, and political values in the approach to community development in Africa. The need to merge various facets of African community development with historical and theoretical knowledge in the field reinforces the importance of ongoing engagement for sustainable development.

One of the central messages that permeates our book is the pivotal role that the community plays as the driving force behind development. It is imperative that we understand the community as the dynamic nucleus of development efforts. The community is not a passive recipient of external interventions but an active and creative agent in shaping its own destiny. Through the lens of sustainability and cultural values, our contributors have demonstrated that when community development is approached, designed, and implemented in a sustainable manner, it results in the harmonious coexistence and interconnection of the diverse elements within a community, ultimately contributing to its development. These diversities, which were once seen as potential sources of conflict, are harnessed as the very strengths that fuel the community's growth and development.

This book reinforces the relevance of community development in Africa, given the continent's unique history and distinctive social structures. Africa's history is rich and diverse, characterized by a tapestry of cultures, languages, and traditions. This uniqueness presents both challenges and opportunities in the realm of community development. The practical implications of the book are twofold and inherently connected. First, the adoption of an Ubuntu approach—a concept deeply rooted in African philosophy—to strengthen engagement and commitment with the community itself. Ubuntu encapsulates the spirit of togetherness, emphasizing the interconnectedness of all individuals and the importance of compassion and mutual support. When applied in community development, Ubuntu transcends individualism and fosters a sense of collective responsibility. Secondly, the promotion of a strength-based approach that recognizes and embraces the diversities within a community spanning social, political, cultural, religious, economic, and environmental dimensions. Ubuntu, as a guiding philosophy, underscores the importance of wisdom and intuition in shaping the course of community development in African communities. When Ubuntu assumes a central role, community development promotes the well-being of people in harmony with their environment, fostering prosperity. Thus, using Ubuntu to address community diversities highlights the synergies that these diversities contribute to the community's prosperity. As conveyed by all the chapters, it is essential to underscore the uniqueness of each approach and contextualize it within the historical, cultural, and social dynamics of Africa.

Over the past decade, we have witnessed a global shift toward decolonial actions in various disciplines and professions, including social work and community development. These actions involve incorporating alternative forms of knowledge and amplifying voices that were historically suppressed. Community development, too, is part of this transformative process, embracing Ubuntu in action as a way of organizing rooted in the African way of being and doing. Hence, it is imperative, as this book is reaffirming, to continue promoting community development in Africa and incorporating decolonial curricula in educational programs worldwide. Stakeholders are encouraged to actively engage with community development professionals, collaborating to merge knowledge and strategies across governments, civil society, households, and international partners. This can be achieved by reinforcing intra and interregional collaborations, fostering international and transnational partnerships, and building and sustaining holistic, participatory, and sustainable community development approaches. In the spirit of Ubuntu, community development will prioritize just and equitable knowledge sharing, with the community itself remaining at the core of development design and programs. We must continue to promote Ubuntu as a guiding principle in community development, which emphasizes cooperation, compassion, and interdependence, fostering a harmonious and equitable development trajectory.

In conclusion, we reflect on the significance of historical perspectives and the pivotal role of traditions in community development. Decolonial actions have enabled us to uncover suppressed histories and traditions and acknowledge their contributions to community development. This journey leads us to reclaim festivals, ceremonies, spirituality, naming, and community stories as avenues that will continue to enrich community development, both in Africa and globally. We express our profound gratitude to the ancestors who made this book possible and to all our contributors for their unwavering commitment and patience throughout the writing and editing process. The importance of shared knowledge and collaboration in advancing community development in Africa is a journey we must all embark on together. Stakeholders, community members, policymakers, practitioners, scholars, and educators all play integral roles in this journey, with the shared ambition to go far and to embrace the transformative processes within our communities. By continuing to be open to new and innovative approaches, we can collectively contribute to the development and flourishing of communities, both in Africa and around the world.

CONTRIBUTORS

Abdulrazak Karriem is an associate professor at the Institute for Social Development at the University of the Western Cape, where he teaches courses on Migration and Development, Theories of Social Transformation, Urban and Regional Development, and Research Methods. He has conducted field research in Brazil and South Africa and his research interests include social movements, citizen participation, food security, migration and development, and urban agriculture. He has participated in several research projects funded by entities such as the South African government, the European Union, and the German government. He has published journal articles and book chapters on social movements and rural development, food security, and urban agriculture.

Atieno Obara Rebeccah Chawiyah is a passionate Kenyan educator with a focus on Gender and Development Studies. She has held leadership roles as Chief Principal at Achego Girls' High School and Rae Girls' High School, where she focused on enhancing teaching standards, managing finances, and staff development. Her research addresses Gender-Based Violence in Kenyan universities, and she is active in the Mothers' Union and as a Gender Activist. She also has experience as a lecturer at Masinde Muliro University and Kisii University, teaching courses on Disaster Management and Gender Based Violence. She enjoys reading, empowering women and girls, and socializing. Her strength comes from prayer and gospel music, and she stays active with sports like tennis. Committed to both personal and professional growth, she consistently seeks new challenges to make a meaningful impact in the fields of education and gender studies.

Babatunde Ayoola Fajimi is Occupational Social Work and Human Resources Management Consultant with over two decades of professional practice working with nonprofit organizations and MSMEs across West and Central Africa. He is a first-class alumnus of the University of Ibadan and currently a post-graduate scholar in the Department of Adult Education, University of Ibadan, Nigeria. He is a member of numerous professional organizations, including Nigerian National Council for Adult Education and National Association of Social Workers. His areas of research interest include Occupational Social Work and Community Development, Management and Workplace Practices, and Social Entrepreneurship. He has published over 23 papers in local and international journals.

Charles Gyan is an Assistant Professor of Social Work and Social Policy at McGill University, School of Social Work. He holds a PhD in Social Work from Wilfrid Laurier University and a Master of Philosophy degree in Social Work from the University of Ghana. He integrates his academic and research pursuits with a dedicated focus on fostering social policy change, advancing transnational social work practices, and contributing to community development. His research endeavors are rooted in a profound commitment to social justice, driving his exploration of ways to unveil, disrupt, and challenge prevailing dogmas, structures, and discourses that contribute to the perpetuation of subjugation and oppression faced by marginalized groups.

Eunice Abbey is a lecturer at the Department of Social Work at the University of Ghana. Prior to her appointment at the University of Ghana, she was a lecturer at the Methodist University College Ghana. She earned her PhD from Hong Kong Polytechnic University. Eunice has presented her research papers at international, national, and regional conferences and has published in leading journals such as *Global Social Welfare, Children and Society, Social Sciences* and *Journal of Comparative Social Work*. She is presently leading a research project on health and rural development.

Fred Moonga is a Lecturer and Head of the Department of Sociology and Social Work at the University of Eswatini. Over the past two years, he has been a member of the University's Human Subjects Ethics Committee. Previously, he worked as Lecturer and Head of Department of Social Development Studies at Mulungushi University and a Research Coordinator at REPSSI. He also worked at World Food Program and Government of Zambia as Social Welfare Officer earned his PhD in Social Work from Stellenbosch University, a MSc from the University of Southampton, U.K., an MSW from Gothenburg University, Sweden, and a BSW from the University of Zambia. His scholarly interests encompass social protection, gerontology, ecological social work, and child welfare.

Hanna Nel, an emeritus professor in the Department of Social Work and Community Development at the University of Johannesburg is a passionate researcher and educator. For the past 15 years, her research has primarily focused on community development, with a specific emphasis on asset-based citizen-led development (ABCD) in South Africa. She has a publication list of 59 articles and chapters in accredited journals and books. She was a co-author with two colleagues of a book on community development of which the second edition was published in 2021. Hanna has guided 59 post-graduate students on master's and doctoral levels in graduating.

Irene Ayalo is a Senior Lecturer and Registered Social Worker currently teaching social work and community development at Unitec Institute of Technology/Te Pukenga in Auckland, New Zealand. She migrated to Auckland from Kenya in 2006 and obtained her PhD from Auckland University of Technology in 2012. She has presented research papers at global, national, and regional conferences with her primary interest lying in community impact research and bridging the traditional gap between theory and practice. Over the last four years, her research has focused on issues impacting ethnic migrant communities. Some of her research findings have been published in leading national peer-reviewed journals, such as the *Aotearoa New Zealand Social Work Journal*.

Linda Kreitzer is a Professor Emerita at the University of Calgary, Faculty of Social Work having taught for 15 years in the Faculty of Social Work. Her research work has centered on social work curriculum in Africa. She has authored one book called *Social Work in Africa: Exploring Culturally Relevant Education and Practice in Ghana*. She has co-authored three other books. Her present research continues to support the decolonization of social work curriculum in Africa through a document analysis of African social work documents from the 1970s–80s and a case study of an African woman's fight against British Imperialism in 1900.

Matthew Mabefam is a lecturer in Anthropology and Development Studies in the School of Social and Political Sciences at the University of Melbourne. He has expertise in international development and specializes in anthropology of development, care, education, inequality, and development. His work contributes to the decolonization of development epistemes, knowledge bases, and practices. His research has been published in a range of International Development journals, including *Development in Practice*,

Forum for Development Studies, Critical African Studies, Int. J. Gender Studies in Developing Societies, and *Energy Economics*. He is an executive member of Development Studies Association of Australia and a Thematic Editor for *Development in Practice Journal*.

Meinrad Lembuka holds an MA in social work and MA in International Cooperation. He possesses extensive experience as a multi-disciplinary and multicultural expert in the area of social work, health, public policies, international relations, gender, key populations and Ubuntu. He has worked in Twining Centre Project for seven years under Tanzania Association of social workers and American International health where he participated in a number of national task forces in development, assessment and review of a number of policies and guidelines in Tanzania. Presently, Meinrad is an Assistant Lecturer of social work at The Open University of Tanzania, and he has specialized in African Ubuntu research and practice.

Paula Ugochukwu Ude, is an Assistant Professor of Social Work at Concord University, Athens, West Virginia. She holds a Master of Social Work License and Doctorate in social work education and leadership from Millersville University of Pennsylvania, United States. Paula has extensive experience in community and hospital case management in various rural cultural settings. Her passion lies in advancing innovation in practice among diverse populations and advocating for the integration of a "cultural competemility and professionalism approach" to enhance the effectiveness of social work education and interventions. Her work has been presented at local and international conferences and published in various journals, including *International Social Work,* and *Journal of National Association of Social Workers*.

Atieno Paul Okello is a High School Principal and PhD candidate at Kisii University. He has 29 years of experience in teaching, mentoring, coaching, and training both learners and teachers. His interests lie in education management, project management, conflict management and community development. He is a full member of The Kenya Institute of Management, Red Cross Society of Kenya, Gusii Mediators' Association, and International Association for Community Development. His research has been published in refereed journals, including *Research on Humanities and Social Sciences, Journal of Studies in Social Sciences, World Scientific Research, World Journal of Advanced Research and Reviews, International Journal of Research and Innovation in Social Sciences* and *Lambert Academic Publishing* among others.

Oino Gutwa Peter, is a senior lecturer and the current Dean of the School of Arts and Social Sciences at Kisii University. He has been awarded over

10 research grants (both individual and collaborative) on various thematic fields such as food security, culture, leadership and development, climate change, mobility and livelihoods, morality and wellbeing and disability. He has extensive knowledge in mixed method research and has published widely. He has consulted for county governments, national and international NGOs. He is the founder of Genesis of Development Foundation (2012) and Elevate, Livelihood, Peace, and Advocacy (ELPA), national NGOs working towards improving the lives of vulnerable populations in Kenya.

Rosemary Anderson Akolaa is a lecturer at the University of Environment and Sustainable Development, Somanya, Ghana. With over two decades of experience, she is not only a passionate academic but also a fervent advocate for community development and health. Holding a PhD in Endogenous Development, alongside degrees in Public Health Informatics, Education, and Agricultural Science, she embodies a synthesis of in-depth knowledge and practical expertise. She played a pivotal role in the transformative Access to Healthcare Campaign in Ghana and is renowned for her contributions to community nutrition, public health, gender issues, and food security. Energetic yet seasoned, she remains at the forefront of impactful research and advocacy.

Senkosi Moses Balyejjusa is a lecturer in the department of Social Work and Social Administration at Kyambogo University, Uganda. His previous work focused on the wellbeing of refugees using a human needs framework. Currently, he is focused on researching and developing social needs framework for social work practice. He has presented at both global and regional conferences and has published in peer reviewed journals such as *African Development, Social Change, Journal of Science and Sustainability,* and in edited book volumes such as the Ubuntu practitioner. He earned a PhD in social change from the University of Melbourne (Australia) and holds a Master of Social work from McGill University, Canada.

Shakespear Hamauswa holds a PhD in Development Studies from the University of KwaZulu-Natal, an MSc in International Relations, and a BSc Hons in Political Science, both from the University of Zimbabwe. He is currently a Member of Parliament in Zimbabwe. He taught Political Science and International Relations at University of Zimbabwe and Mulungushi University in Zambia. He has published more than 25 book chapters and journal articles in the field of governance and development.

Shamiso Mandioma has a master's degree in development studies from University of the Western Cape. She is a PhD student in Development

Studies and lecturer at the Institute for Social Development at the University of Western Cape, where she teaches Community Development Theory and Practice and Research Methods. She has conducted research in South Africa and Zimbabwe and her research interests include food security, community development, citizen participation, gender inequality, rural and local governance. She has participated in research projects funded by the European Union and South African government. She also served as a project coordinator for the Germany Academic Exchange Service from 2021–2022.

Sheilas K. Chilala is a lecturer in the School of Social Sciences at Mulungushi University, Zambia. She previously worked as a lecturer at National College for Management and Development Studies (NCMDS), Zambia. She has presented research papers at international conferences. She has also published in refereed journals. She holds a Master of Social Work Degree (MSW) from the University of Botswana; Bachelor of Social Work Degree (BSW) from the University of Zambia. Her research interests encompass women and youth empowerment, social protection, and community development.

Somnoma Valerie Ouedraogo, Associate Professor at MacEwan University School of Social Work (Canada) holds a PhD in Social Work from the University of Kassel (Germany). She has focused on the pedagogy of social work education and analytical inquiry related to local knowledge, culture, and conflict. Dr. Ouedraogo has conducted research concerning remigration experiences and social service delivery to adults due to forced return migration from Côte d'Ivoire to Burkina Faso and is committed to building social work local knowledge mobilization in Burkina Faso. Her current works are about the impact of political conflict on the organization and delivery of social services to adults in Burkina Faso (The British Academy Fellowship), Afrocentric Social Work scholarship (Canadian Social Sciences and Humanities Grant–SSHRC) and local understanding of Environmental Sustainability in relation to Social Work role in Canada (Internal Project Grant MacEwan University).

Thembelihle Brenda Makhanya is a senior lecturer at the University of Mpumalanga. She previously worked as a lecturer at the University of KwaZulu-Natal, in the discipline of Social Work. She is the founder and chairperson of Imbewu Youth Empowerment Centre. She previously offered professional services to the Department of Correctional Services, as a facilitator and a coordinator for Victim Offender Mediation Dialogue (VOM-D). She has presented papers at international, national, and regional conferences. She has produced several peer reviewed publications in areas around decolonization, higher education access, social justice, climate change, fatherhood and ubuntu. She has received several awards, including Working Groups Programme research funding from the National Institute for the Humanities and Social Sciences (NIHSS), Emerging Social Work Educator of the Year 2021 from the Association of South African Social Work Education Institutions (ASASWEI).

Venesio Bwambale Bhangyi is assistant lecturer in social work at Kyambogo University, Uganda. He also works as a public health social worker with Uganda's Ministry of Health. He served on the board of the National Association of Social Workers of Uganda (NASWU) from 2011 to 2016. His research has been featured in peer-reviewed journals, including *International Social Work* and the *African Journal of Social Work*. His work has also been included in edited book volumes that explore themes in public social services, social policy, social development, eco-social work, and social work theory. He holds an Erasmus Mundus master's in advanced development in social work (ADVANCES). He earned his BSW from Makerere University.

Victor Chikampa is a lecturer of Psychology at Mulungushi University in Zambia. He graduated from the University of Stellenbosch with a Master and Honors Degree of Commerce in Industrial Psychology and a bachelor's degree in psychology with education from the University of Zambia. He has 15 publications under his name in refereed journals. He has also presented research papers at regional and national conferences. His area of research includes psychometrics, traffic psychology, human resources, career psychology, consumer behavior and child psychology. He is currently pursuing a PhD in Industrial Psychology with the University of Stellenbosch.

Vyda Mamley Hervie is a lecturer at the University of Ghana, Legon. Prior to her appointment at the University of Ghana, she served as an Associate Professor/Senior researcher at the Norwegian Social Research (NOVA), Oslo Metropolitan University, Norway. She holds a PhD in Social Work and Social Policy from Oslo Metropolitan University, Norway. Her core research interests include elderly care/ageing, disabilities, child welfare, gender, health, and migration. She has attended several expert conferences and published in peer-reviewed journals, including *International Psychogeriatrics*, *Global Social Welfare*, *Social Inclusion*, and *Children and Youth Services Review*.

William Abur is a lecturer and researcher at the University of Melbourne. He has extensive experience in working with refugees and migrants, both in his research capacity and as a social worker. His PhD thesis, titled "Settlement Strategies for the South Sudanese Community in Melbourne: An Analysis of Employment and Sport Participation," delves into the nuances of settlement strategies for refugees and migrants. He has a wide range of publications in peer-reviewed articles, book chapters, and books. Notably, his work includes *A New Life with Opportunities and Challenges: The Settlement Experiences of South Sudanese Australians*, published by Africa World Books. He has worked on several research projects where he managed projects and grants. He is a member of the ethic committee who reviews research ethic applications at the University of Melbourne.

INDEX

A

ABCD: 67, 68, 69, 70–74, 76, 78–80, 228, 249
Abloh: 8, 13, 17, 118, 127
Accountability: 5, 10, 18, 88, 120, 123, 159
Action plans: 5, 14
Adamtey: 127
Africa: 3–7, 12–14, 23–28, 31–35, 42, 51–55, 58, 60, 61, 67–70, 78–83, 85, 86, 88, 89, 90 95, 127–129, 131, 145, 146, 149, 150, 154 160–163, 181–183, 186, 193–198, 201, 202, 211, 216, 224, 227–229, 231, 236, 238, 240, 243–245, 247–249, 252, 254
African: 3–5, 7, 8, 13, 14, 23–26, 102, 107–110, 118, 120, 121, 126, 127, 154, 163, 164, 174, 181–187–192, 198, 202, 228, 229, 231, 233 – 237, 243, 244, 247, 249–253
African centered: 99, 101, 102, 105, 108, 110
African Cultural Values: 51, 52, 61
African culture: 3, 5, 9, 69, 74, 79, 80, 101, 105, 188, 231
African identity: 186

African nationalism: 7
African Socialism: 53, 55
African societies: 4, 24, 25, 99, 102,
African traditional community development: 14
African traditional knowledge: 23, 27
African Worldview: 68, 69
Afriyie: 5, 121, 126, 128
Afrocentric: 99, 100, 105–107, 109, 252; Context: 106, 107, 109, 110; Conscientization:
 106; myths, 106; culture: 101, 103, 105, 106, 107, 110
Agencies: 41, 44, 45, 95, 119, 122, 135, 136, 144, 168, 170, 175, 197, 201, 237, 238
Agency: 43, 70, 80, 107, 131, 139, 142, 168, 198
Agrarian livelihood practices: 36, 47
Agricultural: 45, 56, 60, 87, 92, 123, 131–139, 141, 143, 144, 199, 218, 251
Agriculture: 8, 12, 40, 56, 57, 70, 88, 89, 132, 133, 135, 137, 139, 155, 165, 198, 218, 219, 223, 247

255

256 INDEX

Aid: 5, 8, 12, 23, 46, 131, 133, 135, 139, 183
Amoah-Mensah: 121, 126, 127
Anand: 89, 96
Anderson: 90, 96
Anyidoho: 152, 154, 157, 160
Apartheid: 101, 102, 107
Arusha Declaration: 55, 56, 58, 121
Asante: 6, 105, 106, 107, 110, 216
ASPEF: 137
Asset-Based Community Development model: 67, 68, 101, 104, 105, 106, 107, 109, 110;
Asset-based: 67, 68, 72, 99, 101–107, 109, 110, 228; Phases of, 67, 68, 72, 73, 76, 78; Connecting and discovering 67, 72 –75; Dreaming/vision 67, 72, 73, 75–76; Designing 78, 73, 76; Delivery, 67, 73, 77–78; Disconnecting 67, 72–73, 77–78; Departing 67, 72–73, 77–78; Participatory Monitoring & Evaluation, 68, 72, 78; Techniques of, 67, 68, 72, 78: Storytelling, 67, 74; Mapping, 67, 68, 74–75; Head, heart and hands, 74; Leaky bucket, 67, 75; Venn diagrams, 75; Community visioning, 75; Participatory Monitoring and evaluation (PERT), 67, 72, 73, 75, 76, 77, 78; Gannt, 76; gathering and activating assets, 76; autonomy, 77; questionnaires, 78; interviews, 78; group discussions, 78; photo, 78; drama, 78
Assets: 38, 39, 67, 70–78, 80 99, 100, 102, 105, 107, 109, 110, 134, 136, 138, 152, 170

Atieno: 85, 87, 90, 96, 247, 250
Autoethnography: 117, 121, 122, 127

B

Baishya: 94, 96
Baldwin: 150, 160
Ballem: 94, 96
Bandewar: 140, 145
Bangladesh: 87, 88, 91
Barnett: 153, 160
Barreteau: 108, 110
Bartel: 121, 126
Bataka: 41, 45
Belonging: 57, 103, 205
Benevolence: 11, 187
Bharamappanavara: 90, 96
Bhattacharyya: 141, 143, 145
Bikpakpaam: 117, 118, 121, 122, 123, 124, 125, 126, 127
Bimbilla: 124, 125
Binib gbaan kpa Kimɔkbaan pam: 123
Birmingham: 101, 111
Block: 70, 74, 76, 80
Bolni: 123, 124
Bondarenko: 18
Bonye: 5, 14, 18, 213, 214, 224
Botho: 69
Bottom–up: 8, 16, 23, 26, 28, 29, 30, 36, 46, 47, 100, 101, 131, 132, 136, 153
Bratton: 12, 18
Braun: 74, 80, 122
British colonial rule: 53
British education system: 7
Brody: 86, 88, 96
Brons: 69, 81
Brooks: 77
Building blocks: 37, 67, 68, 80, 135
Bulungi Bwasi: 41, 46
Bunhu: 69

Bureaucracy: 172, 175
Burkey: 134, 135, 145

C
Capabilities: 38, 39, 68, 70, 74, 75, 105, 136, 141,
Capacity building: 12, 80, 89, 105, 132, 135, 139, 152, 154, 235
Capital: 40, 56, 118, 126, 132, 163, 164, 167, 169,170,174
Capitalism: 5
Cavaye: 152, 160, 170, 176
Chambers: 135, 136
Chaskin: 152, 160
Chauya: 100, 108, 111
Chawane: 104, 105, 111
Chazovachii: 136, 145
Chereni: 69, 82
Chief: 6, 151, 155, 156, 158, 160, 211, 215, 216, 220, 222, 226, 229, 231, 234, 247
Chieftaincy: 7, 171, 217, 220
Chitere: 89, 97
Civil society Organizations (CSOs): 3, 16, 203
Civil war: 41
Climatic: 132
Collaborative: 16, 38, 46, 71, 75, 100, 103, 134, 140, 143, 163, 164, 207, 213, 220, 221, 223, 224, 251
Collective: 3, 4, 5, 28, 35, 36, 41, 52, 53, 54, 57, 69, 72, 76, 77, 79, 85, 90, 91, 92, 93, 104, 105, 109, 110, 122, 128, 134, 139, 143, 152, 164, 175, 182, 184, 188, 193, 200, 211, 244
Collective Farming: 54
Collier: 121, 126, 128
Colonial legacy: 8
Colonial: 3, 6, 7, 8, 16, 52, 53, 54, 55, 72, 101, 109, 118, 119, 121, 122, 137, 183,184

Colonialism: 3, 5, 6, 7, 8, 101, 102, 107, 110, 119, 188
Colonization: 28, 29, 69, 120, 127, 189
Communal: 3, 4, 5, 6, 13, 17, 25, 52, 54, 55, 56, 123, 125, 126, 164, 188, 189, 213
Communal Labor: 5, 6, 8, 9, 13, 14, 16, 17, 125,
Community: 67–70, 72–80, 85, 86, 87, 88, 89, 91, 93, 95, 99, 100–110, 134, 135, 136,
149, 150, 151,163–175; Systems: 211, 212, 214, 215, 216, 243, 244, 245
Community–Based Organizations (CBOs): 3, 9, 16, 41, 42, 75, 104, 184, 212
Community Development Associations (CDA): 163, 164, 165, 166, 167, 168, 170, 171,172, 173, 174
Community Development: 1–17, 23, 28, 30 –39, 42, 51, 53–65 56, 58, 85–89, 91, 95, 99, 100–110, 117–127, 131–137, 149, 150, 151, 153, 154, 159, 160, 163–174, 181–193, 197, 198, 199, 202, 211, 213, 215, 220, 223, 227–238, 243, 244, 245; dynamic: 120; Actors: 9; Approaches: 28–30, Depoliticization: 44, 45, Politicization: 42, 43, 45, Collaborative effort: 25; Human needs: 38, 39, Cultural aspects: 4–5; Principles: 149, 151, 153, 154, 159, 160; problems, assets, mobilizing, 153; planning and vision, 153; implementation, 153; monitoring and evaluation, 153
Community–driven: 67, 68

Community Elders: 25, 31, 222, 231
Community Engagement: 30, 106, 131–137, 139, 140, 142, 143, 144, 223
Community Initiatives: 57
Community involvement: 119, 198
Community Needs: 35, 36, 37, 41, 108, 229, 236
Community Organizing: 117, 118; Design: 118, 119; Planned: 118; Implemented: 118
Community Services, 40, 41, 124
Conflicts: 85, 86, 93, 95, 96, 186
Cooperative labor: 3, 4, 14, 16
Cornwall: 154, 157, 160
Corporate sector: 67, 68
Corvée: 6
COVID: 101, 200
Critical: 87, 93, 95, 103, 104, 106, 110, 181–187, 190, 191, 192, 212, 215
Cultural Competemility: 227, 228, 229, 230, 231,232, 234, 235, 263, 237, 238, 241, 250
Cultural Institutions: 40, 41
Culture: 3, 5, 8, 28, 37, 42, 46, 51, 68, 69, 72, 74, 77, 79, 80, 89, 101, 103, 105, 106, 107, 110, 150, 159, 188, 193, 212, 215, 216, 221, 227, 228, 230–233, 235, 237, 238, 251, 252
Customary Arrangements: 5
Czech: 92, 97

D
Dabo: 121, 126
Dagbani: 154, 216
De Beer: 74, 83, 134, 135, 136, 145
Decekura: 154
Decentralization: 3, 9, 10, 16

Decision-making: 5, 10, 16, 24, 30, 33, 42, 119, 136, 153, 167,169, 186, 187, 190, 191, 193, 211, 222, 223, 230, 234, 236
Decolonization: 53, 58, 60, 61, 101, 106, 249
Decolonial: 100, 102, 106, 244, 245
Decoloniality: 68, 105, 106
DeJonckheere: 139, 145
Democracy: 57, 69, 72, 102, 182, 185, 189, 190, 220
Demonstration: 131, 139, 140, 143
Desai: 92, 97
Development: 4–7, 9–14, 67, 68, 70–72, 74, 76, 77, 79, 80, 94, 95, 96, 99, 100, 101, 103–110, 121, 123–127,131–138, 142–145, 149, 150–157, 159, 160; approaches: 16, 23, 45, 104, 117, 118, 120, 121, 127, 244, Human development: 16, 25, 27, 40, 206, Policies: 13, 42, 55; Politics, 36, Plans, 35, 36, 42, 43
Development Aid from People to People (DAPP): 131, 133, 135, 138, 139, 140, 142, 143
Dias: 155, 160
Digital divide: 15
Dinbabo: 152, 153, 154, 157, 160
Discrimination: 29, 102, 110
Dogbe: 143, 145
Dogbevi: 156, 160
Dube: 135, 146
Du Sautoy: 7,8, 19

E
Economic: 7, 12, 13, 15, 26, 39, 53, 54, 55, 68, 71, 75, 79, 85–90, 92, 93, 94, 95, 101, 103, 122, 125, 126, 134, 150, 152, 154, 166, 169, 170, 185, 186, 187, 190, 198, 205, 206, 211,

212, 213, 219, 223, 228, 231, 232, 233, 235; Challenges: 13, 132, 235; Disparities: 187, 235
Economic development: 9, 11, 16, 17, 38, 40, 42, 77, 230
Economically: 52, 85, 89, 101
Education: 8, 12, 24, 27, 32, 39, 40, 45, 51, 52, 57, 59, 60, 69, 75, 107–109, 164, 167, 199, 212, 232, 233, 235, 236, 237, 238, 247, 248–252
Effects: 7, 16, 40, 88, 93, 119
Eliasov: 71, 73, 74, 77, 81
Emmett: 68, 81
Empowerment: 24, 32, 37, 38, 39, 40, 41, 85, 86, 87, 88, 91, 99, 100–104, 107, 108, 110, 132, 135, 136, 152, 154, 156, 206, 236, 252; Women empowerment: 12, 40
Engagement: 24, 46, 67, 69, 70, 73, 95, 99, 102, 106, 108, 122, 131, 132, 133, 135, 137, 138, 139, 140, 142, 143, 149, 150, 152, 155, 160, 191, 205, 237, 243, 244,
Ennis and West: 79, 81
Environmental: 27, 54, 59, 60, 152, 170, 188, 223, 244, 252
Environmentally sustainable: 86
Environmental management: 31
European: 99, 101, 107, 181, 182, 185, 186, 247, 252
Exposure: 14, 108, 139, 140, 142
Extended Family: 54, 57
External: 41, 58, 61, 68, 72, 74, 76, 77, 79, 88, 91, 117, 118, 119, 120, 124, 127, 164, 167, 168, 169, 172, 174, 175, 213, 243

F
Fairfax: 109, 111
Faith-based: 41, 100

Families: 24, 26, 28, 38, 40, 57, 69, 87, 94, 126, 144, 190, 193, 197, 203, 229, 236
Family helping systems: 41
Familyhood: 56, 121
FAO: 132, 146
Farmers: 13, 91, 93, 122, 125, 131–133, 135–145, 154
Farming: 24–27, 31, 54, 122, 125, 131, 132, 134, 139, 142, 143, 144, 154, 158, 223
Festivals: 4, 5, 8, 9, 14, 171, 217, 220, 245
Fonchingong: 154, 157, 160
Food Security: 12, 89, 132, 133, 137, 141, 223, 247, 251, 252
Foot: 79, 81
Forced labor: 3, 6, 16, 28
Forced Villagization: 59
Fostering systems: 46
Foundation: 33, 36, 41, 61, 69, 70, 80, 90, 155, 156, 157, 158, 159, 182, 230, 251
Frediani: 68, 81
Friedli: 79, 81
Fundraising: 5, 26, 163, 164, 168, 169, 170, 171, 172, 173, 175

G
Gade: 69, 81
Gender: 12, 36, 37, 41, 43, 85, 119, 124, 165, 167, 186, 188, 191, 214, 215, 218, 222, 226, 247, 250, 251, 252, 253
Ghana: 3–21, 117, 118, 119, 121, 122, 123, 124, 126, 127, 149–151, 154, 157, 158, 159, 211–216, 220, 248, 249, 251, 253
Global: 8, 11, 24, 60, 86, 99, 100, 101, 110, 185, 188, 189, 199, 212, 227, 228, 237, 244, 248, 249, 251, 253
Globalization: 8, 15

Goel: 100, 103, 104, 105, 108, 109, 111, 152, 160
Governance: 6, 41, 94, 155, 166, 173, 174, 223, 251, 252
Government: 3, 4, 7, 9, 10, 12–17, 28, 29, 30, 35, 36, 37, 38, 40–46, 57–59, 67, 68, 71, 78, 79, 80, 85, 86, 87, 90, 91, 95, 96, 100, 102, 106, 131–137, 139, 143, 144, 150, 156, 163–175,184, 185, 188, 189, 197, 198, 200, 201, 203, 204, 207, 211, 212, 220–224, 236, 244, 247, 248, 251, 252
Government interventions: 41
Grameen Bank: 87, 88
Grassroots: 12, 13, 85, 86, 87, 95, 99, 100, 110
Group work: 25
Gugerty: 87, 90, 96, 97
Gyan: 3, 4, 5, 13, 15, 19, 119, 126, 128, 248

H

Haines: 38, 39, 47, 70, 71, 74, 75, 77, 81, 105, 111, 161
Hamer: 109, 111
Hearn: 103, 109, 111
Health: 40, 45, 51, 52, 59, 74, 86, 87, 88, 90, 91, 93, 151, 155, 166–168, 191, 203, 206, 212, 214, 218, 222, 223, 233, 234, 248, 250, 251, 253
Historical: 16, 35, 36, 37, 46, 109, 110, 243, 244, 245
HIV/AIDS: 41, 200,
Homan: 70, 71, 74, 77, 81
Households: 42, 85, 94, 95, 219, 244
Human development: 16, 25, 27, 40, 206
Humanitarian: 40, 41, 155

Human Needs: 35, 37, 38, 39, 44, 103, 251
Human Rights: 24, 38, 39, 40, 41, 68, 102, 182, 185, 186, 187, 188, 201, 236
Hustedde: 103, 104, 111

I

IASSW: 103, 228, 230, 237
Ife: 38, 47, 70, 71, 75, 81, 184, 194
IFSW: 103, 111, 228, 229, 230, 231, 232, 235, 236, 237, 238
Imbewu: 99, 100, 101, 107, 108, 110, 252
Implementation: 7, 12, 13, 26, 45, 78, 104, 118, 119, 132, 133, 137, 138, 144, 149, 153, 155, 159, 160, 167–170, 181, 202, 207, 217, 227, 233, 234
Inclusiveness: 103, 107
India: 88, 89, 90, 91, 94, 200
Indigenous: 24, 29, 35, 38, 42, 43, 44, 45, 51, 52, 55, 58, 61, 72, 101, 102, 117, 181, 182, 185, 211, 215, 220
Indigenous knowledge: 31, 32, 68, 101, 136
Indigenous philosophies: 189
Informal: 38, 41, 44, 45, 70, 72, 78, 88, 89, 95, 164, 165, 175, 215
Informal Community Development: 45
Infrastructure: 4, 6, 15, 40, 60, 104, 166, 170, 188, 212
Infrastructure development: 175
INGOs: 12, 16
Institutions: 4, 14, 17, 40, 41, 75, 77, 88, 90, 91, 95, 96, 100, 101, 108, 134, 136, 150,156, 171, 185, 187, 190, 193, 201, 217, 219, 253, 252, 253

Interests: 28, 29, 35, 37, 47, 93, 105, 107, 118, 134, 137, 143, 165, 174, 188, 201, 202, 203, 205, 229, 234, 247, 249, 250
International community development: 28, 29, 119
International Monetary Fund (IMF): 12
Interventions: 36, 37, 38, 39, 41, 42, 43, 44, 45, 46, 47, 68, 71, 78, 80, 85, 91, 95, 99, 100, 106, 107, 110, 119, 125, 139, 143, 153, 155, 205, 206, 221, 229, 230, 234, 243, 250
IYEC: 99, 100, 105, 107, 108, 109

J
Japan's Official Development White Paper: 155, 161
Jatropha: 149, 150, 151, 154, 155, 156, 157, 158, 159
Jimbira: 133, 146
Jobra: 87
Johar: 76, 81
Justice: 99, 110, 150, 181–193, 197, 198, 200
Justice system: 12, 200, 201, 202, 205
Juvenile delinquency: 199, 200, 207
Juvenile justice system: 13, 200, 201, 203, 207

K
Kachim: 122, 128
Kariuki: 150, 161
Karriem: 131, 136, 141, 143, 146, 247
Kenny: 108, 111, 152, 161
Kenya: 85, 86, 90, 140, 181, 185, 186, 187, 188, 191, 192, 249, 250, 251
Kenyase: 119

Kilimo cha Ujamaa, 56
Kimɔkbaan: 123, 124, 126
Kiting aa mumuun: 123
Knowledge sharing: 139, 140, 244
Knowledge Transfer: 140, 144; Storytelling, 31, 67, 74, 235
Konkomba: 117, 122
Kramer: 70, 81
Kreitzer: 3, 103, 105, 111, 151, 161, 187, 188, 196, 249
Kretzmann: 70, 71, 81, 104, 111, 228
Kuhudzayi: 133, 146

L
Labone: 155
Labonte: 154, 156, 160
Landry and Peters: 68, 72, 77, 81
Leader: 94, 120, 140, 141, 151, 158, 221, 226
Leadership: 6, 24, 27, 29, 31, 33, 46, 69, 71, 72, 76, 77, 104, 120, 134, 135, 149, 150
Livelihoods: 16, 38, 52, 74, 85, 86, 90, 131, 132, 133, 139, 142, 143, 144, 193, 251
Local community groups: 24, 27, 28, 29, 30
Local economic development: 11, 38
Local governance: 252
Local Government: 3, 5, 9, 10, 16, 36, 38, 41, 43–46, 79, 150, 165, 171, 172, 212, 220
Local knowledge: 28, 29, 31, 109, 134, 153, 154, 158, 159, 252
Localities: 47, 231, 236, 237

M
Maasole: 122, 128
Mabefam: 117, 120, 121, 122, 128, 129, 249
Mabovula: 120, 126, 129

MacLeod & Emejulu: 79, 82
Makhanya: 99, 100, 101, 102, 104, 105, 107, 108, 109, 112, 252
Mansuri: 12, 20
Mansvelt: 68, 70, 82
Maphosa: 69, 82
Marginalized: 15, 38, 85, 86, 87, 89, 103, 135, 184, 192, 193, 248
Mass Education: 3, 7
Masuku: 102, 112
Mattessich: 105, 112, 136, 143, 146
Mathie: 68, 70, 71, 75, 80, 82
Mawere: 150, 161
Mazowe: 131, 133, 138, 139, 142, 143, 144
Mbiti: 5, 20
McKnight & Block: 70, 81, 82
McMillan: 136, 146
Meehan: 89, 97
Mensah: 141, 146
Mfoafo-M'Carthy: 119, 126, 128
Microfinance: 12, 88, 91
Millennium Development Goals: 126, 184
Mion: 154
M-muumuu: 122, 123
Mobilization: 4, 9, 35, 37, 45, 70, 107, 110, 163, 167, 169, 170, 186, 219, 243, 252
Modernization: 13, 14, 134, 153
Mole-Dagbon: 212, 215, 216
Moniruzzaman: 155, 161
Morse: 70, 82
Mugumbate: 24, 25, 26, 27, 28, 29, 30, 31, 32, 33, 34, 52, 53, 54, 55, 57, 62, 69, 82, 121, 126, 129
Mukute: 137, 142, 146
Multilateral Humanitarian Organizations: 41
Mutual aid: 5, 8, 21, 46
Mupindu: 137, 147
Mutami: 137, 147

Mutisi: 133, 137
Murove: 121, 129
Mutual aid groups: 46
Mwongozo: 56, 57

N
NABARD: 89, 90
Nanton: 154
Narayan-Parker: 136, 137
Narrative: 99, 122
National Development Agenda: 60
National Development Plan (NDP): 38, 43, 44
Ndima: 150, 161
Ndlovu–Gatsheni: 101, 106, 112
Nel: 67, 68, 69, 70–72, 74–78, 82, 100, 101, 103, 104, 105, 107, 108, 109, 112
Network: 39, 141, 206
NGOs: 12, 13, 17, 40, 41, 89, 90, 91, 92, 95, 105, 107, 108, 109, 112, 121, 123, 125, 126
Nhongonhema: 137, 147
Nichols: 88, 97
Nigeria: 163, 164, 165, 166, 167, 168, 169, 171, 172, 173, 216, 248
Nkpawiin: 121, 123, 125, 126
Nnoboa: 5, 8, 9, 117, 121, 126
Non-state actors: 87
Nossal: 150, 161
Noya: 154, 161
Nukunya: 4, 14, 16, 20

O
Odell: 90, 97
Offenders: 197, 199, 201–207
Offiong: 154, 161
Ohayo Ghana Foundation: 155
Okia: 6, 7, 20
Okoth: 102, 112
Okubo: 104, 112
Olson: 92, 93, 97

Organization for Economic Cooperation and Development (OECD): 20, 97, 213
Ornellas: 103, 112
Ouedraogo: 243, 252
Ownership: 13, 16, 24, 31, 68, 70, 72, 76, 77, 80, 100, 123, 124, 125, 154, 156, 214

P

Paradza: 150, 156, 161
Parish Development Model: 42, 43
Participation: 7, 9, 10, 16, 17, 24, 25, 38, 74, 78, 85, 86, 89, 92, 94, 95, 100, 103, 108,
109, 110, 119, 132, 135, 136, 140, 142, 143, 149, 150, 151, 153–159, 163, 164, 165, 167, 168, 170–175, 182– 185, 187, 189, 190, 193
Participatory: 10, 67, 68, 72, 75, 78, 91, 109, 131, 132, 133, 135, 137, 138, 139, 140, 141, 144, 149, 150, 151, 153–157, 159, 160, 181, 188, 190, 228, 244
Partnerships: 11, 12, 16, 38, 69, 136, 137, 213, 219, 221, 223, 224, 244
Pastoralists: 59
Patel: 68, 83, 102, 112, 206, 208
Pindiriri: 133, 147
Political Development: 51, 56
Political economy: 37, 42, 47
Poor: 12, 52, 56, 86, 87, 88, 90, 95, 103, 132, 136, 143, 152, 171, 187, 216, 222
Post-Colonial Africa: 53, 58
Poverty: 4, 7, 38, 40, 41, 44, 45, 57, 59, 68, 73, 85, 86, 87, 89, 90, 95, 103, 107, 144, 186, 188, 198, 199, 200, 207, 221, 223, 229, 236,

Power: 6, 7, 9, 11, 29, 32, 40, 56, 59, 69, 72, 73, 76, 77, 80, 101, 104, 106, 136, 150, 153, 154, 174, 185, 187, 188, 190, 191, 205, 232, 236
Pre-Colonial Africa: 52
Preece: 71, 76, 77, 83
Professionalism: 227, 228, 229, 230, 231, 232, 233, 234, 235, 236, 237, 238, 241, 250
Public services: 40
Puriya: 149, 150, 151, 154, 155, 156, 157, 158, 159

R

Racism: 29, 101
Rahim: 156, 162
Rahman: 153, 162
Ramose: 107, 113
Reflective/reflections: 15, 117, 121, 122, 127, 132, 138
Rehabilitation: 171, 198, 199, 203, 204, 205, 206, 207
Reintegration: 199, 205, 206
Relationships: 11, 15, 16, 67, 68, 69, 70, 71, 72, 73, 74, 75, 79, 174, 190, 205, 217, 220, 222, 227, 230, 232, 238, 248, 253
Resettlement: 56
Resources: 4, 5, 8, 9, 10, 13, 14, 17, 26, 35, 36, 38, 39, 40, 45, 46, 51, 52, 55, 59, 67, 70–77, 80, 85, 89, 100–103, 105, 108, 132, 134, 138, 141, 151–157, 159, 160, 163, 164, 166–171,173,174,175, 185, 187, 188, 213, 214, 218, 221, 223, 230
Resilience: 68, 89, 104, 143, 227, 229, 230
Responsibility: 6, 14, 27, 41, 88, 103, 104, 108, 109, 120, 123, 124, 125, 126, 132, 138, 152, 175, 199, 200, 227, 228, 244

ROSCAs: 90, 91
Rose: 152, 162
Rural communities: 4, 13, 14, 101, 132, 163, 164, 166, 168, 170, 173, 231
Rural development: 4, 12, 45, 52, 56, 89, 90, 135, 137, 163–172, 174, 175, 247, 248
Rural Socialism: 55, 60
Rural-urban migration: 14

S
Sambu: 151
Sampson: 152, 162
Sang: 154, 157
Savelugu: 154
Scancar: 151, 159, 162
Self–help: 8, 21, 40, 41, 44, 45, 85, 86, 87, 131, 139, 140, 141, 150, 163–173, 175, 190, 193; SHGs: 85–96; Savings groups: 75, 89, 90, 91, 93; women's health groups: 90, 91, 93; farmer's groups: 91; privileged ones: 93
Self-Reliance: 55, 58, 60, 68, 154, 157, 170
Siddiqui: 153, 157, 162
Simba: 69, 83
Sister cities: 9, 10, 11
Social capital: 88, 91, 105, 127, 140, 143, 169, 170, 184, 230
Social change: 13, 72, 169, 182, 251
Social development: 9, 16, 26, 36, 37, 41, 43, 44, 95, 96, 108, 165, 188, 247, 248, 252, 253
Social justice: 26, 33, 99, 198, 206, 248
Social Services: 12, 36, 38, 40, 51, 52, 58, 59, 168, 202, 231, 238, 252, 253
Social Transformation: 36, 38, 247

Social Work: 24, 25, 27, 37, 99, 100, 101, 102, 103, 104, 107, 109, 188, 228, 229, 230, 232, 235, 236, 237, 238, 244, 248, 249, 250, 251, 252, 253
Socioeconomic: 38, 42, 51, 56, 77, 87, 88, 89, 95, 135, 188
South Africa: 67, 68, 76, 78, 79, 80, 102, 107, 247, 249, 252
South Asia: 86, 88, 95
South Coast Natural Resource Management: 137, 147
South Sudan: 27
Stakeholders: 4, 12, 14, 16, 68, 73, 79, 80, 96, 100, 104, 105, 119, 132, 137, 144, 153, 164, 168, 169, 172, 175, 203, 207, 213, 223, 224, 227, 228, 231, 233, 234, 237, 243, 244, 245
Structural adjustment programs: 12
Suburbia: 163, 164, 174
Sustainability: 13, 16, 45, 52, 67, 68, 71, 77, 78, 80, 100, 104, 108, 109, 126, 135, 138, 150, 152, 154, 160, 211, 212, 223, 227, 229, 234, 243, 251, 252
Sustainable community: 39, 89, 227, 228, 230, 231, 235, 236, 237, 238, 244
Sustainable Development: 14, 39, 44, 52, 61, 133, 211, 212, 213, 215, 221, 223, 224
Sustainable Development Goals (SDGs): 42, 44, 87, 126, 163, 164, 223
Sustainable farming: 132, 139, 142, 144,

T
Tacconi: 136, 147
Tagarirofa: 134, 136
Tamale: 154

Tanganyika: 52
Tanzania: 51–60, 89, 121, 126, 198, 250
Tembo: 93, 97
Theory of change: 211, 212, 213, 214
Thornhill: 150, 156, 162
Tikkoo: 155, 162
Togo: 122
Tönnies: 152, 162
Tootoo: 124
Top-Down: 8, 13, 16, 23, 26, 28, 29, 30, 33, 100, 134, 137, 138, 153, 181, 182, 183
Traditional: 3, 5, 6, 8, 14, 15, 23, 27, 31, 41, 46, 57, 58, 122, 134, 149, 150, 151, 154, 155, 156, 157, 158, 159, 160, 164, 166, 171, 173, 174, 211, 216, 217, 219, 220, 221, 222, 223, 224, 243, 249
Traditional governance: 6
Traditional leaders: 5, 14, 134, 149, 150, 151, 154, 155, 156, 159, 160, 211, 221, 223, 224, 243
Transformation: 4, 9, 16
Tribal pride: 41
Tribalization: 60
Trotter: 103, 109, 119, 113
Trust: 32, 67, 68, 69, 71, 72, 75, 94, 152, 173, 174, 189, 222
Tshitangoni: 151, 162
Tsotsi: 101, 102, 113

U

Ubuntu Philosophy: 23, 24, 25, 26, 27, 28, 29, 32; Ubuntu Theory: 51, 54; Ujamaa
Policy: 53, 54, 55, 56, Ujamaa: 51, 54, 55, 56, 57, 58, 60, 121, 126; Ujamaa Vijijini: 55, 57, 60; Dignity: 26, 28, 33, 53, 56, 58, 104, 182, 189, 202; Humanity: 24, 25, 26, 33, 69, 206; Humanism: 54, 69, 198, 206, Reciprocity: 26, 71, 75, 152, 189, Collectivist: 56; Community harmony: 25, 26; Community gatherings: 25; Vhuntu: 69; Compassion: 25, 26, 33, 202, 244, 245
Uganda: 35, 36, 37, 38, 39, 40, 41, 42, 43, 44, 45, 46, 47, 251, 253
Unemployment: 68, 95, 109, 199, 207
United Nations: 41, 44, 88, 90, 136, 198, 201
United Nations Development Programme: 90, 97
Urban: 4, 13, 15, 36, 47, 57, 60, 86, 163, 164, 166, 174, 198, 199, 247
Urbanization, 59
Utindaan: 123, 125

V

Values: 13, 23–28, 32, 33, 38, 51–58, 61, 67, 68, 69, 70, 104, 105, 110, 132, 138, 142, 150, 152, 155, 157, 159, 189, 213, 216, 220, 221, 230, 231, 233, 243
van Hulst-Mooibroek's: 89, 97
Vijiji vya Ujamaa: 51, 55
Village Communes: 51, 52, 55
Village saving groups: 46
Villagization: 51, 52, 53, 54, 55, 56, 57, 58, 59, 60, 61
Vincent: 103, 104, 113
Voluntary: 13, 55, 56, 57, 58, 70, 89, 92, 93, 165, 171
Vulnerable populations: 23, 29, 251

W

Waisbord: 153, 162
War and conflict: 25
Wealth: 31, 118, 124, 126, 127
Weingärtner: 94, 97
Welfare: 7, 8, 9, 24, 25, 26, 37, 40, 51, 52, 54, 79, 90, 102, 103, 107, 118, 151, 164, 166, 183, 187, 197, 201, 203, 207, 228, 238, 248, 249, 253
Wellbeing: 36, 38, 44, 46, 47, 69, 99, 109, 151, 199, 202, 251
Western: 5, 7, 11, 15, 26, 42, 79, 99, 101, 102, 105, 106, 120, 127, 134, 153, 173, 216, 229, 247, 252
Weyers: 4, 21, 72, 77, 83
Wheeler: 109, 113
Whitney: 74, 77, 81, 83
Willer: 93, 97
World Bank, 12, 13, 86, 87, 88, 97, 132, 147
World Conference on Agrarian Reform and Rural Development: 135
Wrona: 159, 162

Y

Yendi: 151, 154
Yeneabat: 77, 83
Youth: 25, 26, 32, 40, 42, 79, 90, 99, 100, 101, 107, 108, 110, 120, 184, 188, 193, 215, 225, 229, 234, 252, 253
Yunus: 86, 87, 88, 97, 98

Z

Zambia: 197, 198, 199, 200, 201, 202, 203, 204, 206, 207, 248, 251, 252, 253,
ZAPF: 132, 133
Zibane: 101, 102, 112, 113
Zimbabwe: 8, 131, 132, 133, 137, 138, 141, 142, 144, 198, 251, 252